CAROL CARTER ▪ MAUREEN BREEZE

LEADERSHIP
FOR TEENAGERS

From Ancient Times to the 21st Century

D0033311

LifeBound
DENVER, COLORADO

President/Publisher: Carol J Carter - LifeBound, LLC

Editorial Director: Maureen Breeze

Developmental Editor: Chelsey Emmelhainz

Assistant Editors: Heather Brown, Elizabeth Fritzler, Cassie Buccio, Miriam Evangelista, Angelica Jestrovich, and Kristen Fenwick

Copyeditors: Julie Carter, Kristin Kelly, and Don Cameron

Review Process Editors: Bill Knous and Cynthia Nordberg

Cover and Interior Design: John Wincek

Printing: Data Reproductions

LifeBound
1530 High St.
Denver, Colorado 80218
www.lifebound.com

Copyright © 2011 by LifeBound, LLC

ISBN 978-0-98-205882-4
ISBN 0-98-205882-9

10 9 8 7 6 5 4 3 2 1

PRINTED IN THE UNITED STATES OF AMERICA.

Leadership
CONTENTS

v

Leadership

PREFACE

O ur goal is for you to see yourself as a leader today and tomorrow. *Leadership for Teenagers* will help you develop a personal vision for your leadership and the skills to excel as a leader in the 21st century. Each chapter includes the following features to illustrate these leadership skills in action:

- **Pioneering Young Leaders**—introducing teens like you taking extraordinary steps to make a difference.
- **Enduring Leaders**—showcasing men and women whose leadership has and will continue to influence humanity for years to come.
- **Leadership Then and Now**—comparing tactics used by Cyrus the Great, ruler of the Persian Empire in the 6th century B.C., to strategies used by leaders today across the disciplines.

This book is an interactive tool to help you reflect and think about leadership in expansive ways. The activities at the end of each chapter give you a chance to create specific action plans to make a difference in your life and school, and ultimately prepare you to address some of the world problems that will require leadership from bright and energetic students like you.

We are always looking for ways to improve our student success resources. If you have any suggestions or ideas about how you and your school can use this book, please send us your thoughts. Here's how to contact us:

E-mail:	**contact@lifebound.com**
By phone, toll free:	1.877.737.8510
Snail mail:	Carol Carter and Maureen Breeze
	LifeBound
	1530 High Street
	Denver, CO 80218

NOTE: Curriculum to accompany this book is available for classroom use. It includes analytical, creative, and practical leadership activities, along with questions for discussion, PowerPoint slides, and test questions.

Special thanks to the following people for reviewing the manuscript and offering feedback:

Sandra B. Ameel, *Comprehensive Guidance Specialist,* Salt Lake City School District

Patrick Bassett, *President* National Association of Independent Schools (NAIS); Washington, D.C.

Donna Bontatibus, *Professor of English* Middlesex Community College; Middletown, Connecticut

Rebecca B. Emerson, LPCA, *Director of Counseling* Henderson Community College; Henderson, Kentucky

Mark Hauserman, *Director* Muldoon Center for Entrepreneurship at John Carroll University; University Heights, Ohio

Jaimie Humbert, *Affiliate Director* Indiana Future Problem Solving Program; Indiana

Melanie Isenhour, *Gifted Education Regional Consultant* Colorado Department of Education; Colorado

Debbie Lubrano, *Guidance Counselor* Academy of the Holy Names; Tampa, Florida

Pamela Nevills, *former Teacher Supervisor* University of California, Riverside and author, Corwin Press; Fallbrook, California

Joanna Peters, *College Connection Director* The Classical Academy Schools; Colorado Springs, Colorado

Karin Reynolds, *Executive Director for Secondary Education* Academy District 20; Colorado Springs, Colorado

Amy Slothower, *Executive Director* Get Smart Schools; Denver, Colorado

Kitty Thuermer, *Director of Publications* National Association of Independent Schools (NAIS); Washington D.C.

Melissa Vito, *Vice President for Student Affairs* University of Arizona; Tucson, Arizona

Ed Wierzalis, *Professor of Counseling,* UNC Charlotte

LEADERSHIP
FOR TEENAGERS
From Ancient Times to the 21st Century

WINFREY

Oprah .... launched the Oprah Winfrey Leadership Academy to educate South African girls from economically disadvantaged backgrounds and help them to become tomorrow's leaders.

■ How can you use your interests, talents, and abilities to make a difference?

■ Where can you shine and contribute as a leader?

Chapter 1
BECOMING... a Leader

What does it take?

Teens from Tennessee traveled to Huehuetenango, Guatemala, where they used their hands and improvised tools to build homes for local families. As part of Habitat for Humanity's Global Village Youth Program, they mixed mortar, shoveled gravel, and laid cement blocks to fulfill a basic human need for shelter. They felt connected, valuable, and alive as they worked with these Guatemalan families for two weeks. While making important contributions, they also improved their Spanish, and learned about the ancient Mayan culture.

In Washington State, high school teens collected iTunes gift cards, books, DVDs, and other small gift items to fill two hundred *Brady's Bags*. They distributed these bags to teens enduring chemo- therapy at the local cancer treatment center. Their goal: to honor their fellow classmate Brady who recently died from brain cancer. Their pledge: to keep his memory alive for both his family and peers.

In Lake Tahoe, Hannah Teter snowboard- ed for Africa. Teter, who won the Olympic gold medal in 2006, the silver in 2010, and six World Cup victories in the women's halfpipe event, donated all her prize money from 2009 to improve the water system and infrastructure in a Kenyan village. Proceeds from the Ben & Jerry Ice Cream flavor, Hannah Teter's

Maple Blondie, were also pledged to the cause. Currently, she serves as a spokesperson for Boarding for Breast Cancer, sells underwear to support Doctors Without Borders, and raises funds for war-torn Darfur.

W hat do these stories have in common? They all feature young leaders taking initiative to make a difference. Whether they are lending their time and efforts to support a cause, rallying others to step up and get involved, or using their talents to make a better life for others—they are leading. You might think, *I can't travel to Central America, I don't know anyone who has died from cancer, and I'm not an Olympic athlete*. It doesn't matter. You can lead from wherever you are. The best place to begin is right now in school. This book will show you how.

You may not be an Olympic athlete, but maybe you're on the soccer team and challenge your team's rival to a match, sell tickets to the game, and use the proceeds to offer a skills clinic for young players in a low-income neighborhood. Perhaps you're in the cast of the spring musical and organize an extra performance where you invite business owners from your community to attend and earmark the money from these ticket sales to upgrade the lighting equipment for your theater. If you've experienced the loss of a student at your school, you might plant a garden on campus and have students in an art class collaborate on a special bench to be placed in the garden. Or, you might start a college scholarship in his name so his legacy can live on.

You can lead in a variety of ways. It all comes down to taking initiative, making an effort, and seizing opportunity.

Over the years you've probably learned about great leaders such as Abraham Lincoln, Susan B. Anthony, Martin Luther King, Jr. and Eleanor Roosevelt. These men and women identified problems and took a stand. They had visions for the future in the face of adversity and created unique solutions to overcome obstacles. They built strong coalitions and provided opportunities for others to be involved. Most importantly, they served.

They served both their vision and their followers. They dedicated their lives to such service, often responding to the demands their work before attending to their own personal interests. It is this act of service before self that marks great leaders.

Such traits of service and dedication do not belong exclusively to politicians, but to leaders from all walks of life. Leadership exists beyond politics. Studying the great minds in the arts, sciences, business, society and philosophy offers insights into what constitutes great leadership, and hopefully gives you ideas of where you might lead one day. You never know, someday your name might be among the great leaders written about in this book, and students in high school, decades from now, might read about the achievements you made in your lifetime.

Here is a list of extraordinary leaders from different fields. Research and list each of these leaders' contributions. In addition, add the names of two other leaders and describe their contributions.

Extraordinary Leaders

LEADERS IN PHILOSOPHY

- Socrates— _____
- Simone Weil— _____
- _____
- _____

LEADERS IN SCIENCE

- Louis Pasteur— _____
- George Washington Carver— _____
- _____
- _____

LEADERS IN MATHEMATICS

- Archimedes— _____
- Maria Gaetana Agnesi— _____
- _____
- _____

LEADERS IN ART

- Martha Graham— _____
- Zora Neale Hurston— _____
- _____
- _____

LEADERS IN SOCIAL MOVEMENTS:

- *Caesar Chavez—*
- *Septima Poinsette Clark—*
-
-

LEADERS IN TECHNOLOGY:

- *Steve Case—*
- *Steve Jobs—*
-
-

LEADERS IN BUSINESS:

- *Richard Velazquez—*
- *Mary Kay Ash—*
-
-

Keys for Leadership

PURPOSE: Leadership without purpose is like a boat lost at sea. What is your purpose? What are you resolved to do? Knowing your intention—whether to initiate change, help others in need, or bring awareness to a problem—will inform the choices you make and the actions you take. Once you know your intention, you can focus your attention on making your dreams a reality.

Just as this list illustrates leadership from various walks of life, you can explore leadership in a variety of areas in your own life. Are you on student council or a leader on an athletic team? Are you involved with an after-school club? Do you stand up for what you believe? Do you lead your family by helping your parents and siblings think about things from different perspectives?

You may not see yourself as gregarious, capable of speaking in front of others, and mobilizing them to buy into your ideas. But there are other, more subtle ways to lead. If you have a purpose—whether it is to increase awareness, put a stop to injustice, celebrate excellence, open doors of opportunity, create community, foster involvement—you can learn to lead. If you don't yet have a purpose, keep your mind open. Our goal is to help you do this and give you examples to guide you. The first step is to understand the basic skills of leadership and identify your strengths and weaknesses with respect to these areas.

THE SKILLS AND STYLES OF LEADERSHIP

I n this text, we've identified six areas that create a foundation for effective leadership. These elements are the "what" of leadership. They are the ingredients that leaders use to turn ideas into action. The next six chapters cover these elements in depth.

The "how" of leadership then becomes the style one adopts to implement these ingredients. In the late 1930s, the famous social psychologist, Kurt Lewin, was one of the first researchers to study leadership styles. What he found was that at one end of the spectrum there are leaders who exercise complete control over decision making, who command from the top and give direct orders. These are known as *autocratic* or *authoritarian* leaders. At the other end of the spectrum are leaders who give their followers free reign to make decisions and they empower their followers to take charge. This style is known as *empowering* or *laissez faire* (French for letting people do as they

The foundation of leadership. FIGURE 1.1

choose). In the middle of the spectrum are leaders who spend time communicating with their followers, listening to input from team members, and building coalitions to make joint decisions. These leaders rely on a democratic style.[1]

The best leaders are able to use a variety of styles. Certain instances require quick action and demand a more autocratic approach, while other situations work best when the leader uses a democratic or empowering leadership style. The following table describes the three styles and the conditions that make each most effective.

TABLE 1.1 Leadership styles.

AUTOCRATIC	DEMOCRATIC	EMPOWERING
Leader makes most of the decisions alone	Leader facilitates discussion and tries to build a consensus among followers	Leader empowers followers to take charge and make decisions
Often used in emergencies or when action must be taken immediately	Demands time for discussion; can be challenging when members of the group have differing opinions	Works well when members are committed, have access to necessary information, and are highly capable

1. Do you appreciate teachers who lead the classroom with an autocratic, democratic, or empowering style? Give an example from your experience and explain why you prefer the style you identified.

_____

_____

_____

_____

2. Give an example of a leader who used(s) an autocratic leadership style when a democratic or empowering style might have been more effective. Explain why.

_____

_____

_____

_____

3. Which style feels most comfortable when you lead? Which are you most comfortable with when you follow? Why?

---

4. What impact do you think culture has on leadership style? Think about a nation's culture, military culture, rock-and-roll culture, school culture, and so on.

Regardless of the style a leader uses, he or she must still have a vision, communicate well, command and give respect, possess critical and creative thinking abilities, work well with teams, and uphold ethical standards—all the skills from the pie chart shown earlier. Rather than focus on styles of leadership in this text, we'll explore these six critical elements in depth. As you read profiles of leaders from all ages, you'll witness different styles of leading. From these examples you can begin to formulate your own leadership philosophy.

A special leader that you will be learning about throughout this book is **Cyrus the Great,** the founder of the Persian Empire in the sixth century B.C. Scholars, philosophers, and politicians have studied his approach to leadership for centuries. His story is part legend and part fact. The Greek philosopher and historian, Xenophon, recorded Cyrus the Great's story in writing one hundred years after Cyrus's death, which was recently translated in 2006 by military historian Larry Hedrick. The direct quotes you'll read come from this translation.

Some of the greatest minds in business and politics today refer to Cyrus the Great as a guru in leadership strategy. His ideas have influenced such greats as Julius Caesar (controversial yet powerful leader of the Roman Empire), Benjamin Franklin (one of the founding fathers), Peter Drucker (leading scholar of business and management practices) and Steve Forbes (publisher, businessman and U.S. Presidential candidate).[2] We will weave aspects of his story through each chapter, and compare his tactics with those used by more contemporary leaders. You can witness leadership skills in action—then and now.

LEADERSHIP *then & now*

CYRUS THE GREAT (ca. 580–529 B.C.) and **FREDERICK DOUGLASS** (1818–1895)

In the sixth century B.C., Cyrus the Great united the Medes and the Persians, the original tribes of Iran, and with keen leadership tactics and military success, he overtook the Assyrians to build the great Persian Empire. His kingdom ultimately reached from India to the Mediterranean Sea. When his army conquered Babylon, he became known as one who ruled in the most humane ways, liberating 40,000 Jews from captivity, and promoting peace and goodwill for both his people and those he conquered. His empire thrived peacefully for two centuries until it was overtaken by Alexander the Great.[2]

When Cyrus the Great first set out to challenge the King of Assyria, his opponent who was threatening to take over Persia and Media at the time, his army paled in comparison. He didn't have the large number of soldiers, nor the horses and weaponry that the King of Assyria had. But Cyrus the Great had studied diligently, disciplined his mind and body, and possessed an exemplary work ethic, all of which ultimately led to his victory.

He believed that his journey as a successful leader was as much of an inward self-exploration process, as it was one of building military strength and might. In fact, he placed great value on self-knowledge and said, "Truly, men often fail to understand their own weaknesses, and their lack of self-knowledge can bring terrible disasters on their own heads."[4]

Over two thousand years later, a different leader emerged. One equally dedicated to self-knowledge and discipline of the mind and body, but with a different battle to fight. Frederick Douglass, the first famous African American orator, was born into slavery in 1818 in Eaton, Maryland. At six, he was sent to Baltimore to live as a house boy, where the mistress of the home taught him the alphabet. However, her husband forbade her from teaching him to read and write, so he traded food with the poor white boys in the neighborhood in exchange for lessons. Douglass read everything he possibly could with the belief that reading and writing would be the key for positive change in his lifetime.

During his teen years, he was sent to work on a plantation managed by a cruel slave breaker. The man beat the slaves, and Douglass received more than his fair share of whippings. At one point the slave breaker attempted to tie Douglass to a post for a beating. Although Douglass's spirit was broken, something shifted inside him. "At that moment—from whence came the spirit I don't know—I resolved to fight."[5] They battled for almost two hours before the slave breaker walked away.

Douglass never quit fighting. He eventually escaped and made his way by train and boat to New York City. He attended anti-slave meetings and began speaking and writing about his experiences. He soon learned that his voice was his greatest strength and strongest weapon. He traveled and gave speeches, fighting tirelessly for Constitutional amendments that guaranteed voting rights and other civil liberties for blacks. He published an autobiography in 1845 and started a newspaper, *The North Star,* soon after. Douglass also attended the famous women's rights convention in Seneca Falls, New York in 1848 where he spoke out for women's rights. Because of his self-knowledge, discipline to study, and willingness to fight the difficult battles, Douglass became an advisor to Abraham Lincoln and is remembered as one of the most influential leaders of his day.

Cyrus the Great was born into royalty as the King of Persia's son. He grew up with wealth and abundance. Frederick Douglass was born a slave who had to fight for his life. But they both became great leaders through self-discipline. They studied, learned all they could, took risks, and stood up for what they believed. You may come from a life of privilege where money, family support, well-funded schools, and access to incredible experiences are at your fingertips. Or, you may come from an environment of hardship, where there is little money, resources are scarce, and you have little or no support at home. The bottom line is that you can become a leader regardless of your circumstances if you learn the skills and do the work.

The Cyrus the Great and Frederick Douglass examples emphasize the importance of learning about yourself and assessing your strengths and weaknesses. The following tool will help you do this. Know that even the most honored leaders aren't strong in every category. Be honest with your responses, and you'll discover your greatest opportunities for leadership development.

ASSESSMENT

Discovering your leadership strengths and weaknesses

VISION. Place a check mark on the line that best describes you.

1. I look for new ways of doing things.

    ○ ALWAYS   ○ USUALLY   ○ SOMETIMES   ○ NEVER

2. I set goals.

    ○ ALWAYS   ○ USUALLY   ○ SOMETIMES   ○ NEVER

3. I thrive in ambiguous situations where I don't know the exact outcomes.

    ○ ALWAYS   ○ USUALLY   ○ SOMETIMES   ○ NEVER

4. I anticipate trends in the future.

    ○ ALWAYS   ○ USUALLY   ○ SOMETIMES   ○ NEVER

5. I prefer creating my own solutions to a problem rather than following set procedures.

    ○ ALWAYS   ○ USUALLY   ○ SOMETIMES   ○ NEVER

6. When working with others, I generate the ideas.

    ○ ALWAYS   ○ USUALLY   ○ SOMETIMES   ○ NEVER

7. I see challenge as an opportunity for creativity.

    ○ ALWAYS   ○ USUALLY   ○ SOMETIMES   ○ NEVER

8. I am creative.

    ○ ALWAYS   ○ USUALLY   ○ SOMETIMES   ○ NEVER

CRITICAL AND CREATIVE THINKING.   Place a check mark on the line that best describes you.

9. I ask why problems exist.

    ○ ALWAYS   ○ USUALLY   ○ SOMETIMES   ○ NEVER

10. I have strong observation skills.

    ○ ALWAYS   ○ USUALLY   ○ SOMETIMES   ○ NEVER

11. I ask probing questions to better understand problems.

    ○ ALWAYS   ○ USUALLY   ○ SOMETIMES   ○ NEVER

12. I compare and contrast information to increase my understanding.

○ ALWAYS   ○ USUALLY   ○ SOMETIMES   ○ NEVER

13. I invent imaginative solutions to problems.

○ ALWAYS   ○ USUALLY   ○ SOMETIMES   ○ NEVER

14. I evaluate my solutions and/or responses to problems and situations.

○ ALWAYS   ○ USUALLY   ○ SOMETIMES   ○ NEVER

15. I enjoy wrestling with a problem even if I can't find an immediate solution.

○ ALWAYS   ○ USUALLY   ○ SOMETIMES   ○ NEVER

16. I enjoy word games and number puzzles.

○ ALWAYS   ○ USUALLY   ○ SOMETIMES   ○ NEVER

RESPECT.   Place a check mark on the line that best describes you.

17. My peers respect me.

○ ALWAYS   ○ USUALLY   ○ SOMETIMES   ○ NEVER

18. I follow people I respect.

○ ALWAYS   ○ USUALLY   ○ SOMETIMES   ○ NEVER

19. I acknowledge the success of others.

○ ALWAYS   ○ USUALLY   ○ SOMETIMES   ○ NEVER

20. I'm capable of getting people to commit to a cause.

○ ALWAYS   ○ USUALLY   ○ SOMETIMES   ○ NEVER

21. I work well with people from diverse backgrounds.

○ ALWAYS   ○ USUALLY   ○ SOMETIMES   ○ NEVER

22. I build positive relationships.

○ ALWAYS   ○ USUALLY   ○ SOMETIMES   ○ NEVER

23. I'm a role model for others.

○ ALWAYS   ○ USUALLY   ○ SOMETIMES   ○ NEVER

24. People listen to me when I speak.

○ ALWAYS   ○ USUALLY   ○ SOMETIMES   ○ NEVER

COMMUNICATION.   Place a check mark on the line that best describes you.

25. I adjust what I say and how I say it, depending on whom I'm addressing.

   ○ ALWAYS   ○ USUALLY   ○ SOMETIMES   ○ NEVER

26. I'm a good listener.

   ○ ALWAYS   ○ USUALLY   ○ SOMETIMES   ○ NEVER

27. I enjoy speaking in public.

   ○ ALWAYS   ○ USUALLY   ○ SOMETIMES   ○ NEVER

28. I express myself well when I write.

   ○ ALWAYS   ○ USUALLY   ○ SOMETIMES   ○ NEVER

29. I like to engage in conversation with people I don't know well.

   ○ ALWAYS   ○ USUALLY   ○ SOMETIMES   ○ NEVER

30. I read others' nonverbal communication cues accurately.

   ○ ALWAYS   ○ USUALLY   ○ SOMETIMES   ○ NEVER

31. People understand me when I communicate.

   ○ ALWAYS   ○ USUALLY   ○ SOMETIMES   ○ NEVER

32. People read my nonverbal cues accurately.

   ○ ALWAYS   ○ USUALLY   ○ SOMETIMES   ○ NEVER

TEAMWORK.   Place a check mark on the line that best describes you.

33. I enjoy working with others.

   ○ ALWAYS   ○ USUALLY   ○ SOMETIMES   ○ NEVER

34. I easily build alliances with others.

   ○ ALWAYS   ○ USUALLY   ○ SOMETIMES   ○ NEVER

35. I hold myself accountable to commitments I make to groups.

   ○ ALWAYS   ○ USUALLY   ○ SOMETIMES   ○ NEVER

36. I applaud my teammates when they do well.

   ○ ALWAYS   ○ USUALLY   ○ SOMETIMES   ○ NEVER

37. I prefer to work with others rather than by myself.

○ ALWAYS ○ USUALLY ○ SOMETIMES ○ NEVER

38. I hold others accountable for their commitments to a group.

○ ALWAYS ○ USUALLY ○ SOMETIMES ○ NEVER

39. I'm comfortable handling conflicts between people.

○ ALWAYS ○ USUALLY ○ SOMETIMES ○ NEVER

40. I ask others to generate input.

○ ALWAYS ○ USUALLY ○ SOMETIMES ○ NEVER

ETHICS. Place a check mark on the line that best describes you.

41. I challenge myself to succeed through adversity.

○ ALWAYS ○ USUALLY ○ SOMETIMES ○ NEVER

42. I'm honest with myself.

○ ALWAYS ○ USUALLY ○ SOMETIMES ○ NEVER

43. I'm honest with others.

○ ALWAYS ○ USUALLY ○ SOMETIMES ○ NEVER

44. I acknowledge when I am wrong.

○ ALWAYS ○ USUALLY ○ SOMETIMES ○ NEVER

45. I treat others with respect and dignity.

○ ALWAYS ○ USUALLY ○ SOMETIMES ○ NEVER

46. I'm bothered when my actions aren't appropriate in a given situation.

○ ALWAYS ○ USUALLY ○ SOMETIMES ○ NEVER

47. I receive great internal satisfaction when I make ethical choices, even if they cost me in the short run.

○ ALWAYS ○ USUALLY ○ SOMETIMES ○ NEVER

48. I'm comfortable allowing others to see and learn from my mistakes.

○ ALWAYS ○ USUALLY ○ SOMETIMES ○ NEVER

Look at questions 1–8. Give yourself four points for every *always* you checked, three points for every *usually*, two points for every *sometimes,* and one point for every *never*. Add your points and write the total on the line below.

VISION: _____

Look at questions 9–16. Give yourself four points for every *always* you checked, three points for every *usually*, two points for every *sometimes,* and one point for every *never*. Add your points and write the total on the line below.

CRITICAL AND CREATIVE THINKING: _____

Look at questions 17–24. Give yourself four points for every *always* you checked, three points for every *usually*, two points for every *sometimes,* and one point for every *never*. Add your points and write the total on the line below.

RESPECT: _____

Look at questions 25–32. Give yourself four points for every *always* you checked, three points for every *usually*, two points for every *sometimes,* and one point for every *never*. Add your points and write the total on the line below.

COMMUNICATION: _____

Look at questions 33–40. Give yourself four points for every *always* you checked, three points for every *usually*, two points for every *sometimes,* and one point for every *never*. Add your points and write the total on the line below.

TEAMWORK: _____

Look at questions 41–48. Give yourself four points for every *always* you checked, three points for every *usually*, two points for every *sometimes,* and one point for every *never*. Add your points and write the total on the line below.

ETHICS: _____

Plot your points on the circle below. If your score in vision is a twenty-four, draw a curved line through the vision piece of the pie along the twenty-four mark. Follow the same procedure for each of the six assessment categories.

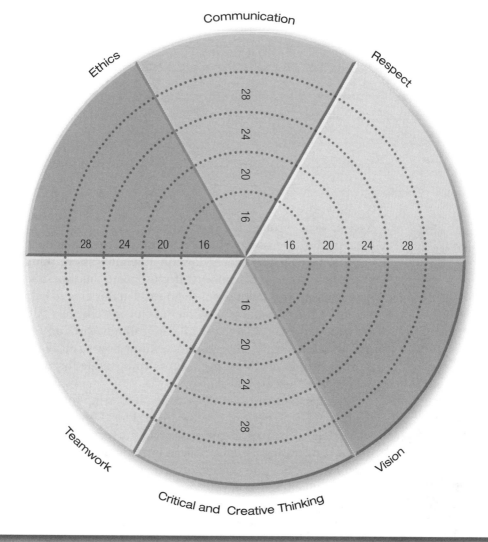

Take a moment to reflect on the diagram you've just plotted. Which pieces of your pie are largest? Which are smallest? Are your pieces similar in size or are there significant differences between them? In other words, what are your greatest strengths? Where are your weaknesses?

Write a paragraph summarizing what you discovered about yourself from this exercise.

_____

_____

_____

_____

_____

_____

_____

_____

_____

As you read through the text, pay particular attention to the chapters discussing areas where you can make the most improvement. If you scored low on communication, think about how you can become an effective communicator, and how you can work with people who excel in this area to help minimize your weaknesses. When reading the chapters that discuss your areas of strength, take note of how you can optimize your abilities. The best leaders know how to make the most of their strengths, using them to compensate for other areas where they are less skilled.

You may not see yourself assuming leadership roles, and figure there is no need to develop these skills. However, you will be called to lead at some point in your life. You may not end up creating national policies or running international corporations, but you certainly could end up leading initiatives at your church or in your community, managing a group of employees, or guiding your family through adversity. It is critical to understand the elements of leadership, to know your strengths and weaknesses in these areas, and to work to improve your abilities because you never know what life might ask of you.

In each chapter you will read about a young leader. This chapter features Ishmael Beah from Sierra Leone, whose courage and perseverance renders him a true hero. He never set out to be the leader he's become. Life called him to the task.

PIONEERING young leaders

ISHMAEL BEAH, author and founder of the Ishmael Beah Foundation

At age thirteen, Ishmael Beah was forced to become a soldier in Sierra Leone's civil war. The war, which began in 1991, was started by a rebel army that tried to overthrow the country's government. The rebels burned down Beah's village, killing his family and friends. Beah escaped and wandered with a group of boys for a period, scavenging what he could from other ravaged villages. When the government army picked him up, he believed he had found a safe haven.

The government camp proved to be anything but a rescue. For a time, Beah and his thirteen peers (all orphaned boys) simply helped with the cooking in exchange for food and shelter. However, the boys were eventually recruited to fight for the army. Before long, Beah had been brainwashed and given drugs, and was coerced to kill people and burn villages the same way he had seen others destroy his own home.

When he was removed from the fighting by UNICEF three years later, Beah had become a completely different person from the young, innocent boy he once was. At UNICEF, he spent eight months rehabilitating and reclaiming his humanity. Despite his drug addictions and haunting memories of his terrible past, he began to recover and eventually left Sierra Leone for the United States at eighteen.

In the United States, Beah graduated high school from the United Nations International School in New York and earned a political science degree from Oberlin College. He also served as a representative at the United Nations First International Children's Parliament, relating the horrors of Sierra Leone's war and his experiences as a child soldier.

Beah published *A Long Way Gone: Memoirs of a Boy Soldier* in 2007, and the book has since received critical acclaim. Starbucks partnered with Beah and UNICEF, donating $2 from each book sale to UNICEF's programs addressing child welfare in war.

Beah also started the Ishmael Beah Foundation, which, according to the organization's website, "aims at creating and financing educational and vocational opportunities for children and youth who have been affected by war, so that they can be empowered to choose a life free of conflict."[6]

Ishmael didn't wake up one day when he was a young teen and decide to be a leading advocate for the treatment and rehabilitation of children soldiers. It was probably the furthest thing from his mind. But by conquering the overwhelming challenges and adversities he faced, he developed a vision for a different kind of world. His vision and leadership work with the United Nations will hopefully save other children from many of the tragedies he endured.

Many other leaders have shared their vision, their gifts, and leadership abilities with the United Nations, whose mission is to provide leadership that promotes international peace, security, social progress, better living standards, and human rights. In fact, Cyrus the Great still plays a role in the United Nations' efforts today.

In 1879 an archeologist excavated a baked clay cylinder from an area in ancient Babylon known as Esagila, or the Marduk temple of

Babylon, which is now Nineveh, Iraq. The cylinder is 23 centimeters long and 11 centimeters wide and contains forty lines of writing. The writing, in cuneiform script, documents Cyrus the Great's promises to his people in 539 B.C., illustrating his respect for people of all races and backgrounds.[7] Recorded on the cylinder are three overlying principles that he subscribed to:

1. People of different racial, linguistic, and religious backgrounds should be treated the same.
2. Slaves and all deported people should be allowed to travel back to their homes.
3. All temples previously destroyed in the city should be rebuilt.

Today the cylinder is kept at the British Museum of London, and a replica is kept at the United Nations headquarters in New York City. Because the document sets standards for humanity that world leaders still wrestle with today, many scholars have declared Cyrus' writings as the first human rights charter. The United Nations translated the writings on the cylinder into the six official U.N. languages. Cyrus's vision and respect for humanity has endured and continues to serve as a guidepost for world leaders today.

In each chapter of this book you will read about different people throughout the ages who illustrate how you can better lead yourself in your own life, as well as lead others in your school and community. For this chapter we chose to profile Confucius. This ancient philosopher offered wisdom that was as applicable to leaders during his time as it is for you today.

ENDURING leaders

CONNECTING YESTERDAY TO TOMORROW

CONFUCIUS (551-479 B.C.)

Confucius was born in China in 551 B.C. and is known as one of the greatest thinkers and philosophers of all time. His teachings greatly influenced the people of Asia and are still highly regarded today, especially in China, Korea, Japan, and Vietnam. There is still some debate whether Confucianism is a philosophy or a religion, as many of his ideas are based on rules for moral behavior and ethics, rather than on religious concepts.[8]

Confucius never claimed to have come up with his teachings on his own, but instead believed he was a transmitter of such ideas from antiquity, which he then dedicated his life to sharing. He taught that humans are responsible for their actions and treatment of others and believed that compassion should be the cornerstone of all human interaction. He is thought to have introduced one of the oldest versions of the golden rule—*Do not do to others what you do not want done to yourself.*

With the highest regard for education, Confucius believed a person could reach his or her ideal self only through dedicated learning, self-discipline, and self-reflection. He encouraged his followers not to simply adopt his teachings, but think deeply for themselves and reach their own conclusions. He also believed that leaders who lead by example can motivate followers to do the same, but leaders who lead only by laws and restrictions while failing to live by example, most often resort to punishment to keep followers in check.

Confucius, Cyrus the Great, and Ishmael Beah all had a vision of how people should be treated. This vision then shaped their life's work. What are you willing to commit to? What do you envision for tomorrow, for the next year, or the next century? How can you make a difference and best prepare for what life may ask of you? In the next chapter we will discuss how you can create a vision and set goals, imagine possibilities, and initiate action to make a difference.

SUMMARY

L eadership is about believing in yourself and your abilities to make a difference. This book will help you learn basic leadership skills. It will also help you explore your purpose as a leader so that you can make an impact at home, at your school, in your community, and later, in the world. Open your mind to the powerful examples provided in this book and see what they can teach you about your leadership potential.

building leadership skills

FOR THE TWENTY-FIRST CENTURY

Success and Failure

ANALYZING LEADERSHIP IN ACTION

Think of someone you consider to be a strong leader, and someone you think is a weak leader. These leaders can be people you know personally, people you've read about, or examples from history.

Ask yourself these questions:

- What strengths did each leader have?
- What weaknesses did they demonstrate?
- Is there any way in which their leadership styles were similar?
- How did they differ?
- What kept your weak leader from succeeding (loss of respect, poor choices, failure to communicate, etc.)?
- What can you take away from these observations?

Leading in Your Own Life

Successful leaders have a purpose, and they pursue this purpose with passion and vigor. Ishmael Beah has a purpose: to keep other children from harrowing experiences he faced. His leadership is motivated by this purpose. Hopefully you'll never face the challenges Ishmael Beah did, but you certainly will encounter adversity from time to time, and these experiences may help you define your purpose.

Ask yourself the following questions:

- What do you care deeply about?

  _____

  _____

  _____

- What brings you joy?

  _____

  _____

  _____

- What angers you?

  _____

  _____

  _____

- What leaves you feeling frustrated or concerned?

  _____

  _____

  _____

- What makes you feel hopeful and inspired?

  _____

  _____

  _____

Your answers can lead you to your purpose. Once you know your purpose, begin to look for leadership opportunities where you can pursue it.

If you don't have a clear cut, well-defined purpose right now, it's okay. Experiment. Get involved. Try your hand at different leadership opportunities. Think about your school, your extra-curricular activities, your part-time job, or other areas where you spend time each day. Where can you take on leadership roles? You might try out for a leadership position at school and, in this position, create a campaign to get all students to attend class everyday, or establish a committee to collaborate with the faculty to determine school policies. You might take a stand against a bully or drug use at your school.

Now ask yourself the following questions:

- Where can you help to make changes that are needed?

- Where do you see things that are average that with your leadership, could be improved?

- Where do you see things that are good that could be great?

- Where are you being called to lead?

- What purpose you can bring to this leadership?

Teamwork for Effective Leadership

Get into groups of three or four. As a team, brainstorm several problems or areas of opportunity at your school that call for effective leadership. Next, choose one that interests your group the most. Define why you group feels it is important.

Here are some examples of problems or opportunities for leadership to get you started:

- Lack of interaction between students of different ethnic groups.
- Few opportunities to learn about higher education and career choices.
- Students' poor attendance rate.
- Shortage of funds for music and theater productions.
- Low involvement in extra-curricular and sports activities.
- Need for recognizing outstanding teachers.

Now discuss the following questions and prepare responses to share with your class.

- What is the problem or cause you would like to address?
- Why is it a problem or an area for opportunity?
- Who is affected by your issue?
- How does it relate to other school problems or needs?
- What will be the consequences if the problem or cause is ignored?
- Who, if anyone, is currently addressing the problem or cause?

WEIHENMAYER

Erik ... the only blind person to summit the tallest peak on each continent, challenges the ideas of what a blind person can do or not do.

- Where do you see a need for greater awareness about a problem?
- What vision can you create to increase this awareness?

Chapter 2

BECOMING
...a Champion of Excellence

How can you create a vision?

stella, Marcus, and Reed knew they were lucky. With closets of clothes and stocked refrigerators, they'd never been without the basic comforts. This was true for most students at Overland High, but not for many teens at their neighboring high school.

These three students wanted to help other teens less fortunate than them. They hosted a canned food drive at homecoming to help their neighbors, but few students at Overland High participated. Everyone was wrapped up in the game and dance, and it seemed that no one wanted to recognize hunger in their own backyard.

To raise awareness of the issue, Estella, Marcus, and Reed came up with an idea. They'd host a hunger banquet in the cafeteria at lunch to help students understand the scope of hunger on the international, national, and local fronts. With the support of the principal and teachers, they advertised their event as a global lunch instead of a hunger banquet to achieve the greatest impact.

As students entered the cafeteria, they drew a number from a hat to determine where they'd be seated. In the center of the room were two beautifully decorated tables with linen tablecloths, china plates, silverware, candles, and flowers. To the right were several traditional cafeteria tables, bare except for paper plates, plastic silverware, and cups. On the other side of the cafeteria were rows of blankets spread out on the floor.

For students lucky enough to sit at one of the center tables, waiters served them spaghetti with meatballs and sausage, heaps of fresh green salad, toasted garlic bread, sparkling apple juice, and brownies with ice cream for dessert. The students assigned to the traditional cafeteria tables walked through a buffet line to help themselves to rice, beans, water, and crackers. The students on the blankets were each handed a cup of water and small bowl of rice to be eaten with their hands.

While everyone ate their lunch, Estella, Marcus, and Reed shared the following statistics. According to the World Bank indicators of 2007, 15 percent of people across the globe have high incomes and access to the best food, 35 percent have average incomes, and 50 percent have very low incomes with little access to fresh, healthy food.[1] They then shared similar statistics from their own city, explaining that many students at their neighborhood schools were going hungry.

The impact was great. Although most of the teens left the cafeteria with grumbling stomachs, their minds were full. The student body rallied together to make the canned food drive a success. But they didn't stop there. With the leadership of Estella, Marcus, and Reed, they launched a program where groups of students picked up leftover food from restaurants each evening that would have otherwise been thrown away and distributed these meals to shelters and food lines in their city.

These three students saw a need in their community. They had a vision for increasing others' awareness of the problem. Then they took initiative and made a difference. That is leadership.

L eadership isn't about being meek and small-minded. It's about being bold and courageous. It's about thinking big and envisioning possibility.

In 2560 B.C., the Egyptians built the Great Pyramid of Giza as a temple for the Pharaoh Khufu. This pyramid, which weighs approximately 6.5 million tons, is still structurally intact and was the tallest man-made structure on Earth for more than 4,000 years! The creators of this temple had a grand vision that certainly stood the test of time.

How it was built is still beyond comprehension. It's estimated that a team of 14,000 to 360,000 men worked to cut, move, fit, and cement 2 million blocks of stone into place. The Egyptians then encased the entire pyramid in limestone (though this casing was later stripped away by invaders), smoothing its surface to reflect sunlight. Moreover, the pyramid's four sides are aligned perfectly with each of the

four compass points and, most notable of all, the ancient Egyptians erected the pyramid at the precise center of the Earth's land mass. Few places on Earth could have accommodated such weight, and it appears that the Egyptians knew exactly where to build it.

What kind of thinking was required thousands of years ago to create such a structure or envision a wall that stretched long enough to protect an entire empire? China's Great Wall, made of stones and wood, extends for approximately 5,500 miles. That's 2,500 miles more than the distance from the east to west coasts of the United States! With guard towers and watch stations, it was designed to protect the Chinese Empire from nomadic invaders descending from the north. Work on the wall began under the Qin Dynasty's rule (221–206 B.C.) and was modified and extended during the Ming Dynasty's rule (1388–1677 A.D.) Do you think the leaders of the Qin Dynasty would have ever thought that their vision would be a major international tourist destination over two thousand years later?

Figure 2.1 lists the Seven Wonders of the Ancient World.[2] As you read, think about the vision these creators had. How did these leaders challenge the knowledge of their day? How did they vpush forward the understanding of architecture, technology, and teamwork? How did they come up with ideas and create structures that were unthinkable at that time?

FIGURE 2.1   The Seven Wonders of the Ancient World.

The Seven Ancient Wonders	Location	Date Built (all dates are approximate)	Description
The Great Pyramid of Giza*	Cairo, Egypt	2560 B.C.	Built as a tomb for the Pharaoh Khufu
The Hanging Gardens of Babylon	Al-Hillah, Iraq	600 B.C.	Used a highly complicated irrigation system (it rarely rained) to bring water from the Euphrates to the vaulted garden terraces
The Temple of Artemis at Ephesus	Selcuk, Turkey	550 B.C.	Honored the Greek goddess of hunting and nature; was built entirely of marble; was 377 feet long and 180 feet wide with 127 60-foot columns
The Statue of Zeus at Olympia	Olympia, Greece	450 B.C.	Ivory statue of a seated Zeus measuring 40 feet tall
The Mausoleum at Halicarnassus	Bodrum, Turkey	353 B.C.	Tomb of the Persian King Mausollos and his wife; stood 135 feet high and was full of statues of people and animals; known for its ornamentation as well as its structure
The Colossus of Rhodes	Rhodes, Greece	280 B.C.	100-foot tall statue of the Greek god Helios that stood at the entrance to the island's harbor
The Pharos (Lighthouse) of Alexandria	Pharos Island, Alexandria, Egypt	280 B.C.	Up to 450 feet in height with a mirror at the top to guide ships into the harbor

*The Great Pyramid of Giza is the only one of the Seven Ancient Wonders surviving today.

What type of thinker do you need to be to see possibility where others see none? What type of thinking will you need live a large life? To pursue excellence in the face of mediocrity? To challenge the status quo and initiate change?

You may not have visions for building pyramids or other magnificent structures, but you can generate ideas for greatness for both yourself and those around you. Our goal for this chapter is to both challenge you and help you become visionary in your thinking.

Visionary thinking is critical for leadership. It helps you to see a better place or way of doing things than what exists today. It gives you a picture of what to work toward. It sets a standard for excellence and serves as a guide-post to bring about change.

Take a moment to refer to the self-assessment in the first chapter. How capable are you of doing the following tasks?

> ### Keys for Leadership
>
> **COURAGE:** To see possibilities when others see none and act on bold visions takes courage. Leaders must possess an undaunted spirit to fight for their convictions despite criticism. They must be willing and courageous to stand in the face of adversity and doubt. How courageous are you?

- Seeing new ways of doing things.
- Setting goals.
- Dealing with ambiguity and unknown outcomes.
- Anticipating trends.
- Seeing adversity as an opportunity for creativity.
- Challenging the way things are usually done.
- Stepping forward with courage.

Some of you may have a knack for visionary thinking. If you don't, it will take practice. It might also require you to challenge your view of yourself. Have courage to think big. The ideas will follow.

Let's return to Cyrus the Great from chapter one, to see how he created a vision for himself and then implemented ideas that changed the world order of his day. We will then compare his journey to that of Erik Weihenmayer, the much celebrated blind mountain climber who conquered Mount Everest.

LEADERSHIP *then & now*

CYRUS THE GREAT (ca. 580–529 B.C.) and **ERIK WEIHENMAYER** (1968–present)

Cyrus the Great was born into royalty, his father being the King of Persia. However, Cyrus didn't let his privileged upbringing become an excuse for a life of laziness and luxury, without a vision for his future. His father taught him that great leaders made sure to meet their people's needs, and that their ultimate responsibility was to help people be the best they could be. As he reflected on these ideas he started to envision himself as a great leader, one who could eventually realign nations and create a great empire. During this time, he prayed that his goals and ambitions would help to make the world a better place for all humans. His vision to serve became his moral compass.

However, Cyrus didn't sit idle and simply reflect on his grand vision. He took action to prepare himself for his time of leadership by learning from adults in his father's court, mastering his own warrior skills, and disciplining his mind to remain clear and strong for the battles that lay ahead.

In the meantime, the King of Assyria had built a strong empire and was threatening to take over Persia and Medes. Cyrus's uncle, who reigned over Medes, contacted Cyrus and asked him to join him in stopping the King of Assyria's troops who were threatening to take over the entire region. Although young, Cyrus decided the time was right for him to seize the opportunity and step into his new leadership role.

To inspire followers to join his army, Cyrus shared his vision of a better world and all the things possible for the Persians and Medes if they conquered the Assyrians. He enticed them by explaining how they would personally benefit from this mission, knowing that many followers like to know this before committing to a leader.

With a modest army gathered, he set out to join forces with his uncle in Medes. When they approached their first battle against the Assyrians, Cyrus yelled, "Brave men out front!" calling others to join him at the front of the battle line.[3] He always led from the front, not from behind, committed to never hiding behind others. Cyrus's army charged their opponents with fierce determination, and the Assyrians quickly retreated from their first round of attack.

Now fast forward to the 20th century. When Erik Weihenmayer was a young boy he too began formulating great visions. But his circumstances couldn't have been more different than Cyrus's. Instead of growing up in a royal family and living in palaces, Erik was battling a rare eye disease, retinoschisis, and by the time he was thirteen, he was completely blind. However, he didn't become a victim of his handicap but instead accepted his father's challenge: to change the perceptions of what a blind person could do or not do. This began his vision to succeed.

Like Cyrus the Great, Weihenmayer spent his adolescence learning all he could—from attending blind youth camps, to participating in outdoor adventures, to wrestling on his high school team to learn about his body's strength and agility, to graduating from college and earning a master's degree in education.

But Erik's vision of breaking through perceived barriers about what was possible for a blind person continued to grow and evolve. It wasn't long before he was trekking through Peru, scaling mountain peaks, and skydiving. Some of his greatest accomplishments include becoming the first blind man to trek

the Inca Trail into Machu Picchu (Peru), biking tandem from Hanoi to Ho Chi Minh City (Vietnam), climbing to the top of Mount Everest, and completing the Seven Summits (reaching the highest peaks on all seven continents). Much of what Weihenmayer has accomplished stems from the vision he began cultivating as a teen to shatter the limitations of blindness.[4]

Neither Cyrus the Great nor Erik Weihenmayer created a vision overnight. They worked hard, resisted laziness, and avoided indulging in privilege or shrinking in the face of adversity. They disciplined their minds and bodies and learned all they could from those around them. It is no different with you. If you too commit to seeking knowledge, resisting laziness, and living a disciplined life, your mind will open to new possibilities.

Consider the word vision. What comes to mind? The act of seeing? A mental picture? An idea? *Webster's II New Riverside Dictionary* defines vision in the following three ways:

1. The faculty of sight
2. A mental image created by the imagination
3. The unusual ability in foreseeing what is going to happen

Leaders exercise vision in all three ways. Some have a keen ability to see the value in something that others overlook. Others know how to take what they see and transform it into something else with the help of their imagination.

A group of students in Alabama did just this when they received permission to turn an old Masonic lodge into a teen center. The building had been empty for years and was rundown and in disrepair. After hours of painting and putting in a sound system and dance floor, these kids opened the doors for business. Their new teen center became the hub of activity every weekend as they hosted dances, slam poetry readings, band jams, and other social events.

Executives from Magnum D'Or Resources, a Canadian company, saw profits where others saw waste.

It's estimated that each year, over one billion tires are disposed of worldwide. Seeing opportunity, Magnum D'Or Resources, Inc. partnered with the Malaysian firm, Sekhar Research Innovations, to develop a state-of-the-art, green recycling process that transforms scrap tires into environmentally friendly products. Their goal is to save the landfills from disposed tires, reduce the hazards of this waste, and add value to the economy by producing environmentally friendly products from the recycled rubber.

When have you seen value in something that others overlooked? If you can't come up with something, write about someone else who had a vision for something others believed was worthless.

_____

_____

_____

_____

_____

Some leaders are able to foresee what will happen in the future and take action well in advance of others. In the early 1950s, Ray Kroc worked as a milkshake machine salesman. Calling on various customers, he met the McDonald brothers, who had opened a burger establishment along with a handful of franchises in San Bernadino, California. Kroc realized the business had enormous potential and tried to convince the brothers to expand their operations. When they resisted, Kroc bought them out for $2.7 million. He took over the operations in 1954 and developed it into the most successful fast food operation in the world. During his lifetime, Kroc created a fortune surpassing $500 million.

List five things that you use practically every day that were once merely a vision of someone who anticipated a trend or need for a convenience:

1. _____

2. _____

3. _____

4. _____

5. _____

This chapter's Enduring Leader both challenged the common agricultural practices of the time while anticipating trends for the future. Our current farming methods result from his visionary work.

ENDURING leaders

CONNECTING YESTERDAY TO TOMORROW

SIR ALBERT HOWARD (1873–1947)

In the early 1900s, Sir Albert Howard traveled from England to India to share the latest Western agriculture methods with the Indians. But, as visionary leaders often find themselves from time to time, he became the student. Now that he was out of the laboratory, he was able to spend time on the land, studying how crops could grow in typical field conditions, not the ones made up for scientific experiments indoors. Howard spent the next twenty-five years of his career learning and fine-tuning the traditional Indian farming practices that became the basis for the modern day organic movement.

During his years in India, he built upon their composting methods and developed the Indore method, which allows for biodegradable waste to fertilize the soil as it decomposes. This return to traditional farming methods came from his observations that insects and plant diseases indicated the poor health of the soil. By working to improve the soil's condition, he effectively warded off insects and unhealthy plants without the use of pesticides and chemicals.

In the 1940s, Sir Albert Howard wrote two books: *An Agricultural Testament* and *The Soil and Health,* which outline the philosophies behind organic agriculture. Today, he is universally regarded as the father of the organic movement, and his ideas continue to inform the practices that we now consider cutting edge.

The agricultural industry is far different today than it was sixty years ago because of Sir Albert Howard. For many leaders, a vision isn't an instant picture in the mind or a clear-cut idea that suddenly appears. Often, it is an accumulation of experiences or ideas that blend together—a mosaic of thought—that leads to a picture of what might be possible. Cyrus the

Great didn't start out knowing exactly what his empire would look like. Instead, he spent years studying and learning about the world outside of Persia as he created what he called "his empire in his mind."[5]

Actor and activist Christopher Reeve, who at the peak of his career played Clark Kent in the *Superman* movies, suffered a devastating horseback riding accident that damaged his spinal cord and left him completely paralyzed. Reeve brought his role as Superman to life again in a much more poignant way. Although he was in a wheelchair and breathing with the aid of a ventilator, Reeve mobilized people and resources to discover a cure for spinal cord injuries. He successfully focused international attention to this cause and developed significant support for much of the groundbreaking scientific research being done today. Reeve didn't have a vision as a teenager, or as a famous actor, that he'd be called to this leadership role. But as he moved through life, he accumulated experiences and knowledge that he later used to create a vision for positive change.

What experiences have you had in your life that might one day influence your leadership vision?

_____

_____

_____

_____

TRANSFORMING GOOD TO GREAT

hile adversity and tragedy inspire some leaders, others are motivated when they see a good situation that, with vision and hard work, could be transformed into a great situation.

Have you ever heard of the Miracle on Ice? Perhaps you've seen the movie with the same title. The term was coined after the coach, Herb Brooks, led the 1980 U.S. Olympic hockey team to a gold medal victory. Mr. Brooks started with a group of college and amateur players who were good, but not nearly as great as the Soviets, who dominated the sport at the time. Known for his hard tactics, Brooks pushed his team, working them to near exhaustion. He forced them to face their weaknesses, both on and off the ice, and pulled them together as a cohesive team.

When it came time for the Olympics, people underestimated all the hard work Brooks had done with the team, and they didn't believe the U.S. had a chance of winning. Their first big game was against the Soviets, who were expected to sweep the competition. A columnist for the *New York Times* wrote, "Unless the ice melts, or unless the U.S. team or another team performs a miracle . . . the Russians are expected to easily win the Olympic gold medal."[6]

The U.S. team played with skill and determination, moving ahead of the Soviets four to three. With only five seconds remaining in the game, the broadcaster announced to the cheering crowd, "Do you believe in miracles?" As the final buzzer sounded, the crowd roared back, "YES!" *Sports Illustrated* voted this victory the best sports moment of the twentieth century.

The 1980 U.S. Olympic hockey team went on to win the remaining Olympic Games and capture the gold medal. Brooks' vision and leadership transformed a good team into a great team.

Transforming good to great doesn't happen only in sports arenas. The greatest of leaders are able to observe situations and spot opportunities for improvement. They know where to apply pressure and make changes to elevate good results to great ones.

Business expert Jim Collins wrote the book *Good to Great* to help business executives transform average performing companies into great ones. He based his work on these leadership principles:

- Lead with humility and do what's best for the organization.
- Be honest about the difficulties you face.
- Know what the organization is best at doing. Pay attention to what the team and leaders are passionate about doing.
- Create a disciplined culture.
- Avoid being distracted by too many smaller goals. Keep focused on the main mission.

How do these principles relate to you as a student? Take a moment to write down how each of these ideas can be applied to your leadership, whether it is at home, in school, at a part-time job, or in your community.

_____

_____

_____

_____

_____

Whether your goal is to transform a good situation into a great one, increase awareness about an issue, or initiate change, you can look to the following suggestions to help you create a bold vision.

Developing Your Visionary Skills

Keep Your Mind Turned On and Your Eyes Wide Open

Cyrus the Great shunned laziness. He didn't let a life of luxury distract him. He kept his mind focused on possibility. Christopher Reeve didn't allow himself to wallow in his tragedy. Instead, he kept his eyes on the future. A future made better by science and research.

Keeping your mind turned on and your eyes wide open is perhaps the single most important thing you can do as a teenager. This means focusing on what you are passionate about and what is important to you. It means avoiding the things that cause you to check out, disengage your mind, and prevent you from seeing what's possible.

How do you check out and disengage? How many hours a day do you spend watching TV or playing video games? How much of your time is spent text messaging friends or hanging out at the mall? Do drugs or alcohol interfere with your vision for yourself and the world around you?

Everyone needs downtime. Knowing how to relax from the pressures of day-to-day living is critical for success. But there is a fine line between relaxing and shutting down, or in other words, putting blinders over your eyes.

By keeping your eyes and mind open, you can envision possibilities.

What distracts you and keeps you from seeing all that is possible? Is it a negative attitude? Too much time in front of the TV? A limited circle of friends? What commitments are you willing to make to keep your mind open?

_____

_____

_____

_____

_____

Take a Risk

Experience is the best teacher. You can read about vision and study great leaders, but in the end, your experiences will teach you the most. Go ahead and take a risk. Run for office, assume a leadership role in your clubs, and take part in political campaigns in your community.

When you land a leadership role, or if you are already in one, think about how you can make the greatest impact. Try something that's never been done at your school. Push yourself out of your comfort zone. There is no better way to learn.

When you are working on a team, step up to the plate and help your group embrace a vision—whether it's an idea for the science fair, a story concept for your group video project, or a strategy for getting people to sign up for your talent show. Doing this is especially valuable when there is not a designated leader. However, it can be challenging. Without an appointed leader, you'll have to be sensitive to the group dynamics so you don't come across as overbearing. You've probably all worked with a group that's had a hard time getting focused and deciding what to do. Be the leader, come up with a vision, and get the momentum started.

You don't need a formal title or team to develop your visionary skills. You can practice with your group of friends. Start a program or host an event on your own. Put yourself out there. Stand up, imagine what's possible, suggest ideas, make plans, and rally others to join you. Four young women from Colorado did just this when they began making wallets from duct tape. With weaving patterns and bright colors, their creations were such a hit that they began selling them at young entrepreneur markets. From here, they branched out and began making belts, purses, and bookmarks, among other things. Soon, they had their duct tape items for sale on the Internet. Their vision of making wallets blossomed into a business.

By taking a risk, you give yourself new opportunities to impart your vision.

What risks are you willing to take?

_____

_____

_____

_____

_____

Learn All You Can

Learn all you can about the world around you. You can start today. Books are perhaps the most accessible, inexpensive gateway to new cultures and new ideas. Nothing will help you increase your awareness like challenging yourself to read about things foreign to you.

Ask questions. It is one of the best habits you can cultivate for yourself. Raise your hand in class. Be curious and you'll quickly increase your learning. Most toddlers possess an insatiable curiosity and move through their days asking "Why?" Remain curious. Ask why.

Enter into new situations. Where can you gather new experiences? Traveling is a terrific way to learn about the world. Yet it is not always an option. If you can't see the world in person try watching foreign films, eating foods from different cultures, studying religions from around the world, and cultivating friendships with people from different backgrounds. The more you widen your circle of influence, the more aware you'll become. With increased knowledge, you'll have greater perspective about bold and unique possibilities for yourself and your world.

Finally, surround yourself with other visionaries. Stay in the company of those who are inquisitive, willing to learn all they can, and challenge themselves and their thinking. Who can you turn to for guidance, direction and knowledge? Seek out role models and mentors to help you sift through ideas you might already have in mind.

By learning all you can, you are better able to think big about your leadership potential.

How can you remain curious? What actions are you willing to take today to learn all you can about the world around you?

_____

_____

_____

_____

_____

Think about the Future

Great leaders are able to envision the future and anticipate the needs and demands that will surface in years to come. In the 1950s, Ray Kroc of McDonald's anticipated the trend of fast food and led a revolution in the restaurant industry. Today, engineers developing solar energy products, technology experts creating applications for handheld computer devices, and scientists inventing new medicines to fight cancer are all leaders whose work will certainly change the way we live fifty years from now.

One of the best ways to anticipate future trends is to practice looking at a situation and then imagine how it could be improved. It wasn't long ago that travelers carried their heavy suitcase by a small handle. Then, one day someone had the vision of rolling a suitcase on wheels. This person anticipated that most people would pay for such a convenience, and the roll-aboard suitcase was born.

A second way to think about future trends is to look at what is popular now and ask how it can be combined with other ideas and transformed into something new. For example, in many developing countries, poverty prevents people from attending school. However, many people in these places have cell phones. Lessons and curriculum are currently being developed to transmit over cell phones so that these people can learn on hand-held devices! Many leaders in the sciences, business, politics, and the arts have achieved greatness by developing this ability to think about the future.

By being able to anticipate future trends, you set yourself apart from others and lead the way for new solutions.

What trends do you anticipate for the next five years? What about for the next fifty years?

_____

_____

_____

_____

_____

Dream Big

Unleash your imagination. *What if* you had all the resources you needed to go to college and graduate school? *What if* you could travel the world or live in a foreign country? *What if* people in your community had access to nutritious food? *What if* a source of energy existed that was inexpensive to produce and created no pollution? *What if* a vaccine could be created to eradicate cancer?

Many people resist envisioning big ideas. Not knowing the "how" of bringing an idea to life keeps them from ever entertaining the "what." It's much like embarking on a path without a road map, which can be overwhelming. But leaders learn to trust that if they keep focused on their vision, they can learn to live with this ambiguity and know that a path will unfold before them. Being able to move forward despite uncertainty is a hallmark trait of great leadership.

The construction of the Italian cathedral, Santa Maria del Fiore, began in 1296 with just a vision. The plans included an octagonal dome on top of the building, but no one had any idea how to build it. They began construction despite not knowing how it would be finished. In 1419, over a century after construction had started, they were ready to build the dome. A contest was held to see if anyone had a vision for engineering such a feat. Brunelleschi, who was known for being a master door maker, won the contest. He claimed he could build the dome with no internal supports. Many people thought he was ridiculous and his ideas were impossible. But Brunelleschi came up with groundbreaking techniques, many still used in engineering today. His plan included building multiple domes of brick and sandstone to fit inside the octagonal dome. He also found ways for oxen to raise and lower the heavy beams and loads. After sixteen years, Brunelleschi completed the dome on top of the cathedral of Florence, bringing the 139-year construction process to a successful close. The structure still survives today, despite hurricane-like winds and earthquakes. And Brunelleschi is now often referred to as the first engineer of the Renaissance.[7]

The top of the cathedral in Florence is currently the largest masonry dome in the world. However, if it weren't for the vision of the Italians in 1296 and their willingness to get started in the face of uncertainty, the dome wouldn't exist.

It was the same for President John F. Kennedy, who envisioned the possibility of putting a man on the moon. In his speech to enlist the support of Congress on May 25, 1961, he said, " ... I believe that this nation should commit itself to achieving the goal, before this decade is out, of landing a man on the moon and returning him safely to the Earth . . ." But he didn't stop with mere words. He stayed focused on the vision, committing resources and implementing a rigorous schedule to transform what was a seemingly impossible idea into reality.

By dreaming big, you push yourself to conquer what was previously believed to be impossible.

What is one big idea you have that seems impossible?

Don't Overlook Small Visions

Many of the greatest ideas that come to being are a conglomerate of smaller ideas. While it is important to think big, it is also imperative to see opportunities in the smaller steps. Visions develop over time. By paying attention to smaller ideas, you'll be better prepared to create grand visions.

Georgia O'Keefe, a master artist, created exquisite paintings of flowers one stroke at a time. Her vision of what she wanted to ultimately portray on the canvas wasn't born in an instant. Paint stroke upon paint stroke, she created her work. A painting of a blossoming flower demanded she envision and then paint the stem, which informed how she painted the petals, which then informed her decisions regarding the background; the painting became a sum of the parts with each smaller vision feeding into the ultimate picture.

Yet it can be helpful to know how small steps dovetail with a grand vision, as this parable illustrates. Once upon a time three men were laying bricks. When asked what they were doing, the first man replied, "I'm laying a brick." The second man replied, "I'm building a wall." When the third man was questioned, he answered, "I'm building a cathedral." All three men were executing the same action. But the third man was able to see his smaller action in terms of a greater vision.

Building upon small ideas can lead you to grand visions.

What small ideas do you have now that might lead to bigger visions in the future?

William Kamkwamba never set out to be a global leader. His goal was simply to help his family with essential needs. Yet with this vision and an innovative spirit he was able to do much more.

PIONEERING young leaders

WILLIAM KAMKWAMBA

Growing up in the African country of Malawi, William Kamkwamba witnessed poverty's devastating effects. When a fierce famine hit in 2002, William was forced to leave school due to financial strains. Armed with curiosity and a vision of a better life for himself and his family, he did not let his absence from the classroom affect his desire to learn. William stumbled across a textbook on agricultural practices at the library. On its cover was a picture of a windmill. Knowing Malawi had plenty of wind, Kamkwamba soon had the vision of a windmill providing energy for his family. Unfortunately, the book didn't offer detailed instructions on how to construct a windmill, so he figured it out himself.

William was fourteen when he built his first windmill using discarded items from neighbors' trash and scraping up money to buy a few essential pieces: a rubber belt, a bike chain ring, a bicycle frame, some bamboo poles, flattened PVC pipes, and a tractor fan. His small, crude windmill generated enough electricity to power a few light bulbs, an old radio, and a cell phone. From there, William set to work building another, larger windmill, making improvements to the electrical output. Word soon spread about the boy's genius, and his windmills became a popular subject within his community and beyond. As a result of his efforts, he was accepted as one of the first ninety-seven students to attend the African Leadership Academy. What's his next move? "My dream is to finish my education and to start my own company making windmills," William says. His vision now involves providing affordable electricity to his community, giving them access to knowledge via the Internet, and powering indoor lights to study in the evenings. "That's what I'm planning to do—to come up with reliable electricity. Yeah, that's what I'm planning to do."[8]

William Kamkwamba's vision was born from saying no to a lack of education, to hopelessness, and to poverty. Perhaps one of the most effective ways to begin crafting a vision is to say no. What do you see in the world that you long to say no to? Climate change? Hunger? Abuse? Illiteracy? When you can identify what fails to serve you or others around you, you can begin to see what needs to be changed. Standing up and saying no to injustices opens doors for opportunity. It is central to the process of becoming a champion of change.

What are you willing to say no to? Your responses can involve your personal life, your community, or world issues.

1. _____

_____

2. _____

_____

3. _____

_____

4. _____

_____

5. _____

_____

6. _____

_____

7. _____

_____

8. _____

_____

9. _____

_____

10. _____

_____

Let's look to Martin Luther King, Jr., who so eloquently spoke about the world he said no to. His words gave birth to a new marching order for the civil rights movement in the United States.

On August 28, 1963, Dr. Martin Luther King, Jr. delivered his famous speech *I Have a Dream*. Read the following lines from his speech and write a few sentences interpreting what you believe Dr. King was saying no to.

". . . I have a dream that one day my four little children will one day live in a nation where they will not be judged by the color of their skin but by the content of their character . . ."

_____

_____

_____

". . . I have a dream that one day on the red hills of Georgia the sons of former slaves and the sons of former slave owners will be able to sit down together at the table of brotherhood . . ."

_____

_____

_____

". . . This will be the day when all of God's children will be able to sing with new meaning. 'My country 'tis of thee, sweet land of liberty, of thee I sing. Land where my fathers died, land of the pilgrim's pride, from every mountainside let freedom ring.' And if America is to be a great nation this must become true."[9]

_____

_____

_____

_____

Dr. King didn't discuss specific solutions to the problems, but he gave a voice to them. And his voice helped millions of people embrace a vision for change—a vision that is still being acted upon today. Great adversity led to this vision for change, and in turn, has sustained the soldiers who've fought for equality in the United States for over forty years.

Vision is born from adversity and becomes the wings to fly above it.

SUMMARY

V ision is at the heart of great leadership. To embrace a bold vision and work toward achieving it requires courage and stamina. As a teen, you can develop your leadership skills by envisioning ways to make a difference. To do this, take a risk, open your mind, learn all you can about the world around you, anticipate what the future might hold, and most importantly, dream BIG!

building leadership skills

FOR THE TWENTY-FIRST CENTURY

Success and Failure

ANALYZING LEADERSHIP IN ACTION

How might your leadership be negatively impacted? Perhaps you fear standing up to your peers, you surround yourself with negative people, you don't have extra time to take on other obligations, or you don't have a vision.

List any fears you have about being a leader today in your school and community.

_____

_____

_____

_____

Look at each fear and come up with several ways you might overcome it. For example, if you fear standing up to your peers, practice taking a stand with your family, trying small steps like writing an anonymous letter to the editor of your school newspaper, or disagreeing with a conclusion your teammates have come to on a science project.

_____

_____

_____

_____

_____

_____

_____

Leading in Your Own Life

DEVELOPING A BOLD VISION

Whether you are a peer mentor, student council member, team leader, or an inspired student without a formal title, think about the differences you can make in the various roles you play with your family, your peers, your school, and in your community.

Take a moment to think big and answer the following questions.

- What would you do if you knew you couldn't fail?

_____

_____

_____

- Imagine you won the lottery and were required to spend half the money on a cause. Which cause would you choose?

_____

_____

_____

- What would you do if you only had one year to live?

_____

_____

_____

- What would you do if no one was watching you?

_____

_____

_____

- What would you do if the whole world was watching you?

_____

_____

_____

Now, answer these more immediate questions that involve your leadership today.

■ When you graduate from school, how do you want to be known (for your ideas, your compassion, your spirit, your can-do attitude, etc.)?

_____

_____

_____

■ Twenty years from now, what do you hope your fellow students remember about you and your contributions to your school?

_____

_____

_____

_____

■ What personal gifts or talents do you have that could benefit your school (your ability to connect with others, your organizational skills, your ability to speak in front of others, etc.)?

_____

_____

_____

_____

■ What is good that, with your leadership, could be great?

_____

_____

_____

■ What is the greatest contribution you can see yourself making to your school?

_____

_____

_____

■ What is the greatest contribution you can make this year?

_____

_____

_____

Now it's time to state a bold vision you have for your leadership this year. Be courageous and go for it!

My bold vision for leadership this year is:

_____

_____

_____

Three people who support my vision are:

1. _____

_____

2. _____

_____

3. _____

_____

Teamwork for Effective Leadership

WORKING TOGETHER TO MAKE A DIFFERENCE

Get together with the same team you formed to complete this teamwork exercise in chapter one.

Think about the problem your team identified in chapter one. Brainstorm several ways you might address the problem. You might plan an event, host a fundraiser, or publish a newsletter. Any project is fair game as long as you are leading the way to address your chosen problem. Remember the students who hosted a hunger banquet and then took leftover restaurant meals to food lines? **Be bold. Stretch your thinking.** (If you are stuck, some examples of projects other students tackled are at the end of this exercise.)

List your ideas here:

_____

_____

_____

_____

_____

_____

_____

_____

Decide on the best project to pursue as a team. Write your team vision for improving your chosen situation on the following lines.

_____

_____

_____

List three people who will support you with your team vision:

1. _____

   _____

2. _____

   _____

3. _____

   _____

For the next five chapters, you will work as a team to plan your project. While you are studying chapter eight, you and your team will implement your vision. In chapter nine, you'll evaluate your results and reflect on your team experience.

SAMPLE PROJECTS:

■ Create an alumni database to track where recent graduates go to college and work. Use the database to establish a peer mentor program where these graduates share insights with current students.

■ Host a drug awareness panel. Invite speakers from rehabilitation centers, juvenile detention centers, the police force, and health clinics to give students the real facts about drugs and alcohol. Also feature a teen keynote speaker who shares his story of drug use and recovery with students.

■ Produce a slam poetry night featuring poems and raps created by students.

■ Sponsor a faculty talent show to raise money for art and theater programs.

■ Create a student "lookbook" for incoming freshmen that includes pictures of everyone in the class, a calendar to be used as a day planner, a listing of school resources available, important dates, a four-year academic plan for completing the necessary courses and tests to apply for college, etc.

■ Set up an attendance rally where grade levels compete against one another for the highest year-long attendance rates. The winning class receives prize money for trips, activities, etc.

YO-YO MA

photo by Stephan Danelian

. . . uses his passion and artistry to build communities world-wide.

- How can you lead the way to think creatively about building a tight-knit student community at your school?

- What obstacles might you face as you work to build community and bridge gaps between people?

Chapter 3

BECOMING

. . . a 21st Century Thinker

How can you think critically and creatively?

O n any given day, Jade could walk the halls of Lake High School
and hear English, Spanish, and Vietnamese being spoken. Her
school could have been the picture-perfect image of the American melting pot where students both grow and meld together.
But it wasn't. Students stuck with those like themselves. Little
mingling took place between the Hispanics, Caucasians, African-Americans,
and Vietnamese. When they did interact, it usually took the form of fighting. Gang membership was on the rise. Diversity divided.
Teachers and school administrators were at a loss.

Jade could see that students were losing the opportunity to learn from one another. She also saw
possibility. She loved filmmaking and hoped to
make it a career someday. But in the meantime,
she thought, Why not take what I'm passionate
about and try to make a difference now in my
school? Soon the idea of hosting a student ju-
ried international film festival came to her. She
envisioned a festival that featured films from other
countries. These students would not only help select
the films but also organize panel discussions to share
insights about the various cultures with the audiences. Using
film to connect people with differences, to share ideas and history, and to
open channels of positive communication could help bridge the cultural
divides she witnessed every day in the hallways of her school.

With a creative vision in place, she went to work. She sent out notices recruiting students to be on the jury. When there were more applicants than she could accept, she decided to form multiple juries, each responsible for one film and panel discussion per month. When the local theater said they couldn't use the space to show the films, she went to a projection company and asked to have the needed equipment donated on those evenings so that they could project the movies in the school auditorium. The company manager was so impressed with her mission that he volunteered to teach students how to set up and run the equipment themselves.

To make sure her festival was well-attended, Jade worked with the faculty to help promote the movies. The social studies, history, and language arts teachers agreed to give class credit for attending the festival and created extra credit opportunities for students to improve their grades.

By combining her passion for film and her desire to make a positive impact on her school, Jade had a creative vision. With her can-do attitude and problem-solving skills, she plowed through potential roadblocks to create her school's first Teen International Film Festival.

The ability to think both critically and creatively about problems is a trademark of successful leaders. Many of the world's greatest inventions come from people who approach a dilemma with ingenuity. Archimedes, a scientist and mathematician from the third century B.C., wanted to access water that pooled in a low-lying reservoir. He created a special screw pump to pull and transfer the water, introducing technology still used in parts of the world today, over two thousand years later! Although water pumps have evolved over time, you can still appreciate Archimedes's creative thinking when you see sprinkler systems watering lawns.

The Framers of the U.S. Constitution exemplify the power of critical thinking. From May to September 1787, fifty-five delegates met in Philadelphia to write the U.S. Constitution. These men labored for four months behind closed doors, analyzing how a government could be shaped to best serve the people. Their belief that a government should serve

We the People of the United

insure domestic Tranquility, provide for the common defence, promote

and our Posterity, do ordain and establish this Constitution for the Un

Article I

and protect the rights of the people, not grant rights to people, was revolutionary. However, they all had different ideas of how to write a document that ensured this belief.

They compared and contrasted different governments in Europe, retaining some of the best ideas and discarding others. They debated how citizens should be represented in the national government and eventually came up with what is called the Great Compromise: A system with two houses of representation, including the Senate where each state has two elected representatives, and the House of Representatives where the number of representatives is determined by the state's population.

The Framers also brainstormed ways to create a government that kept one person, or one ruling body, from having absolute control, and created a system of checks and balances between the executive, legislative, and judicial branches. Endless hours were spent thinking about how the words they were writing would be interpreted to ensure civic welfare and the citizens' rights to "life, liberty, and the pursuit of happiness." After a hot summer of negotiating ideas and evaluating possible solutions, these men created a constitution that has held as supreme law for over two hundred years.

What do water pumps and the U.S. Constitution have to do with you becoming a leader in your school and community? It's all about the skill of thinking both critically and creatively. It's about being resourceful. It's about observing and coming up with new ideas. Some leaders have visions and then need to turn to deeper thinking skills to deal with obstacles they meet along the way. Others have exceptional critical and creative thinking skills and invent new products or see solutions where no one else can. As a result, they become leaders. Either way, critical and creative thinking can bolster your ability to lead.

Keys for Leadership

RESOURCEFULNESS: Leaders must be able to see new ways of doing things. They must think outside of the box, try alternatives, and make use of resources that others might not think of using. How can you be resourceful?

Imagine your class needs to raise money for a trip to New York City. You've sold wrapping paper, hosted bake sales, and staffed car washes. Participation is low, people are bored, and you aren't reaching your financial goals. You decide to put your creative thinking to work. You ask yourself how you can generate money, get people involved, and generate excitement all at the same time.

With some ingenuity, you come up with a plan. You develop an "amazing race" where participants join in teams and pay to play. The teams compete against one another by riding bicycles to various stations you set up across your neighborhood. At each station, participants perform different activities. At one stop, they create a food dish with random ingredients. At another, they sing karaoke in public for tips. At a third, they execute an obstacle course on tricycles. You solicit prizes for the winners from businesses in the community in exchange for giving the companies free publicity. With some creativity, you raise the needed money, have fun, and get people excited—a nice change from run-of-the-mill approaches.

It takes practice to look at an issue and think critically and creatively about it, whether it involves fundraising, improving student attendance, or increasing community involvement. This type of thinking involves making observations, comparing and contrasting information, asking questions and being curious, imagining new solutions, and evaluating outcomes. Look back to your self-assessment from chapter one. How do you rate as a critical and creative thinker? Where do you excel? Where can you improve?

In this chapter, we will go through each of the steps for critical and creative thinking and offer tips for improving your abilities. We'll also give you many examples of how these skills are used for effective leadership. To begin, let's look at how Cyrus the Great used deeper thinking to lead his army in building the greatest empire of his day. Then, we'll show how these same skills came into play as three astronauts set out to conquer a different frontier: the moon.

LEADERSHIP *then & now*

CYRUS THE GREAT (ca. 580–529 B.C.) and
THE ASTRONAUTS OF APOLLO 13 (launch date April 11, 1970)

Perhaps one of Cyrus the Great's most noted strengths was his ability to think strategically about the problems he faced. He resisted making rash decisions based on emotion, knowing that acting impulsively could cost him lives and battles and diminish his ability to lead.

During the early stages of his conquest, his uncle, the King of Medes, outlined a strategy for an upcoming battle that would have revealed the size of their army to their opponents. Cyrus the Great analyzed his uncle's strategy and knew he had to put a stop to it. Despite being nervous to contradict his uncle, he explained how letting their opponents see how small their army was would be a huge mistake. He then offered a better plan of attack.

Cyrus the Great also took great care to anticipate the problems that his army might face and properly prepare his troops. He relentlessly observed and analyzed his opponents' movements. In one battle, he noticed the Assyrians were approaching on horseback from afar in a wide fan formation. He speculated they were planning to encircle his troops and attack from all sides. Instead of panicking, he figured out how he might be able to use their formation to his benefit. With a quick reordering of his men, Cyrus's troops banded together and attacked the Assyrians in a straight line, taking advantage of their opponent's weak center, and as a result, quickly defeated them.

When Cyrus and his allies defeated enemies in battle, he gave all the riches and food to the allies, requesting only the horses for his own. His allies thought he was quite generous. However, he had a greater plan in mind: to strategically transform his army, that was mostly on foot, to an army on horseback, which was faster, stronger, and more agile. He was also known for his creative problem-solving on the spur of the moment. He masterminded a four-poled chariot pulled by horses covered in bronze breastplates and a tower transported by oxen that carried twenty men on a protected platform—all advances in technology that were unheard of at the time![1]

Just as Cyrus relied on ingenuity to conquer new lands, the astronauts of Apollo 13 relied on ingenuity as they saved themselves from disaster while trying to perform

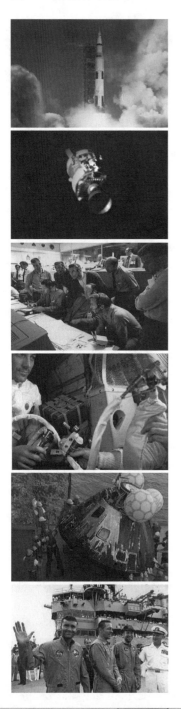

new feats in outer space. In 1970, James Lovell, John Swigert, and Fred Haise were the astronauts chosen to command Apollo 13's mission to the moon. After an oxygen tank onboard ruptured 199,990 miles from Earth, the now famous line, "Houston, we have a problem" was delivered by one of the astronauts to the ground crew in Texas (the astronaut actually said, "Houston, we've had a problem"). These three courageous leaders faced limited power onboard, a loss of cabin heat, little potable water, and the dire need to remove the carbon dioxide building up in the spaceship. They had to make several life-or-death decisions, and most importantly, they needed to use their ingenuity under extreme pressure.

The spaceship consisted of three adjoining compartments: a command module, a service module, and a lunar module. After assessing the damage, they quickly decided that the lunar module would be their best bet for guiding the damaged spaceship back to earth. They moved to this compartment, but many creative adjustments had to be made because the lunar module was not designed for such a task. When they tried to close a hatch to limit the amount of oxygen flooding, they couldn't get the door to latch, so they strapped the lid to a structure in the command module. To remove the buildup of carbon dioxide, they used plastic bags, cardboard, and tape to adapt canisters to do the job.[2] Despite all their training on Earth, they had to think on the spot and come up with creative solutions to power the ship back home. After these leaders safely landed, their flight was hailed as a "successful failure" all because of their resourcefulness in a time of crisis.

DEVELOPING YOUR CRITICAL AND CREATIVE THINKING SKILLS

Here are the basic stepping stones for deeper level thinking:

1. Ask why a problem exists.
2. Observe the problem.
3. Question the situation.
4. Analyze the information.
5. Imagine solutions.
6. Apply the solutions and evaluate outcomes.

Let's look at each of these steps to see how they relate to stellar leadership.

Step One: Ask Why

The first step to deeper level thinking is asking why. Why might a problem exist? Why are things done the way they are? Can things be different? Questions like these help us challenge the status quo—or what currently is. They help us accept a problem, which initiates the thinking required to solve it. Without challenging a problem by asking why, positive change can't happen.

In the 1970s, several scientists began asking why space debris might pose significant problems for space exploration. Before this time, no one paid much attention to the issue, not even cataloging and tracking various explosions that had occurred and left material orbiting around the Earth. But Donald Kessler, John Gabbard, and other researchers decided to track the materials and determine whether a potential problem existed. They discovered that the likelihood of collisions in space, an issue many people thought wouldn't be a problem for a billion years, would be a real threat to space exploration in just decades.[3]

This problem is very relevant today. In February 2009, two satellites collided, with catastrophic effects. For scientists involved with the International Space Station, space debris is a real concern. Imagine a five-inch piece of metal free-floating in space at speeds up to 18,000 miles-per-hour. In March of 2009, there was a near miss when a five-inch piece of debris came within 2.8 miles of the space station—far too close for comfort. These pieces of metal, along with an estimated fifty thousand pieces of debris floating in space, are a significant issue.[4] Hopefully, one day space scientists will be able to effectively deal with this threat to the safety of astronauts and equipment in space.

Where are the opportunities in your life to ask why? How can you emerge as a leader by asking this simple but powerful question? Are there systems in place at your school that don't serve you or your peers? Perhaps it is long hours of standardized testing without necessary breaks for a snack or fresh air. Or, an abundance of junk food sold in your cafeteria with few nutritious or appetizing options for health-conscious students. Maybe it is a lack of support and recognition for students who represent your school at alternative activities such as speech and debate meets or engineering competitions instead of the more traditional activities like football or baseball.

Leaders from a high school in Nevada took initiative for such a cause when their speech and debate team competed at the national championship tournament. They used Skype technology to broadcast the school's team winning a second place award. The cafeteria was packed with students watching their peers on a big screen take the national stage to receive their reward. By asking why some groups of students don't get the recognition they deserve, these leaders were prompted to take the initiative and make a change.

Are there situations with your family or personal life where you can ask why? If you fight a lot with your parents, have problems getting to your first class on time (well-prepared, fed, and rested), or wrestle with jealousy of a close friend, ask why. Think of this step as opening the door to a problem, a door you must walk through to find a solution on the other side. Know that leading yourself by solving basic personal problems will help you develop into a leader who can create solutions to benefit others.

Practice asking why by completing each question below. Use this opportunity to challenge anything you want, from how things are done in your household to how things are managed in your city. Perhaps you'll want to question not only problems, but also why something works exceptionally well. Be curious. Let your mind roam.

1. Why _____ ?
2. Why _____ ?
3. Why _____ ?
4. Why _____ ?
5. Why _____ ?

Step Two: Observing the Problem

Once you identify a problem and ask why it exists, it is time to think about possible solutions. However, the best leaders resist being impulsive and acting right away on their first ideas and instead take time whenever possible to research the problem in detail and explore options for solutions. Taking this time keeps them from being short-sighted and making bad choices.

Think back to a time when you faced a problem and quickly reacted before thinking through things. Perhaps it was a fight with a friend, an exchange with a customer at your part-time job, or a complex question on a science exam. What did acting impulsively cost you?

_____

_____

_____

_____

Imagine the lead paramedic and his team arriving at the scene of a horrible car accident. If he rushes over to the first victim and begins treating this person without taking a brief moment to observe the scene, his decision might cost him precious time and lives. However, if he quickly surveys the scene, looks for the number of victims and their apparent injuries, listens for any cries for help, takes note of any additional threats such as a car fire or the odor of ignitable gasoline, and considers his emergency crew's strengths, he can develop a quick, strategic plan to best use his resources to help as many people as possible in the shortest amount of time.

As you can see from this short example, observing is more than just seeing. The Merriam-Webster Dictionary defines observing as "coming to realize or know especially through the consideration of noted facts." To gather these noted facts requires use of all the senses. It involves looking, touching, smelling, listening, and sometimes most importantly, sensing with your intuition. When you face a problem, ask yourself the following questions:

- What do I see?
- What do I hear?
- What do I smell?
- What do I taste?
- What do I feel?
- What does my gut instinct tell me about the situation?

Here's a fun example that illustrates the power of observation and how it can help you solve problems. In the third century B.C., King Hieron of Syracuse was suspicious that he had been swindled by a crown maker. The king gave the crown maker the exact amount of gold needed for a new crown he was having made. When the crown was delivered, King Hieron suspected that some other metal had been used instead of all the gold he had provided the crown maker. He asked Archimedes, the mathematician and scientist introduced earlier in the chapter, to look further into the matter.

As legend has it, Archimedes was climbing into a tub when he observed water overflowing as he immersed himself in the water. He wondered if the amount of overflowing water was proportional to the weight of an object immersed. If so, he could measure the amount of water that overflowed when he put the crown into the tub and compare it to the amount of water that overflowed when he immersed pure gold into the tub. If the amounts of water were different, he could assume that another metal had been substituted for gold in the king's crown. Archimedes climbed out of the tub and ran home naked, excitedly shouting, "Eureka! Eureka!" which means, "I have found it! I have found it!"

This concept is now known as the the Archimedes Principle. Its definition, in more formal terms, states that an object immersed in a fluid is buoyed up by a force equal to the weight of the fluid displaced by the object.[5] This principle is still used to measure the density of objects and helps explain why steel ships float, while solid steel sinks in water. Archimedes's sharp sense of observation led the way for scientific measurement.

As this story indicates, observation is about more than recognizing a problem. It's about remaining aware of the world around you and making connections between related events. Had Archimedes not been perceptive enough to notice the similarities between his current situation and the problem at hand, he might not have made his groundbreaking discovery.

Your job as a leader is to look at a problem in as many ways as possible and to use what you discover about the problem to generate creative solutions.

For example, imagine you volunteer at a food donation center. You observe that during distribution times, the people in line become irritated and frustrated, which increases everyone's stress levels. You could just accept the situation as something you must contend with on your job. Or, you could take action as a leader and observe what happens in the waiting lines that contribute to the problem. Perhaps you note that most people have young children with them and they easily become bored. You also notice that the distribution times are at 6:00 p.m. when most people, especially the young children, are hungry and tired. Finally you consider that the distributions are held only twice a week, where distributions held more often might ease the crowds. In response, you write up an action plan for your manager that includes: offering sliced apples and orange juice as snacks to people waiting in line; creating a kiddy corner with books, crayons, and paper for children to entertain themselves as their parents wait; and finally, a suggestion for adding two additional morning distribution times each week to accommodate different schedules and shorten the waiting lines.

Now take a moment to think about a problem you currently face. Once again, this problem can be personal, can involve friends or family, or can relate to your school or community. Write down as many observations as you can make about your problem. Don't forget to ask yourself the questions listed earlier to make sure you observe with all your senses.

_____

_____

_____

_____

PIONEERING young leaders

CAROLINE MOORE

Our Pioneering Young Leader for this chapter possesses a keen ability to observe and has made history as a result. Caroline Moore, a fourteen-year-old from upstate New York, loves scanning the night sky and making observations.

In November 2008, Caroline was using a small telescope when she discovered a previously unknown supernova some seventy million light years away. She became the youngest person to discover a supernova in a nearby galaxy. To her surprise, and the surprise of the modern astronomical community, Caroline's supernova, named SN 2008ha by scientists, is actually an extremely rare breed of supernova. In fact, it bridges the long-disputed gap between novas (nuclear explosions on the surfaces of the stars) and supernovas (exploded stars caused by internal nuclear reactions).

When Caroline made her discovery, SN 2008ha appeared to be halted in the transition between nova and supernova. Her

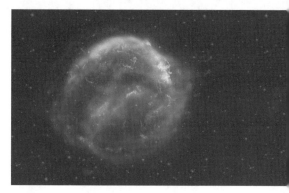

supernova is now prompting astronomers to question further how stars die since their current models fail to explain the behaviors of the SN 2008ha.[6] The result has been, well, astronomical. At just fourteen, Caroline has emerged as a leader. Her findings are living proof that powerful observation skills can lead to exceptional leadership opportunities. After all, what if Caroline hadn't questioned the starry mass in her telescope and led other astronomers to her discovery?

Step Three: Asking Questions

Some leaders rise to prominence because of their insatiable curiosity and need to ask questions. Growing up in school, Jacques Cousteau, the famous underwater explorer, was often bored and got into trouble. It wasn't until he discovered the ocean's underworld that he was able to channel his curiosity into passion and discover how to use his love of questions to make a mark on the world. Always searching for new answers and discoveries, he spent years writing and producing TV shows that enlightened audiences about the ocean's underworld and raised their consciousness regarding water pollution. But that's not all. Cousteau inspired the next generation of marine biologists, oceanographers, and artists.

James Cameron, the Academy Award-winning director, looked to Cousteau's work for inspiration after filming *Titanic*. Cameron and his team left the Hollywood scene for several years after making the blockbuster film and explored Cousteau's world, asking questions and piquing their own curiosity. Much of what they discovered while filming several documentaries underwater fueled their imaginations as they then went on to create the characters for the film *Avatar*.[7] Here, the questions and curiosity of one leader fueled the imagination and creativity of another.

Being curious and willing to ask questions are your best tools for gathering information and jump-starting your thinking. The answers you find can reveal new insights and different perspectives about a situation and boost your problem-solving abilities.

Asking questions can:

- Pique your curiosity.
- Channel your thinking down different paths.
- Motivate you to challenge your assumptions.
- Reveal your limited perspectives about a situation.

Think of a good detective stuck in the midst of a crime scene. He or she will question the witnesses, the credibility of any alibi, the relevance of various clues, and the assumptions made about the case.

When leading, you must also be willing to ask questions to gather as much information as you can about your situation. Imagine you are on student council and in charge of producing a school carnival where proceeds from the event will be donated to a local charity. Your job is to decide to which charity you will donate. Write down several questions you could ask to help you make this decision.

- _____
- _____
- _____
- _____
- _____
- _____

Did you consider which charity might benefit the most from financial support generated from your event? Did you think about which charity might interest your fellow students the most, and in turn get them excited to participate in the school carnival? What about whether or not students from your school have any personal connections with local charities?

Leaders in science are often known for their inquisitiveness. For Galileo Galilei, this quality was the cornerstone of his success.

Born in 1564 in Pisa, Italy, Galileo pioneered an experimental scientific method and was the first to use a refracting telescope to make important astronomical discoveries (including the four largest satellites circling Jupiter now referred to as the Galilean moons). He asked questions about the world around him, including everything from how objects of various masses travel through space to whether the Earth or the sun was at the center of the universe. After years of focusing on this last question (whether the Earth rotated around the sun or vice versa), he publicly supported Copernicus's theory that the Earth orbited the sun. However, the conventional thought of the day was that the sun revolved around the Earth. Galileo was condemned for his views and was forced to spend the remainder of his life under house arrest. However, many of the questions Galileo asked opened the doors to further scientific exploration. As a result, he is often considered the father of modern science.

Galileo asked questions to lead science forward. What questions can you ask about science? Don't worry if these questions have been answered yet or not. Just be curious and write down whatever comes to mind.

1. _____

   _____

2. _____

   _____

3. _____

   _____

4. _____

   _____

5. _____

   _____

Step Four: Analyzing the Situation

Once you've gathered information by observing and asking questions, it's time to analyze the situation. This step might include comparing what you know about your situation with other situations you've experienced. On the flip side, it might require you to contrast your problem with other problems by asking: What's different here? What will prevent last year's solution from working this year? What are you assuming to be true that might not be? Analyzing information might involve looking for patterns or repetitions that offer clues or identifying unusual circumstances that contributed to the situation. Ultimately, it's about making connections between what you know about the problem and what you know outside of the problem.

Imagine you and five classmates are working on a history presentation for a school competition. You've worked with these same students before, and it was disastrous. This time you've been appointed group leader and you want to do all you can to make this project the best that it can be. To do this, you will have to solve the problems that plagued your group the last time you worked together.

By comparing this project with the one your group did last time, you can outline the needs your team will have that are different. Because this project requires the group to do research about a historical topic, write lines for a play, create scenery and costumes, and then perform the play, you believe that dividing and conquering will be a better approach this time. By analyzing what you already know about these students, you realize that two of the members must be separated and assigned to different tasks on the project so that they don't argue and distract the team.

You also now know that one of the members is a great visual artist but struggles with deadlines. As the group leader, you decide to assign this person to do the scenery, but you help your group agree to commit to early deadlines well ahead of when the project is due to ensure that everything is completed on time. By analyzing what you know about the project, and what your experiences were in the past with these same teammates, you'll be able to deal with the problems you've faced in the past and be better positioned to lead your team to success.

Leaders in the working world follow the same process. They study, they analyze, and they compare, contrast, and connect. Consider the lead team of rocket scientists assigned to investigate the Challenger mission that exploded in 1986 just seventy-three seconds after takeoff with teacher Christa McAuliffe, the first civilian to travel in space, onboard. Figuring out what went wrong on the tragic flight was critical for NASA to regain public support and trust.

After much work comparing and contrasting how this attempt differed from so many successful flights before, they discovered that the O-ring, which is a type of gasket, had a seal around it that failed due to cold temperatures. This failure allowed hot gases and flames to leak out and burn a hole in both the external fuel tank and the piece that held the booster rocket to the side of the shuttle. When the booster rocket broke off, it crashed into the external fuel tank, exploded, and tore the shuttle apart. Investigators worked diligently to solve this problem and reconfigure the seal on the O-ring, and for the next eighty-seven flights, NASA went accident free.[8]

Unfortunately, in February 2003, the Space Shuttle Columbia experienced a different technical problem when a piece of foam fell off during launch and hit one of the shuttle's wings. When the shuttle reentered the Earth's atmosphere many days later, it exploded, killing all seven crew members onboard.

The best leaders know how to look for cause and effect relationships, see patterns, and identify differences and similarities. This information helps them to make sound choices when solving problems.

Describe a time when you've faced a challenge and stepped back to analyze the situation. It might have been a disagreement with a teacher, a problem with a coach, or an issue with your parents. How did your actions reflect the thinking you did beforehand about the problem?

_____

_____

_____

_____

Step Five: Imagining Solutions

When solving a problem, don't settle with the first solution that enters your mind. Search for and imagine the best ideas, and then work to bring these ideas to life. This ability to think outside the box, to imagine new and different ways to approach situations, is often what separates a good leader from a great leader. What about the people who brought you the iPod, laptop computers, and cell phones that record videos? Without their creative thinking, you'd still be listening to music on a boom box, typing your papers on a typewriter, and talking to your friends on a phone attached to the wall in your kitchen. Their creative thinking and ingenuity have literally changed the world we live in today.

In San Francisco, three teens competed in a kinetic sculpture race. The goal? To create a human-powered sculpture that could race through a hilly obstacle course. They needed to be able to move their sculpture up and down San Francisco's steep hills, yet it needed to be light and nimble enough to maneuver tight twists and turns on the course. These teens put their imaginations to work. They built a lightweight frame with wire mesh over a tandem bicycle, shaping the mesh into the form of a giant tidal wave. Next, they filled the holes in the mesh with ocean blue crepe paper. Plastic fish dangled from the wave, and a Styrofoam surfboard was anchored on top. The cyclists painted their faces and bodies blue to blend in with the sculpture. As they raced through the course, they blasted music from the 1960s television show *Hawaii Five-O* from portable speakers attached to the handlebars. Although they didn't win the competition, they certainly had fun imagining solutions to their problem.

How can you imagine unique solutions to problems? Next time you face a dilemma and need a brilliant idea, ask yourself the following questions to spur your creativity and let your mind wander:

- What rules can be broken?
- What parts can be added?
- What parts can be eliminated?
- How can the order of things be changed?
- What ideas can I combine?

And the best and perhaps most simple question of all . . .

- What if?

In 1914, the painter Guirand de Scevola was working as a telephone operator for a French artillery unit during World War I. As an intermediary between headquarters and the front lines, Scevola learned that the artillery unit had been attacked only moments after being given their orders. Realizing the unit must have been easily spotted, Scevola wondered how they could disguise the army's troops to protect them from the enemy. He pondered this idea until he finally came up with his brilliant idea for camouflage.[9]

Scevola spent months perfecting his design. When he was ready, he presented the French army with a demonstration. He dressed several men in uniforms streaked with Earth-colored paint. A signal was given and a plane flew overhead with orders to identify the uniformed men on the ground. The plane was unable to locate the team; Scevola's creative solution worked.

Immediately following the demonstration, Scevola was put in charge of the newly formed *La Section Camouflage*, a team comprised of several other painters like Scevola who adopted the style of Pablo Picasso and Cubist forms to incorporate into camouflage design. The large square blotches in Earth-toned hues help the wearer blend into the natural landscape. Art and war are typically not considered similar pursuits, but for Scevola, thinking creatively across boundaries led to an idea now used throughout the world.

How can you come up with the best possible solutions to problems? Brainstorm, ask compelling questions, and search for innovative ideas. Push yourself to think out of the box. Try the following activity: *What if?*

Let your imagination soar as you fill in the lines below. Don't worry about focusing on one topic. Simply ask yourself, "What if?" Have fun. The possibilities are endless.

WHAT IF?

What if you could exercise your body while asleep by simply taking a pill?

What if animals could speak your same language?

What if every country had the same access to water, fertile soil, and other natural resources?

What if there was a global currency?

What if _____ ?

What if _____ ?

What if _____ ?

What if _____ ?

What if _____ ?

What if _____ ?

What if _____ ?

Step Six: Evaluating Outcomes

The final step in thinking critically and creatively is to apply the solutions you've devised and to evaluate how the solutions work. This step is essential to make sure it is the best fit for the problem at hand. In short, to evaluate your outcome, ask whether your solution, in any given circumstance, solves the problem. You can also evaluate your results by asking questions such as:

- Did it bring about the expected results?
- Was it efficient and timely?
- Can the solution be copied and applied again and again?
- Did it cause other problems you hadn't considered?
- Did it make the best use of your resources?
- Can you use it to address other problems?

To deepen your understanding, don't forget to ask why a solution works or fails to work, which brings you full circle. It is especially important to ask why a solution doesn't work so that you can learn from such failures.

Leaders are put on the spot to make choices and deal with difficult situations, and they are certain to fail at times. What differentiates an ordinary leader from a great leader is the ability to evaluate solutions that fall short of expectations, and devise a new plan of action.

The famous scientist and mathematician, Johannes Kepler, often considered the founder of modern astronomy, made his mark by evaluating outcomes—both his and those of his fellow scientist, Copernicus.

As a student of astronomy in the late 1500s, Kepler was among the earliest subscribers to Nicholas Copernicus's theory that planets orbited the sun in a circular pattern, which as mentioned earlier in this chapter, went against the common belief at the time that the Earth was the center of the universe and the sun orbited around it. Because Copernicus's theory was still unpopular, Kepler's support of it damaged his own reputation.

However, Kepler continued to study Copernicus's research and evaluate this scientist's results while performing his own experiments. By the time of his death in 1630, Kepler had discovered a flaw in Copernicus's conclusions. By taking years to refigure complicated calculations, Kepler discovered that planets revolved around the solar system in elliptical orbits, not circular ones like Copernicus had indicated. This discovery changed the face of Copernican thought and the world of astronomy forever.

CULTURES as leaders

CRITICAL AND CREATIVE THINKING

Certain cultures from antiquity stand out as leaders in critical and creative thinking. They are known for their observation skills, ingenuity, and in-depth analysis
of the world around them. The Mayan civilization was such a culture that led the
way with its abilities to study astronomy, create a fully developed written language,
construct complex mathematical systems, and create highly accurate calendars.
The Maya lived primarily along the Yucatan Peninsula in Mexico and flourished from
2000 B.C. to A.D. 1500, but Maya still live in the region today.

When the Spanish conquistadors came upon these people, they found sophis-
ticated agriculture and water management practices. They also discovered that
the Maya people used not just one, but several calendars to track time. One called
the long calendar recorded events in history from a zero point of August 13, 3114
B.C. Their other calendar tracked time in periods of eighteen months, each with
twenty days, along with five supplemental days. At the time, their calendar was
considered to be more accurate than the Julian calendar that was revised in 1582.

The Maya were astronomers, studying both solar and lunar
eclipses in detail. They also studied the visible planets, and took
special interest in Venus. The Maya tracked the sun's passing
overhead, referred to as zenial passages, which were unfa-
miliar to the Spanish conquistadors when they arrived
in the Mayan region. This picture is from Chichen
Itza, where a Mayan temple was constructed
with such mathematical and architectural
precision that two times a year on the
equinoxes, the sunlight overhead
appears as if a serpent is slith-
ering along the steps of
the pyramid.

ENDURING leaders

CONNECTING YESTERDAY TO TOMORROW

HENRIETTA SWAN LEAVITT (1868–1921)

Henrietta Swan Leavitt emerged as a leader in astronomy with discoveries that continue to inform astronomers today about the size and scope of the universe. She was born in Cambridge, Massachusetts and attended Oberlin College and the Society for the Collegiate Instruction of Women (now Radcliffe College).

After graduating, she suffered a serious illness that left her deaf. But this didn't stop her from pursuing her love for the sky. She signed up to volunteer at the Harvard College Observatory, and seven years later, she was hired for a mere thirty cents an hour to study photo images of stars and determine their magnitude. Leavitt was a master critical thinker, questioning all she saw in the sky and analyzing relationships between the stars. During her time at the observatory, she discovered 2,400 variable stars that go from bright to dim and become bright again. More importantly, she found a direct correlation between the time it takes for a star to fade from bright to dim, and the star's level of brightness.

Her discovery is now referred to as the period-luminosity relationship and has been used by many other astronomers, including Edwin Hubble.[11] Hubble relied on this correlation to measure distances in the universe and ultimately discovered that the universe is far larger than ever previously believed. The universe as we understand it today is forever changed by the groundbreaking work of Leavitt.

Without Kepler's commitment to evaluating the conclusions from Copernicus's work, the truth of how our planets orbit in space might not have been revealed. You might ask why this is important and what the implications of Kepler's research are today. For one thing, his research tells us that because the planets orbit in an elliptical pattern, as opposed to a circular pattern, their distance from the sun changes over the course of their orbit. As a result, the velocity in which they travel differs along the course of their orbit as the gravitational pull of the sun changes. Now, in the twenty-first century, scientists rely on this information to solve problems ranging from how to plot the most efficient routes for spaceships exploring planets in our solar system, to launching communication satellites that orbit the Earth.

Many of the brightest scientific minds spend their lives continually evaluating their own thinking. British physicist, Stephen Hawking, who just happened to be born on the 300th anniversary of Galileo's death, is known for his theories regarding black holes. Hawking, who is paralyzed from Lou Gehrig's disease, recently came forward and changed his earlier position that black holes (which occur when stars disappear into a point of infinite density) consumed all matter that was sucked into them. After years of evaluation, he now concludes that these holes eventually open up and release viable information. "I've been thinking about this problem for thirty years," he said.[10] While the physics are complex and beyond the scope of this book, the important issue is that Hawking continued his relentless pursuit to evaluate his ideas—even if it meant changing his argument after thirty years.

Think about a time when a situation turned out different from what you had expected. Some examples include: preparing for an audition, trying out for student council, working with a team on a presentation, or interviewing for a part-time job. Summarize your experience on the lines below. Now come up with four questions you could ask yourself to evaluate the outcome and then answer each of the four questions.

_____

_____

_____

_____

_____

1. _____

2. _____

3. _____

4. _____

SUMMARY

C ritical and creative thinking involves asking why problems exist, observing situations, coming up with questions, analyzing information, imagining solutions, and evaluating results. Leaders rely on these skills to work through obstacles and find new approaches to challenges they face. Pushing yourself to think deeply about the mysteries of the world will help you master this important element of leadership.

building leadership skills

FOR THE TWENTY-FIRST CENTURY

Success and Failure

ANALYZING LEADERSHIP IN ACTION

Think about two leaders who addressed, or are addressing, the same problem. Some examples include:

- Richard William Pearse and Wilbur and Orville Wright's attempts to fly.
- The U.S. and the U.S.S.R.'s race to the moon.
- Germany, the U.S., and Japan's race to build the first atomic bomb.
- Two class presidents at your school working to increase student participation in extracurricular activities.

Compare and contrast their leadership by answering the following questions:

1. How were (are) their approaches to the problem the same? How were (are) they different?
2. How did (do) the leaders demonstrate ingenuity and resourcefulness?
3. How were (are) the leaders' successes and failures directly tied to their abilities to think creatively and critically? Give concrete examples.

Leading in Your Own Life

BECOMING RESOURCEFUL

Take a moment to reflect on yourself as a blossoming young leader. You've already spent some time defining your purpose and embracing a vision. Now write down some of the obstacles you face in this leadership role (getting support for your ideas, having the courage to speak out, being elected to a certain position of leadership, creating the time to dedicate to your cause, etc.).

_____

_____

_____

_____

_____

_____

_____

_____

_____

What resources do you have to help you with your challenges? Do you have a role model or mentor? Do you know people in the community who can help you attain your leadership goals? Can you compare and contrast what others have done who've faced similar situations? What strengths do you have that you can rely on? What creative approaches can you take?

_____

_____

_____

_____

_____

_____

_____

_____

_____

Teamwork for Effective Leadership

WORKING TOGETHER TO MAKE A DIFFERENCE

Meet with your leadership team. Look at the vision statement
you and your team created in the last chapter. What obstacles
do you think you'll face as you address your chosen problem?

Now, think critically about these obstacles by answering the following questions:

1. Why are these obstacles for your leadership?

   _____

   _____

   _____

   _____

2. What observations can you make about these obstacles (are they
   perceptions that people have, are they temporary or permanent
   obstacles, do you observe others facing similar issues, etc.)?

   _____

   _____

   _____

   _____

3. Who has faced similar challenges? What approaches did they
   take that worked and that failed to work?

   _____

   _____

   _____

   _____

4. What are other approaches your team can take to accomplish
   your vision?

   _____

   _____

   _____

   _____

5. Who can help you work through these difficulties?

_____

_____

_____

_____

6. What special advantages do you have that you can rely on?

_____

_____

_____

_____

_____

7. What are three unordinary solutions you can try?

_____

_____

_____

_____

_____

CHAVEZ

César . . . fought tirelessly for farm workers' rights.

- Who has done something recently that you respect?
- What have you done lately to earn respect?

Chapter 4

BECOMING ... **Credible**

How can you earn and give respect?

tudents at a high school in Oregon didn't just talk about the
importance of respect, they acted on it. For their winter dance,
they decided it was time for a new vision of royalty, something
different from the traditional homecoming queen and king determined by good looks and popularity. Instead, the king and
queen for this event would be recognized and honored for acts of compassion and service, and for the respect they earned from their peers.

The idea took hold. The first year, a junior was crowned for helping
his single father raise his four younger siblings. Another year, a senior
was recognized for spending her time every afternoon reading to little
kids at a daycare center. When a young woman returned to school after
suffering from a severe brain injury that resulted from a ski jumping accident,
her peers acknowledged her strength and determination for learning to speak
again and navigate a wheelchair by voting her the queen. Last
year, a brother and sister were crowned for collecting old bicycles
and then revamping and distributing them to children in need.

"What's been great," one teacher said, "is that students
begin looking for examples of their peers performing acts of
compassion, kindness, and service at the beginning of the
year to decide on who they'll nominate for royalty. It's
become an important part of our school culture."

In fact, the idea gained momentum and has
morphed into a month-long celebration honoring students for acts of compassion and

service. Inspired by the *Pay It Forward Foundation,* they created a fifteen-foot-long bulletin board at the entrance of their high school to post notes whenever they experienced or delivered a random act of kindness. If a student arrived at the lunch line cashier and someone had anonymously paid for his meal, he posted a note on the *Pay It Forward* bulletin board. When a student helped an elderly man take his groceries to her car, she posted a note on the board about her own deed.

Whether on the receiving or giving end of a compassionate act, these students acknowledged the effort, showing respect for both what they'd done and had done for them throughout the month. "It's become a fabulous way to both earn and give respect," the teacher said. "They've inspired us. Now we teachers do something similar in our faculty lounge."

The beauty of this project is that students actively looked for opportunities, even in the smallest of ways, to make a difference. In the process, they developed respect for themselves and their peers.

T o be respected means that you are highly regarded, held in esteem, or appreciated. It does not necessarily mean that you will always be well liked. Being liked and being respected are two different things. You may like your friends in your math class but you might not always respect them. You may respect a world-class athlete, but if you went to school together, you might not like him or her. Many of the world's greatest leaders make difficult choices that earn them respect, not popularity contests.

Respect helps you gain trust and earn credibility. The key word is earn, and it is a process that you must continually work to develop and maintain.

How did you rate yourself on respect in chapter one? Do your peers listen to you? Are you capable of getting others to join you in a cause? How well do you motivate others? Are you a role model?

As you read through this chapter, focus on how the featured leaders succeeded in earning respect from their followers and giving it back in return.

Sir Edmund Hillary became the first man to summit Mount Everest on May 29, 1953. He gained world-wide attention and admiration for surviving the treacherous trek that had claimed so many lives and becoming the first person to step foot on the highest point on Earth. However, it was the work he did after conquering this climb that counted the most to him. In the 1960s, he returned to Nepal and dedicated his time and resources to help the Nepalese develop hospitals, schools, and clinics. He also persuaded the New Zealand government to provide funds for protecting the Himalayan environment. Sir Edmund Hillary gained respect and notoriety for his mountaineering achievements. But he was most proud of the work he did for the people of Nepal, who he'd come to cherish.[1]

In spite of all his accomplishments, Hillary was a humble man who remained steadfast to his commitment to creating a better life for the people of Nepal and preserving the beauty of the Himalayas.

Some people earn respect by serving others and remaining humble. Others earn it by persevering in the face of adversity, striving for excellence using a given talent or ability, or by challenging conventional thoughts or ideas. Who do you respect in your life? Is it your mother who works two jobs to keep the family afloat? Or your uncle who overcame alcoholism? It might be a cousin who is going to college at night and working long hours during the day, or a friend who plays the piano for five hours, seven days a week, and just won a national competition.

The following activity gives you an opportunity to reflect on the respect you have for others.

Think about someone you respect and list three specific reasons why he or she has earned your respect.

REASON 1: _____

REASON 2: _____

REASON 3: _____

> ### Keys for Leadership
>
> **HUMILITY:** To be unpretentious and humble, to lack arrogance, and remain modest in the face of great accomplishment is the mark of a great leader. You must be secure with yourself to maintain humility while leading others. If you can marry this humility with an unwavering commitment to your goals, you'll earn the respect of others.

Think about someone you do not respect and give three reasons why. Remember that respect isn't whether you like someone or not but about appreciating what he or she stands for and does.

REASON 1: _____

REASON 2: _____

REASON 3: _____

Take a moment to think about the respect you have for yourself. If you have a strong sense of self-respect, you'll be more likely to earn the respect of others. What is self-respect? It's treating yourself with dignity and honoring your character. It's about being proud of the choices you make. It's about holding onto your values and remaining true to what you believe. It requires healthy boundaries and demands that you stand up to those who don't treat you appropriately. It involves making the most of the gifts you have to give to the world.

List three reasons why you respect yourself.

REASON 1: _____

REASON 2: _____

REASON 3: _____

List three things you can do to develop a greater sense of self-respect.

1: _____

2: _____

3: _____

THE VALUE OF RESPECT

H aving both self-respect and the respect of others is like money in your leadership bank. Nothing can harm your ability to lead more than people losing respect for you. For Charles Hall, the American Arctic explorer, losing respect cost him his life.

Passion and charisma were two words often used to describe the adventuresome Hall. However, his ability to earn and maintain the respect of those working with him was a constant struggle. In 1871, Hall set sail on the USS Polaris to conquer the North Pole. It didn't take long for trouble to brew. Conflicts erupted between Hall and his crew and serious power struggles followed. Tension and dishonesty prevailed onboard. Shortly into their journey, Hall became severely ill and accused the crew of poisoning him. He died days later. The belief at the time was that he'd suffered a stroke. Miraculously, after many harrowing and near-death experiences, the rest of the crew made it back alive. After decades of intrigue, Hall's body was finally exhumed in 1968, and it was discovered that he had indeed died from arsenic poisoning at the hands of a crew that lost respect for him.[2]

It takes time to earn respect, and one mistake, if big enough, can set a leader back for years. Bernard (Bernie) Madoff, a once-admired leader in the financial industry, deceived his investors and lost their respect, the public's trust, and the ability to work in the industry ever again.

As the former chairman of the NASDAQ stock exchange, Madoff was a savvy investor and built one of the most profitable Wall Street firms, Bernard L. Madoff Investment Securities, LLC. However, he also conned millions of people into participating in one of the largest pyramid schemes in history, where he ended up losing between $10 billion and $20 billion dollars of investors' money through false investments. Arrested in 2008, Madoff pleaded guilty to eleven felonies. His clients not only lost their money, but their trust in a financial system that would allow such a calamity to occur. His dishonesty cost him respect and affected the entire industry by creating substantial public doubt. As part of his sentencing, the Securities and Exchanges Commission banned Madoff from ever working in the field again.[3]

Most leaders don't lose their lives or end up in jail when respect is lost, but they certainly lose credibility. As a result, effective leaders work hard to cultivate respect, not only for themselves, but for everyone involved with their cause.

Dorothy Height, who President Obama referred to as the godmother of the civil rights movement, was a driving force behind the civil rights move-

ment precisely because she was able to generate respect for both her efforts and the people involved with the cause. She worked side-by-side with Martin Luther King, Jr. and was often the only woman in his inner circle of leaders.

One of her most noted programs was *Wednesdays in Mississippi*, where she united black and white women from both the north and south to build interracial relations and broker mutual respect as they worked for education and healthcare reform. Getting the opposing sides to respect and understand one another was at the heart of her strategy. Ms. Height went on to serve as the president of the National Council of Negro Women for forty years. She's remembered for saying, "If the time is not ripe, we have to ripen the time."[4] How did she ripen the time? With respect.

The value of respect can be seen every day in your school. What do you think when you see a young woman who struggles with a challenging disability walk down the hall with her head held high? Or when you witness a student stand up for a coach who has been unjustly fired?

How do you feel when a classmate campaigning for student council promises to do things for your school, but when elected to office never acts on his word? Or when members from your baseball team sign contracts saying they'll stay drug and alcohol free, and then you see them drunk at a party? It's hard to regard them the same after you've lost respect.

Think about an example from your own life. Describe a time when you witnessed a leader influence the actions of others because of the respect they'd earned.

_____

_____

_____

_____

Describe a time when others lost respect for you or someone you know. What was the result?

_____

_____

_____

_____

Let's look at two examples of people, one from the past and the other from the present, to see how they earned and gave respect.

LEADERSHIP *then & now*

CYRUS THE GREAT (ca. 580–529 B.C.) and **NYDIA VELAZQUEZ** (1953–present)

As a young warrior, Cyrus knew that to be effective he could not merely rely on his royal status but needed to be credible in his own right. So he worked to be as knowledgeable and fit as possible, committing to studying, learning, and physical training. He was quoted as saying, "A true leader shuns luxury and ease, and once in power, should work harder than ever."[5] Yet, when Cyrus didn't know the best path to take when traveling over difficult terrain, he didn't try to hide it, but showed humility and asked his fellow soldiers for help.

At one point, his army faced a tough battle against the Assyrians who clearly outnumbered his men. As they advanced toward the enemy, he felt the panic sweep across his soldiers. For a moment, he worried they'd be encircled and doomed. But knowing that in crisis his men would look to him for guidance, he kept a positive attitude and exuded confidence by shouting their battle hymn. His soldiers joined in and rallied their energy to overtake the enemy.

Cyrus knew that to lead, he must also show respect for others. He openly thanked his growing troops for their loyalty. After intense battles, he made a point to honor the soldiers who did brave deeds. He also took great measures to protect those who chose to follow him, at times traveling alone at night with few provisions to ensure his men wouldn't fall into enemy hands.

His ultimate act of respect for humanity came when he and his troops finally conquered Babylon and set up their kingdom. At this point, he freed the slaves and established laws based on honor and respect, which helped his empire flourish peacefully for nearly two hundred years.

Today, you can see these same traits in action by looking at Nydia Velazquez, elected to the U.S. House of Representatives in 1992 to serve New York City's twelfth district. Ms. Velazquez was one of nine children in her family, born in Yabucoa, Puerto Rico. Her father worked in the sugarcane fields and was a political activist, taking her to rallies and showing her how to stand up and fight for what was important. She pursued her studies with vigor and became the first member of her family to earn a college degree. Like Cyrus, she pushed to learn all she could by continuing on to earn her master's degree and becoming a college professor.

With a passion to serve, she became the first Latina to join the New York City Council. Velazquez initiated Atrevete, or Dare to Go for It!, a successful Latino empowerment program, and in 1992 she was elected to Congress. In this role, she took time to listen to the needs of the Polish, Chinese, and Hispanic residents in her district. She nurtured relationships with these people and earned their trust. In turn, she has been able to enact important legislation on their behalf.

She confidently speaks out against injustices, having recently confronted a major TV station for airing anti-gay language—a bold move that illustrated her willingness to stand up and demand that all people, regardless of race, gender, or sexual orientation, be treated with respect.

Today, Velazquez spends her time fighting for the rights of others and continues to blaze trails as a role model for young women in her community.[6]

How can you lead like Cyrus the Great or Nydia Velazquez? The following section offers specific ways you can earn the respect of your peers, teachers, and community.

HOW TO EARN RESPECT

Stand Up for What You Believe

Take a stand for what's right. Speak out against what's wrong. Nothing can earn you more respect than acting on what you believe. When someone is being bullied and you step in to his or her defense, others will respect you. They may not have the courage to do the same, but deep down they'll admire you for stepping forward.

When members in your community are suffering and you organize others to help them, you'll earn respect. Plan fundraisers to benefit those whose lives have been affected by earthquakes, hurricanes, or other disasters; collect get well cards from peers to give to a student in the hospital; or, circulate a petition to your classmates to initiate a change in policy at your school. Stand up. Use your voice. Others will respect you for having the courage to fight for what is important to you.

When should you refuse to go along with the crowd? Maybe your friends want to pull a practical joke that you believe is harmful and it's up to you to say they're going too far. Or perhaps you work at a fast food restaurant and your co-workers regularly give food away to their friends that come in and visit. You, however, tell your friends that you must uphold the restaurant's policy and that they must pay for what they order. When you say no to behaviors with which you disagree, you earn respect and become a leader.

Andrei Sakharov, a leading physicist in the former Soviet Union, took a stand by saying no that not only changed his life but contributed to reshaping his country. In the 1950s, Sakharov led the team responsible for the development of the hydrogen bomb, of which he later wrote, "I was working for peace, that my work would help foster a balance of power (between nations)." [7]

Yet, when the U.S.S.R. began testing nuclear weapons in space, Sakharov took a stand. He understood the devastating effects of nuclear fallout and petitioned the government to halt the testing. On September 25, 1962, he phoned Soviet Prime Minister Nikita Khrushchev and said, "This test is pointless. It will kill people for no reason." The prime minister agreed to try and postpone the test. However, the next day, the test continued as planned.

At that moment, Sakharov realized that the ideals he worked for as a physicist and scientist—to create a world of balance where truth, freedom, and compassion could prevail—could not be attained by his work developing nuclear weapons for an authoritarian state. As a result, Sakharov abandoned his post and began speaking out for democracy throughout the U.S.S.R. He was arrested and put into exile, but his leadership fostered the next generation of revolutionaries. His efforts to persuade Khrushchev to halt nuclear tests in the late 1950s resulted in the 1963 United States/Soviet Union treaty to cease nuclear testing in outer space, the inner atmosphere, and underwater. It was clear that Sakharov earned world-wide respect when he was awarded the Nobel Peace Prize in 1975. Today, Sakharov is considered one of the inspiring leaders who started the movement that eventually crumbled the former Soviet Union.

President Kennedy signing the treaty to cease nuclear testing in 1963.

Taking a stand requires courage. You can begin to cultivate this type of courage in your life today. Where do you see injustice? Where do you see abuses of power? Where do you see potential damage and the opportunity to do something about it?

_____

_____

_____

_____

List three things that you see happening in your life with which you disagree.

1. _____

2. _____

3. _____

How can you take a stand against one of these things?

_____

_____

_____

_____

Model the Way

There are some leaders who simply give orders. There are others who share their action plan, then roll up their sleeves and get to work. The best leaders are the ones who work alongside their followers to complete the job. They model commitment, a willingness to do the work, and the way something should be done. Doing this earns them respect.

There is a story about a woman who traveled to see a great sage for suggestions on how to get her son to stop eating sugar. He asked her to return in three days. She questioned why. He replied that he still ate sugar, but he'd give it up and in three days he'd be able to answer her. He believed in modeling the way.

How can you model the way? Do you give one hundred percent on the athletic field and set a standard for your teammates? Do you show up on time and come well-prepared for meetings with your history group? Do you put in the time to memorize your lines and do your research when you're cast in the school play? By doing your best, you model excellence and earn the respect of those around you.

When have you worked alongside a leader and he or she modeled what was to be done? How did this action influence you?

_____

_____

_____

_____

Demonstrate Excellence

Some people are deemed leaders because of an exceptional skill or talent, and the public looks to them as role models. You don't have to look far to see sports figures, actors, artists, and musicians admired because of the excellence they demonstrate.

If you enjoy music and play the piano, you may have heard of the new phenomenon Lang Lang. Born in China in 1982, this rising star has become a dominant force in classical music. Winning competitions throughout Asia and Europe before coming to America, Lang Lang plays the piano with rock star appeal and, as a result, has a huge following of both young and old music lovers. Perhaps you saw him play for the opening of the 2008 Beijing Olympics or at the 2008 Grammy Awards. Known for his kinetic and emotional playing, Lang Lang demonstrates excellence both in his musicianship and ability to connect with audiences. He recently started the Lang Lang International Music Foundation to support aspiring young pianists and was included on *Time* magazine's 100 Most Influential People in the World list.[8]

Wilma Randolph, the first American female runner to win three gold medals at the Olympics, demonstrated excellence, especially due to the fact that she was confined to leg braces until age eleven after a bout of polio and scarlet fever. Her ability to overcome the odds and achieve excellence has made her a leader and role model for more than fifty years.

However, leaders who win the public's attention and admiration because of a skill or ability are then often expected to demonstrate other leadership qualities. If they fail to do so, there is usually public outcry. Think of Tiger Woods, who made decisions in his personal life that cost him his reputation, or swimmer Michael Phelps, who was pulled from advertising campaigns and banned from several competitions because of drug use.

Not all of us have extraordinary gifts and talents that catapult us into leadership roles. However, if you do, you must cultivate the other necessary attributes to maintain your leadership position.

Do you feel that people such as Tiger Woods and Michael Phelps are leaders? If so, should they be held accountable for their personal actions?

_____

_____

_____

_____

Nurture Relationships

Respect is either earned or lost depending on how you relate to others. When have you had the power to persuade your friends to do something because of the respect they have for you? On the other hand, when have you felt that no one listened to you, perhaps because they didn't respect what you had to say? Knowing how to nurture relationships and build alliances with others—whether they are your friends, your co-workers, your teachers, or managers—will not only earn you respect, but also will help you take action as a leader.

Wade Davis, the explorer-in-residence for *National Geographic*, has made a living by cultivating relationships with people from indigenous cultures across the world and then sharing their stories. From the voodoo cults of Haiti to the Inuit tribes in the Arctic regions, Davis has been able to connect with these people, earn their respect, and be treated like an insider. How does he do this? By being curious, embracing their differences, asking questions, respecting their customs, and honoring their traditions. Many of these cultures are closed and do not invite others, especially Westerners who are very different, into their lives. However, with his skill at creating personal bonds, he's been asked to join these people's inner circles and often is treated as one of their own. In fact, he's become an expert on the ancient wisdoms of these cultures and a leading advocate for preserving them. You can read more about his fascinating work in his book, *The Wayfinder: Why Ancient Wisdom Matters in the Modern World*.

Perhaps you've heard about Greg Mortenson and his fight to provide humanitarian aid and education for the poor in Pakistan. You may have even read his popular book, *Three Cups of Tea*, which refers to the Pakistani tradition of drinking three cups of tea in order to establish trust in business dealings. Creating trust and respect through making connections is just what Mortenson has done.

After his sister died from a lifelong battle with epilepsy, he climbed K2, a mountain in Pakistan, in her memory. While recovering from the climb in a nearby town, he discovered some children writing with sticks in the dirt. At that moment, Mortenson made a vow to build a school for them.

He sold his climbing gear and car for money to purchase supplies to build the school. However, the people from the community responded by saying, "We're grateful, but you didn't think this out. Before you build a school, you're going to have to build a bridge."[9] The city's bridge was in terrible disrepair; without a usable one, no child would be able to get to the school. Mortenson realized that in order to help the community, he would have to listen to their needs and address their concerns. As a result, the bridge was built while an even greater bridge of mutual respect between the Pakistanis and Mortenson was created.

Over the next two decades under Mortenson's guidance, one hundred and thirty schools were built, educating more than 58,000 children each year. At first, rallying support for his vision wasn't easy. However, he stayed committed to his belief that through education humans can begin to break down the great barriers of ignorance that separate us and lead to war, destruction, and violence. In time, he earned the respect of both American investors and many Pakistani people who together mobilized efforts to make education a possibility for many Pakistanis. Mortenson received Pakistan's highest civil award, and his book, *Three Cups of Tea*, is required reading for several levels of U.S. military personnel and is used in many schools across the U.S.

Davis and Mortenson made connections and nurtured relationships. Think about the people in your school and community who are different from you. How can you embrace these differences, be curious and ask questions, listen to others' needs, and serve as a connector in your school or local community?

One final point to think about is how being a champion of others earns you respect. You've all experienced the leader who takes all the glory and basks in the limelight after a great accomplishment. However, leaders who are humble and gracious and honor the contributions of others are often well-respected long after the glory of the accomplishment has passed.

When you are asking people to put their time and energy into a cause, the best way to reward them is by acknowledging them both privately and publicly. A thank you, a pat on the back, or even better, a public statement about their contributions goes a long way.

When Captain Sullenberger crash-landed a US Airways jet in the Hudson River in 2009, he didn't take all the credit for every passenger surviving the ordeal. Instead, he told the press that it was due to the quick actions of his crew and the early responders that everyone was safely rescued from the wreckage.[10]

When have you helped with a cause and been acknowledged by the leader? It might have been on a sports team, working on the school play, or helping in a classroom as a teacher's assistant. How did the acknowledgment affect your motivation to give your best and how will this influence you as a leader?

_____

_____

_____

_____

The abilities to embrace diversity, make connections with people, and be a champion of others helps leaders to build lasting relationships and earn respect. With respect, they can then inspire people to donate time, money, and energy to causes and mobilize much-needed resources to accomplish their visions.

Think of a leadership role you now have or could have in the near future. What relationships do you need to cultivate to be effective in this role? How will you make these connections? What can you do to acknowledge their roles in your efforts?

_____

_____

_____

_____

Be Dependable

When leaders fail to be dependable, the relationships they've nurtured are damaged and respect is lost. Being dependable means keeping your word. It involves following through on your commitments and knowing the limits of your promises. It means being committed to finding the best possible solutions, even if you don't know what these are right away.

If you show up to class every day, on time, with your work done, your teacher will be much more inclined to nominate you for leadership opportunities knowing that you are reliable. If you commit to taking home and finishing the video project that you and your group have filmed, and you bring it to school the next day fully edited and labeled as promised, your group will trust and respect you. People who keep their word are respected.

In Bhutan, King Jigme Singye Wangchuck did just this. Wangchuck, once the world's youngest monarch, made headlines when he announced his promise to voluntarily give up his throne and turn his country into a democratic state. Many doubted his sincerity. After all, what kind of leader gives up his own power in favor of the power of his people?

Some thought it was a publicity stunt designed to draw favor or increase popularity. But Wangchuck kept his promise. In the last year of his rule, he sent every household in the country a new draft of the constitution outlining his impeachment. On December 14, 2006, he graciously stepped down from the throne, leaving his son in power with an order to hold a parliamentary election for a democratic government two years later. The move startled politicians around the world. [11]

Wangchuck made a bold promise and kept his word. As a result, he was named as one of *Time* magazine's "100 People Who Shape Our World."

If you are a leader, people want to know that they can rely on you, trust you, and count on you to be there in times of distress. On December 26, 2004, disaster struck the countries of the Indian Ocean as a massive earthquake shook the area, unleashing deadly tsunamis across the region. By the end of the day, the devastation had taken the lives of more than 150,000 people while destroying the homes of millions more, making the tsunami one of the deadliest in history.

In the following weeks, amidst the devastation, Dina Astita, an assistant English teacher in Indonesia, took a stand. While she didn't have a formal leadership title, her vision and dependability made her a true leader. Ninety percent of her village was dead or missing, including her own three children. But Astita knew that the children left alive, many of whom were orphaned, were in need of protection and a place to go, so she restarted a school. Resources were scarce. Undeterred, Astita took to the demolished streets. "I asked for help wherever I could get it: the soldiers, the non-government organizations, anyone, over and over again. Sometimes my colleagues complained I pushed too hard." [12]

Determined to make a difference, Astita persuaded people to give their time and energy. She convinced an Austrian firm to donate dozens of tents and secured other donations for desks and school supplies. Within weeks, school was in session. Exactly eight hundred and one students, ranging in age from five to eighteen, attended classes each day. In a time of crisis, these children were able to depend on Astita's leadership.

When have you depended on a leader and had them fail to follow through with promises? What was the result?

_____

_____

_____

_____

On a scale of one to ten, one being low and ten high, how dependable are you? How do you think your dependability influences your ability to lead?

_____

_____

_____

_____

Hold On to the Bigger Vision

Wangchuck's and Astita's success as leaders stemmed from their ability to follow through and be dependable. It also resulted from their ability to see the big picture and hold on to the bigger vision. For Wangchuck, the big picture included his people being free to choose their leadership. For Astita, it involved the children having a safe haven during crisis.

When have you witnessed students at your school work toward a long-term goal that required patience, perseverance, and fortitude? Maybe it involved a student having to ice-skate at 5:30 a.m. every day for a chance at making the Olympic team. Or perhaps you've seen a group of your peers work for over two years and save money to join a Habitat for Humanity group building houses in Costa Rica. Or you might have witnessed your school's basketball team over the course of several years go from a losing record to having an undefeated season.

Leaders who are able to hold on to a bigger vision, especially during times of adversity, are able to make the seemingly impossible possible. Whether it is changing the fate of a nation or achieving a far-fetched goal, respect is earned.

When Beryl Markham set out to be the first pilot to successfully fly nonstop from Europe to North America, people thought she was crazy. Not only did she want to be the first to fly the route nonstop, she wanted to be the first woman to fly solo from east to west across the Atlantic, a feat that several people had died trying to do.

Markham, who grew up in Kenya, began her flying career as a bush pilot, spotting animals from the air and signaling their locations to safaris on the ground. She also delivered supplies, passengers, and mail to remote areas of Kenya. Soon, Markham became aware of long-distance piloting opportunities and set out to accomplish her goal.

Both her friends and seasoned pilots warned her against the treacherous flight. But she kept her eye on the prize. On September 4, 1936, Markham took off from Abingdon, England in her small private plane without a radio or a life vest. During the twenty-hour flight, the fuel tank vents froze and Markham was forced to crash-land at Baleine Cove in Nova Scotia. Though she fell just short of her goal, Markham claimed both titles: the first person to fly from England to North America nonstop and the first woman to cross the Atlantic solo.[13] Though adjustments had to be made to her goals mid-flight, Markham's determination earned her the role as a respected aviation pioneer. Had she listened to those who tried to keep her from attempting her dream, she may never have inspired others to follow in her footsteps.

Where in your life do you need to hold on to a bigger vision despite challenges and adversity?

_____

_____

_____

_____

_____

_____

The Pioneering Young Leader for this chapter illustrates what is possible by having an unwavering commitment to a goal regardless of the difficulty and the respect earned in the process.

PIONEERING young leaders

JESSICA WATSON

Jessica Watson, a sixteen-year-old sailor from Australia, took the lead, quite literally. Her dream was to become the youngest person ever to sail solo, nonstop, unassisted around the world.

In late 2009, Watson set sail on her voyage. She spent Christmas Eve and New Year's in the South Pacific Ocean alone on her boat and homesick. That's not all. Watson endured freezing temperatures and forty-foot swells during her journey. Critics doubted whether she'd return alive. But she proved them wrong. Two hundred and ten days after departing, she returned to the Sydney Harbor, successfully fulfilling her dream. Watson stepped foot on land and was greeted by the New South Wales Premier Kristina Keneally, along with a cheering crowd.[14]

Watson's determination is an essential trait for leaders, and a trait that has brought her respect and a strong following. Hundreds of thousands of people followed Watson's voyage and blog through the Internet. She had hosts of corporate sponsors funding her expedition and countless volunteers assisted her efforts. Her courage inspired and engaged both those near to her and those far away. With her adventurous spirit and determined outlook, she resembles others profiled in this chapter who've led by gaining credibility and earning respect.

Know When to Question Authority

Beryl Markham and Jessica Watson both challenged friends and naysayers and, as a result, made their mark on history. Great leadership depends on knowing how and when to challenge authority. It is not that you should question every rule and every person, but there will be times in your leadership that you'll need to challenge conventional thinking and look for different ways of doing things. You may see opportunities that someone who has authority over you might have missed. Having the courage to express your ideas in these situations is essential for great leadership.

When you challenge a boss or person in a leadership role, make sure that you've done your homework. If you are questioning the way things are done, be prepared to offer a better solution so that you don't come across as simply complaining. If you offer suggestions for improvement, include why your ideas might be effective and how you could implement them. It is important to take a stand when you don't agree with how things are done, but being prepared and tactfully approaching the person in charge can earn you much respect.

Failing to question authority can be costly, even deadly. Korean Air, the thirteenth largest international carrier, was plagued by a series of accidents and mishaps that spanned for over twenty years. By 1999, the carrier had seen near- ly seven hundred fifty deaths as a result.

In one of the most tragic accidents, a plane descending into Guam crashed, killing two hundred twenty-eight people. The cause: the copilot failed to warn the pilot that the plane was nearing a ridge during its descent. After lengthy investigations, it was determined that many of the accidents weren't a result of faulty planes or bad weather but the reluctance of copilots to question their captain's authority.

An important part of Korean culture is a deep respect for senior- ity. To question one in authority can be frowned upon. But to make the airline safer, a new cockpit culture was implemented where copi- lots were not only encouraged, but trained, to question their captain's decisions.[15] As a result, many lives have been saved, and the airline now flourishes.

For these pilots, learning when and how to challenge authority became a true lifesaver. Several clients who paid to climb Mount Everest in 1996 still wonder what might have happened had they challenged their leaders and questioned the decision to pursue the summit.

It was after two o'clock, the time the leaders had previously told the climbers they'd be coming down the mountain whether or not they'd reached the top. An established turnaround time was critical for getting off the face of the mountain before nightfall, when dangerous storms usually moved in. The climbers were never to question this decision to turn around.

However, for some reason, the team's leaders continued the summit pursuit—past two o'clock. Several of the clients noticed that one of the leaders seemed out of sorts. But the rule to never challenge the leader's decision had been ingrained. They continued on to the top, without questioning. After they reached the summit and began to descend, the team encountered a fierce blizzard. Darkness soon fell. A treacherous night followed as the climbers tried to make it back to their tents. Tragically, five died during the descent, two of whom were the highly trained and experienced team leaders. Journalist Jon Krakauer writes about the expedition in his book *Into Thin Air*. While many twists and turns of fate contributed to the fatal climb, one cannot help but wonder what might have happened had the clients taken the lead, questioned the authority of the expedition guides, and pushed to begin their descent at two o'clock.

Leaders must know when questioning authority will produce the desired effect and must be strategic in how they do it. Determining the right moment to challenge someone is a tricky process. You can start by taking advantage of situations where your ability to observe can be helpful to superiors. If you encounter an opportunity to voice a concern, do so with grace and humility. Offer the solution as a benefit to all, acknowledging the effort of others. Even when questioning authority, be humble, gracious, and dedicated to the well-being of those around you. You will be respected for your leadership.

Write a brief response describing how you would challenge authority in the following three scenarios.

1. *You belong to your school's community service club. Your club wants to host a hundred-mile cycling trip to raise money for breast cancer awareness. Your principal feels you are thinking too big and wants you to scale back your vision. He suggests you consider doing a 5K run on school grounds. How can you challenge your principal?*

_____

_____

_____

_____

2. *You are a class representative on your student council. The council has been raising money the past four months for a sculpture to be built on school grounds to honor a fellow student who recently died in a car accident. A carnival is planned next month to raise the additional funds needed. The president of the council wants to hire a band for the carnival and use the funds raised the past four months for the sculpture to pay for the band. She believes that the money spent will be made up with ticket sales and that having the band will make the carnival more successful and profitable. You do not believe the funds earmarked for the sculpture should be risked and used to pay the band. How can you challenge her authority?*

_____

_____

_____

_____

3. *You and four other teenagers are riding in your friend's car. It is snowing, the visibility is poor, and the roads are icy, but your friend continues to drive faster than the speed limit. You've asked him once to slow down, but he's ignoring your request. How can you confront your friend and question his judgment behind the wheel?*

_____

_____

_____

_____

ENDURING leaders

CONNECTING YESTERDAY TO TOMORROW

SIR ERNEST SHACKLETON (1874–1922)

Sir Ernest Shackleton, an Anglo-Irish explorer, wanted to be the first person to cross the Antarctic continent on foot. In early December 1914, he set out on his expedition with twenty-seven men and one stowaway who was discovered a few days after setting sail.

Though many warned the explorer about the treacherous ice floes along their path, Shackleton was not deterred. *The Endurance,* his Norwegian-made ship, was specially designed to batter through huge packs of ice. For six weeks, the ship and its crew fought through the icy waters of the Weddell Sea toward Antarctica.

In January 1915, the boat came to a slow halt at the foot of a massive floe. Shackleton and his captain decided to hold the boat for a better opportunity to slip through the ice packs. However, harsh winter gales hardened the ice pack, trapping the boat at a thirty-degree angle. Shackleton and his crew realized the grim reality: the boat would be stuck until the following spring's thaw.

To keep his crew's spirits up, Shackleton kept them focused on daily tasks. The men trained the large collection of sledding dogs brought along for the trek across Antarctica and wrote about the situation in personal diaries. Shackleton, a believer in mixing social classes, encouraged the men to engage in sports, entertainment events, and ship duties with equal responsibility. When the weather became harsher, Shackleton made sure the sailors, not the officers, got the warmest clothing.

In October 1915, nine months after becoming trapped in the floes, the pressure of the ice began to compress the ship and they were forced to abandon it. The crew was stranded on the ice floes of Antarctica eight hundred miles from the nearest

whaling station with limited supplies and only a few lifeboats. They all loaded into the tiny boats and ventured into the open sea toward a tiny sliver of land one hundred miles north called Elephant Island. After seven days on the treacherous, heaving seas, they all arrived safely on the desolate shores.

Once the men were safe, Shackleton knew he needed to go for help. Selecting five of his strongest sailors, Shackleton bid the other men farewell and left them with nothing more than a promise to return with help. He and his five-man crew gathered into one of the ragged lifeboats and began their journey back to the whaling stations of South Georgia, some eight hundred miles away.

The tiny lifeboat rose and fell in the surging waves for seventeen days. The men, exhausted and nearing starvation, were deteriorating. When they finally landed on the outskirts of South Georgia Island, the men were forced to rest for ten days before setting out across the jagged landscape. They marched nonstop for the next thirty-six hours before reaching the nearest whaling station and nearly collapsing. Under Shackleton's perseverance, they had made the treacherous journey and could now gather a team to rescue the twenty-three men left behind. How many were still alive, Shackleton did not know.

Over the next four months, Shackleton attempted four separate rescue missions, each ending unsuccessfully due to weather or ice. Finally, on August 30, 1916, Shackleton succeeded in rescuing his shipmates using a tugboat loaned by the Chilean government. As he neared the shore, the castaways ran onto the beach waving their arms. Shackleton counted them through binoculars and reportedly exclaimed through his tears, "They are all there!" After spending four hundred ninety-seven days on the ice in freezing temperatures with no supplies, Shackleton's twenty-eight men were all finally safe.[16]

Sir Ernest Shackleton's heroic expedition is one of the greatest tales of leadership against all odds. Despite hazardous obstacles, exhaustion, starvation, and perilous terrain, the explorer led his crew to safety, ensuring their trust and their respect.

SUMMARY

E arning respect and being credible are essential ingredients for leadership. To do this, stand up for what you believe and model excellence in what you do. Be dependable with both your words and actions. If you give respect to those who deserve it, hold on to your vision while maintaining humility, and have the courage to question authority when needed, you'll receive respect from those around you.

building leadership skills

FOR THE TWENTY-FIRST CENTURY

Success and Failure

ANALYZING LEADERSHIP IN ACTION

Pick two people from pop culture, one who you consider to be a strong leader and one you consider to be a weak leader. Some examples include: Angelina Jolie, Lady Gaga, Carmelo Anthony, Tiger Woods, Kathryn Bigelow, Henry Santos Jeter, Lindsey Vonn, Jennifer Lopez, Zac Efron, Derek Jeter, Shawn White, and Flo Rida.

_____

_____

If you need, research your two leaders and then answer the following questions.

1. Does the person stand up for what he/she believes to be important? Explain.

_____

_____

_____

2. Does he/she serve as a role model? Explain.

_____

_____

_____

3. Does he/she nurture positive relationships and build alliances? Explain.

_____

_____

_____

4. Is he/she dependable? Explain.

_____

_____

_____

5. Does he/she hold on to a bigger vision of what is possible? Explain.

_____

_____

_____

6. Do you respect him/her? Explain.

_____

_____

_____

7. Do you feel the two people you've chosen to consider have a responsibility to lead? Why or why not?

_____

_____

_____

Leading in Your Own Life

EARNING RESPECT

Close your eyes for several minutes and imagine yourself
as the leader you hope to become in the next three to five
years. Think specifically about what you will be doing and how it will
affect you.

Now answer the following questions from this perspective.

Who respects you?

_____

_____

_____

Why do they respect you?

_____

_____

_____

_____

How do you show them respect?

_____

_____

_____

_____

_____

How do you show your humility?

_____

_____

_____

_____

Teamwork for Effective Leadership

WORKING TOGETHER TO MAKE A DIFFERENCE

Meet with your leadership team and review your vision for dealing with your chosen school problem. Whose respect do you need to earn to execute this vision?

If you want to produce a school-wide event, you'll need to earn the respect of your peers so that they participate in your plan. You'll need the respect of the school administration if you need them to sign off on what you are doing or grant permission for your event. If you want a local newspaper to run an article about what you are doing, you'll need to impress them and earn their respect as well.

Think about the various things you'll need to do to execute your vision. Who is involved? Whose help do you need? Who do you want to participate? Whose attention are you trying to get? As you go through this process, write down how you as a team will earn the respect of those you are trying to get involved with your vision and those you are trying to influence.

MANKILLER

Wilma

. . . served as the first female Chief of the Cherokee Nation, where she significantly improved relations between the Cherokee Nation and the U.S. Federal Government.

- If you were responsible for getting others involved in an activity or club, how would you communicate your message with passion, creativity, and conviction?

- When has someone enthusiastically communicated what they do, and in turn, inspired you to get involved?

Chapter 5

BECOMING

Influential

How can you communicate your ideas?

A principal at a small urban high school understood that students involved in extracurricular activities are more likely to stay in school, graduate, and do better academically. To make this happen, he challenged his students to get as many incoming freshmen as possible to sign up for a club, team, or school activity. He offered this proposal: If ninety percent or more of the incoming students joined a club, team, or activity, the entire student body would be taken on a two-day raft trip with all expenses paid. If eighty to ninety percent of new freshmen signed up, a music festival featuring two local rock bands would be held on the first Friday in April in place of regular classes. If fifty to eighty percent of the new students signed up, all students would be admitted free of charge to a movie screening once a month at the local theater.

The proposal inspired a group of juniors to take action and meet the challenge. They developed a booklet, *Passport to Sundale High,* which featured every club, team, and organization at the school. Instead of creating a traditional brochure, each organization submitted a short, compelling description of their group, along with a vibrant photo and a URL that students could use to connect to a YouTube video clip showcasing their organization in action. They mailed the *Passport to Sundale High* to incoming students several weeks before school started.

At the orientation, booths with representatives from each club and team lined the cafeteria walls. At one booth, members of the baseball team recruited students interested in playing, managing the team, keeping stats, or announcing plays at the games. At another booth, members played a DVD with funny bloopers from students rehearsing, designing sets, hanging lights, and creating costumes for the annual school musical. The yearbook committee had several laptops at the booth where members introduced new students to the latest computer technology used to create a digital yearbook, while members from the choir performed a rap song about last year's concerts.

The students' goal: to get incoming freshmen to join in by promoting what they do in a way that generated enthusiasm and excitement.

Passport to Sundale High was a great success. The first year, eighty-two percent of incoming freshmen joined an organization. Each year the figure has steadily increased. "These students developed an amazing program that generated excitement and involvement on a level I've never seen," the principal said. "I knew they'd be creative and rise to the challenge, but I underestimated their ability to communicate what they're passionate about with such creativity and conviction."

Y ou may have amazing ideas, but if you can't express them effectively, you will struggle as a leader. Knowing how to listen to others, read people's body language, and speak with conviction are just a few skills you'll need in your tool box.

Have you ever had someone listen to you with great attention and make you feel as if what you were saying at the moment was the only thing that mattered in the world?

Maybe you know someone who is so observant that he can tell what another person is thinking by simply noting a change in the person's posture, a shift in the eyes, or a furrow in the brow.

Or perhaps you even have a friend who, when she speaks, everyone seems to listen. It might be the way she combines just the right words, how she knows the best time to say something, or her tone of voice that creates a sense of intrigue. However, it might simply be her passion for what she's saying.

Leaders who communicate passionately about what they believe attract attention and use this skill to connect with others.

You might be thinking that you aren't charismatic, you'll never be a passionate speaker, or that writing with conviction will not be your strong suit. Don't worry. You can improve your communication skills and develop your own sense of style that will dovetail with your leadership needs. But it does take awareness and know-how.

How did you rate yourself as a communicator in chapter one? Are you usually understood by others? Are you a good listener? How well do you pick up on nonverbal cues? Do you prefer writing to speaking?

Think about your friends. Do you know someone who easily brings people together with the bubbly way she communicates? Or do you have a friend who can tell exactly how you feel about something without you ever saying a word? Maybe you know a boy who doesn't talk much, but when he does you take it seriously. To connect with others, read people's emotions, and make an impact are all results of effective communication.

> ### Keys for Leadership
>
> **PASSION:** Communicating with passion brings your vision to life. To lead, infuse your ideas with enthusiasm to incite action. Bring emotion to what you are saying. The intensity and fervor you express for a cause will rally others to join in your fight.

Keep them in mind as you read through the examples of good communicators in this chapter. See what these leaders have in common and how you can develop similar skills.

We'll begin by looking at how Cyrus the Great capitalized on his ability to speak to his soldiers and comrades, and how activist Christine Stevens used these strategies over 2,000 years later to introduce legislation and become one of the foremost advocates for animals.

LEADERSHIP *then & now*

CYRUS THE GREAT (ca. 580–529 B.C.) and **CHRISTINE STEVENS** (1918–2002)

We've mentioned how Cyrus the Great spoke to his first army, inspiring them to join him on his quest. With powerful words and a confident tone, he convinced the troops of his worthiness to lead. But this was only his first communication challenge as a leader.

While in battle, Cyrus didn't have the luxury of technology to pass along orders to his growing army. Instead, he developed chains of command for communicating messages to retreat, charge ahead, or quickly move into hiding. Cyrus appointed special messengers on horseback who would approach a division of soldiers, give the message to the group's leader, and then continue on to another division. The messengers would gallop down the line passing Cyrus's orders on to each division leader as quickly and concisely as possible. Cyrus the Great won many of his battles by being able to communicate his directives so effectively to such large numbers.

Outside of battle, Cyrus was frank about communicating the challenges he and his soldiers would meet. He understood that by being dishonest or covering up news of dangers and troubles ahead, he'd put his people in harm's way and lose their trust. However, when speaking to his men about battle plans or strategic decisions, he kept his messages brief and concise. Too many words, he believed, took away the power of what he was saying and made him sound less confident.

Finally, when upset with his soldiers for their wrongdoing, Cyrus didn't yell or scream but made the effort to express his anger or frustration in a mild, tempered way. He believed that by maintaining his composure he'd come across to his followers with greater command and authority.

This quiet yet powerful and persuasive communication style can be seen in action by the twentieth century animal activist, Christine Stevens, also referred to as the mother of the animal protection movement.

Stevens founded the Animal Welfare Institute in 1951 with a mission to end inhumane treatment of animals. Today, the organization publishes books and newsletters to communicate on behalf of animals. She also created the Society for Animal Protective Legislation (SAPL) and helped pass countless laws on behalf of animals everywhere.

Her skills of persuasion were not lost on the politicians. For nearly fifty years, senators, representatives, and even presidents were aware of her influence. In a letter to Supreme Court Justice Abe Fortas, a writer admitted Stevens's strength: "Dear Abe: I surrender. Mrs. Stevens and I visited at some length yesterday on the humane slaughter bill. She is as persuasive as she is charming."[1]

Stevens's ability to listen was only strengthened by her talent for speaking. Even Dr. Jane Goodall, the famed chimpanzee researcher, recognized Stevens's influence: "Passionate, yet always reasoned, she took up one cause after another and she never gave up. Millions of animals are better off because of Christine's quiet and very effective advocacy."[2] Passionate, reasoned, quiet, and effective. These are the communication skills of a leader like Christine Stevens—the skills that gave a voice to millions of animals.

Cyrus the Great and Christine Stevens used effective communication to both inform people and call them to action. The best leaders know that communication is truly a two-way street. To be able to effectively inform and motivate, they must also be able to pick up on what others are thinking and saying by listening, observing, and noticing nonverbal cues.

Leaders such as Christine Stevens, who advocate for those without a voice, have an even greater need for these communication skills. When a group is unable to stand up against injustices done to them, leaders must rely on their own abilities to listen and observe, and then convey a vision of a better life for them and convince others to join the cause. You'll find many examples in this chapter of leaders standing up for those who cannot fight injustices on their own.

Look around your home, school, and community. What injustices do you see? Where are leaders needed to speak up on behalf of those with no voice?

EFFECTIVE LEADERS COMMUNICATE IN FOUR WAYS

Let's examine the four ways effective leaders communicate:

- Speaking
- Listening and Observing
- Understanding Nonverbal Cues
- Writing

As we discuss each of these points and share stories of leaders who excel in these areas, think about how you can fine-tune your own abilities to be a better student leader.

Speaking

What makes a speaker powerful? His or her tone? A careful choice of words? Saying enough but not too much? Direct eye contact? In fact, it's all of these things. For some, speaking powerfully comes naturally. For others, it must be practiced.

The best leaders don't impulsively say whatever is on their minds. Instead, they think first about what they'll say, how they'll say it, when they'll speak, and why they are speaking. In short, they make conscious choices about the words, the tone, the timing, and purpose of their messages. It is a lot to think about. But with practice you can learn to speak with impact. Here are a few points to remember as you develop your speaking skills.

Speak with confidence. If you get stage fright easily or find that your voice shakes when you have to speak in front of others, know that this is normal for many people. Studies have shown that many rank public speaking as one of their greatest fears. Here are some suggestions that may help you gain or maintain your confidence while speaking to others:

- *Take a deep breath.* Remembering to breathe can calm you down and help you focus on what you want to say.
- *Prepare and practice.* Know what you want to say beforehand and practice it alone in front of the mirror before you stand in front of others. Being certain of your facts and viewpoints can go a long way in building your confidence.

■ *Seek out opportunities to try your skills.* Practice talking to others whenever you can: during lunch, at social functions, or in front of the class. Consider joining a speech and debate team where you'll have opportunities to get objective feedback on your skills and progress.

Keep messages brief and clear. If you ramble, you lose your power and effectiveness as a speaker and leader. Consider the following two examples of teen leaders speaking to their fellow students about raising money for an animal rescue shelter:

LEADER ONE

"So guys, you know we need to help this place out, right? I was there this one time and I saw this puppy and he looked so sad. I was going to cry if I kept looking at him. He was one of those little white dogs, you know? They're kind of fluffy and they don't bark a lot. Actually, they kind of look like this pillow I had in my room when I was a kid. It was really big and green and super soft. I wonder what happened to that thing. Now that I think about it, I haven't seen it in a long time! Anyway, we should really help this place out 'cause it has cute dogs and stuff."

LEADER TWO

"The Happy Homes Animal Rescue Shelter needs our help. Every day, five animals are put to sleep as a result of overcrowding. That's 150 loving animals every month! If we can raise $5,000 with this fundraiser, we will have enough money to help the shelter expand. Let's work together to make sure that no animal is put to sleep just because there isn't enough room. Every animal deserves a roof over its head and a chance at a better life."

Which leader inspires you more? Why?

_____

_____

_____

_____

Audiences generally respond to shorter, concise messages that make sense and include relevant details. The first speech was too informal and included irrelevant information that could be distracting. The second message was direct, with a clear focus of attracting support for the fundraiser.

When you are asked to speak for a cause, remember to keep your message brief and focused, and don't forget to choose your words carefully.

Time the message for the greatest impact. You've probably heard the old adage "timing is everything." When it comes to getting the most out of every word, nothing could be more important. What happens when you ask a teacher about a bad grade you received when she is in a hurry to begin her next class? How effective is it to talk to your principal about having a spring dance when she's just cancelled the school carnival due to students' poor behavior? Knowing where your audience (or the person you are speaking to) is coming from before you attempt to communicate is essential to your success. To do this, ask yourself these questions:

1. What are my audience's needs at this moment?
2. Is my audience in a place, both mentally and emotionally, to best absorb my message?
3. When would be the best time for my audience to receive my message?
4. How can I make my message relevant to their immediate situation?

By answering these questions before you speak, you'll be better positioned to get the most out of your communication.

Think about a time when a challenging conversation with someone (a parent, teacher, principal, etc.) went particularly well. How did the timing of your conversation influence its effectiveness?

_____

_____

_____

_____

Use powerful words. Carefully choose your words for the greatest impact. Make your stories rich with metaphors and images that spark interest. Use words such as we, ours, us, instead of I, mine, or me, to include the listener. And don't forget words that generate positive feelings, hope, and excitement, as opposed to words that create a sense of doom and gloom.

Let's look at a simple example of a student trying to generate support for an upcoming fundraiser. Consider the following two announcements. Which one would you choose to use?

ANNOUNCEMENT 1

"The junk sale I'm doing to raise money for the shelter will be on Saturday and Sunday. Everybody should bring their stuff to sell even if it's beat up and old. Ask your mom and dad if they have anything they want to throw away. Meet me at nine in the morning to set up and make signs. The posters should be pretty big and just say something about the sale and the shelter. If you have any extra markers, bring them."

ANNOUNCEMENT 2

"Our campaign to save the animals starts on Saturday and continues through Sunday night. Since we're doing a community yard sale, talk to your parents, friends, and neighbors for donations. We need everything: old furniture, used toys, clothes, and books. This event is going to cause quite a stir, so we'll need to meet at 7:00 a.m. on Saturday in front of the school to get a jump-start. Bring neon-colored poster board, bright markers, glitter, paint, and anything else that will catch people's attention. Think big!"

In the second announcement, the speaker includes specific words such as old furniture, neon-colored poster board, and glitter to give the audience a better visual of what is being said. Because the announcement includes words such as we and our instead of I and me, it comes across as more inclusive, making it sound like a community event designed for everyone's participation as opposed to the leader's sole effort. Finally, the second version is upbeat and positive, encouraging the listeners to get involved and think big about the possibilities.

These same rules apply when you are having one-on-one conversations. If you need to speak to a teacher about an upcoming conflict, choose a time when he or she isn't rushed or distracted. Use your words wisely, remain calm and confident, and offer solutions rather than simply expounding on the problem. Teachers, managers, and those with authority will respect you for taking the initiative to communicate.

Where do you need to have a one-on-one conversation that will require good communication skills (with a teacher, a friend, a boss, your parents, etc.)? Write down what you want to say in this conversation and what skills you need to practice to be as effective as possible.

Using Spoken Language to Lead

There is a long list of famous leaders who've given eloquent speeches: Sojourner Truth, Abraham Lincoln, and Martin Luther King, Jr. quickly come to mind. One can never underestimate the power these speakers had to inspire people to action. But there are also leaders who've used spoken language in different ways for the benefit of many. One example is the Navajo American Code Talkers in World War II. The Navajo Indians living in the southwest region of the United States in the 1930s were not allowed to use their own language in the government-operated schools. However, their ability to speak their native tongue became a huge asset during the war as the Allied troops battled in the Pacific. Twenty-nine Navajo American Code Talkers developed a series of code words from their language that stood for each letter of the English alphabet. They then used code words to spell out secret messages to military leaders during battle. They also came up with words from their language to represent common military terms often used in war operations. Because these Navajo American Code Talkers could communicate messages with incredible speed and accuracy, they played a critical role in bringing World War II to an end.

Listening

For effective communication, speaking is only part of the equation. Knowing how to listen is equally important.

There are many reasons leaders need finely-tuned listening skills:

- To help accurately assess various problems at hand
- To gauge the level of commitment of their followers
- To understand why people support or fail to support their visions

- To gather invaluable feedback to determine whether their messages are being accurately heard and understood

You spend much of your time in school learning to speak and write well, yet little attention is given to listening. To improve your listening skills, try the following suggestions.

Stop and make time to listen. Commit to taking the time to be present in the conversation. Avoid distractions such as checking your cell phone or thinking about what you have to accomplish next. Give your undivided attention.

Make eye contact. Look the other person in the eye. This step helps you to do more than just hear words. It allows you the opportunity to observe what is being communicated through facial expressions and gestures. Maintaining eye contact is also a sign of respect and communicates that you are paying attention to what's being said.

Practice empathy. As you listen, try to understand the speaker's perspective. Doing this can help you better understand what you are hearing and assist you in making emotional connections to what is being said. If you treat each conversation as a chance to learn more about the other person, you'll be in a much greater position to lead.

Ask questions. True listening often results in new questions being generated. So listen carefully, be curious, and ask questions, even if they're simply rephrasing what was just heard to ensure that you understood it correctly.

Using Listening Skills to Lead

For Dr. Heini Hediger, known as the father of zoo biology, effective listening and observation were instrumental as he led the way for new thinking about the designs and structures for wild animals held in captivity. After years of listening to animal experts and observing how animals interact and inhabit various spaces, he began publishing his ideas about how these animals should be kept in human care. He coined this study zoo biology. He believed animals living outside of their natural element should not be regarded as captives, but as owners of their own property or territory.[4] As a result, he set out to help people create such dwellings in zoos and national parks that simulated this idea of an animal's own property.

Hediger's suggestions went beyond the space itself and included how to furnish the enclosures. He emphasized that the size of the enclosure was not nearly as important as the quality of the structure and its ability to meet the animal's individual needs. By the 1950s, Hediger's design recommendations were attracting attention. His publications gave a voice to wild animals and influenced the construction of enclosures and development of new zoos. Today, Hediger's influence can be seen in hundreds of cities and in the four main objectives he set forth for all zoos, which are still regarded as the standard today: recreation, education, research, and conservation.

To lead, listen with an active mind, make eye contact, practice empathy, and commit to being curious. If you are receiving directions in class, pay attention to what's not being said. Missing information often holds the key to solving problems. If you are working with a group, listen to who's talking and who isn't. Your job as a leader is to gather ideas from everyone. If you are working on a part-time job, notice what frustrates your manager. Your ability to take note of such things and offer solutions will set you apart from your co-workers. Listening skills help you determine what is needed in a situation. Once this is identified, you can take action.

However, listening is a skill that goes far beyond hearing words and forming a response. As the Hediger example illustrates, listening involves observations. Observations will help you hear what is said, and what is not being said. Observations also allow you to note many of the nonverbal cues that are an integral part of communicating. We'll look more closely at how leaders make the most of nonverbal communication in the next section.

You've certainly witnessed politicians who failed to listen to voters' concerns and, as a result, were not elected or re-elected to office. Where else have you seen leaders fail to listen, and in the process, lose credibility? At home? In the classroom? On the soccer field? On the job? In a student council meeting? How could improved listening have changed the outcome?

Nonverbal Communication

Nonverbal communication involves messages without words that are relayed through facial expressions, gestures, eye contact, posture, and other body language. Leaders depend on their abilities to read nonverbal communication clues to know whether people responding to them are interested, resistant, inspired, confused, or cynical. They might look at the people they are addressing and question: are they smiling; are they leaning forward when listening; are their brows furrowed; or, are they sitting back with their arms crossed? Leaders must also be aware of the nonverbal cues they send as they communicate. The way they stand, gesture, or simply appear gives off messages about them, and hopefully these messages are in line with their leadership vision and goals.

You communicate nonverbally through many channels including:

- *Face.* Your smile, eyes, eyebrows, and forehead all work together to make expressions which communicate your feelings. A furrowed brow might indicate confusion while a smile might suggest you want to hear more. A nod may mean that you agree with what is being said. And your ability and willingness to maintain eye contact communicates a message as well.

- *Posture.* The way you sit, stand, hold your arms, and use your hands all communicates messages. A tilt of your head might indicate confusion or doubt, while uncrossing your arms and leaning your torso forward might reveal you are open to what is being communicated.

- *Gestures.* Pointing, waving, and shrugging your shoulders are basic gestures that communicate without words. A common gesture in one culture might have a different meaning in another, adding to the challenge of correctly interpreting nonverbal communication.

- *Appearance.* The way you dress, style your hair, accessorize with jewelry, etc. sends powerful nonverbal cues. As much as we all like to believe that we are open-minded and do not judge a book by its cover, how someone appears makes a strong first impression on us—an impression that many leaders work hard to use to their advantage.

How does body language affect your ability to communicate and interpret messages? Imagine this scenario: You are walking downtown with your family and a dirty young woman approaches you. Her hair is matted and tangled, and you suddenly realize that the warm, salty scent you smell comes from her. She's carrying a plastic jar stuffed with coins and dollar bills. There's a wrinkled picture of a shark sloppily taped to the jar. She immediately launches into a pitch about saving the great white sharks, which are becoming endangered due to changes in their ecosystem. While her information is compelling, you find yourself distracted by her looks and smell. When she finally walks away, you realize you hardly remember a word she said.

While it probably wasn't intentional, the woman's poor hygiene made it difficult for you to focus on her message. When obstacles like these interrupt the flow of a message, you experience interference. Interference can keep you from hearing, understanding, or caring about the messages being communicated to you.

Make sure the nonverbal cues you are sending don't interfere with your message. Instead, be clear about what your facial expressions, body language, movements, and appearance say about you so that you can persuade, motivate, and inspire others. Sometimes it is challenging to assess ourselves in these ways of communicating. Ask a trusted mentor for honest feedback.

Using Nonverbal Communication to Lead

Mastering nonverbal communication can take years. Horseman Monty Roberts has dedicated his life to it.

As a child, Monty Roberts was around horses all the time. He spent endless hours observing feral mustangs interact in the wild. It wasn't long before he began to recognize patterns in the horses' behaviors signaling affection, annoyance, fear, and many other emotions. By watching their nonverbal communication, he believed he had come to understand the language of horses.

Roberts put his new-found experience to the test when it came time for him to follow in his father's footsteps and train young horses. Appalled by the violent, cruel nature of traditional horse breaking, Roberts tried a new approach: using the nonverbal cues he'd observed in the pack of mustangs to communicate and ultimately tame a wild horse.

There were plenty of skeptics, though. Traditional methods of horse breaking had been in place for thousands of years, and few people believed his method could be as effective as what had been used for so long. But much to their surprise, Roberts accomplished just what he claimed he could do. Time and again, Roberts has proven that he can take "a wild, high-strung horse who has never before been handled and persuade that horse to accept a bridle, saddle, and rider in thirty minutes," all by understanding and communicating nonverbal cues.[5] The traditional process to tame a horse normally takes up to two weeks with the intention of breaking the horse's independent spirit.

Roberts's success has been so widespread that he was asked to train the equestrian team of Queen Elizabeth II in London. After seeing his methods in action, the queen encouraged Roberts to write a book and spread his message further.[6] Today, Roberts can be found at juvenile detention centers speaking to troubled teens, at demonstrations gentling a 1,200-pound horse, advising Fortune 500 company executives, or teaching his methods to students at his equestrian academy in Solvang, California. By mastering the intricacies of equine nonverbal communication, Roberts blossomed into a worldwide leader responsible for the humane treatment of thousands of horses and is a much sought-after speaker about the positive benefits of understanding nonverbal communication.

Though you may not be heading for a career in the stables, you can still learn from Monty Roberts. Be aware of the nonverbal messages you're sending to others and think through those you receive in return. Understanding the impact of both will help you make conscious choices in communicating, which, in turn, will bolster your ability to persuade and influence others.

Write about a time when someone's nonverbal communication did not match the words he or she was saying. What was the effect of the message?

Writing

People have been using the written word to lead for thousands of years. Writers including the Scottish economist, Adam Smith, who authored *The Wealth of Nations*; the Italian philosopher and one of the first contributors to modern political science, Niccolo Machiavelli, who wrote *The Prince;* and Charles Darwin, the English naturalist who wrote *On the Origin of Species,* influenced thinkers around the world through their use of the written word.

You may not have interest in writing a book to revolutionize the way people think, but your ability to make an impact will be enhanced if you can write well. Learning how to use words successfully can help you empower, inspire, motivate, and drive others to accomplish amazing feats. But it takes practice. Here are some basic ideas that can help bring your writing to life.

Use powerful words to evoke emotions. Your writing teachers have most likely instructed you to use powerful, active words as opposed to weak, passive ones. Nothing could be more true for leaders who communicate through writing. Consider someone composing a letter to the editor of the local newspaper, hoping to inform the public about dangerous pesticides being used in public parks and inspire them to take action. Which short excerpt impacts you more?

EXCERPT #1

. . . It is important to reconsider the ways the weeds are dealt with in our local parks. The pesticides used currently are dangerous for pets and children . . .

EXCERPT #2

. . . It's now time we demand city officials put a stop to toxic chemicals being sprayed in our parks. These dangerous pesticides not only kill weeds, they can harm our children and pets! . . .

The first excerpt asks the reader to consider and think about the problem. The second excerpt uses powerful words and phrases such as *It's now time*, *demand*, and *toxic* to create a sense of urgency and motivate the reader to take action immediately. For most leaders, time is vital. The best leaders convey this by keeping their writing concise and using the most powerful words possible.

Sharpen your skills of persuasion. Every leader must possess the ability to persuade. When it comes to writing, this task takes on a greater challenge as you typically are not present to deal with your audience's objections. To make your writing convincing and able to overcome doubts and objections, you need to present a solid case, supporting evidence, and answers to questions your readers are likely to have. Let's take a look at persuasive writing with this example of a flyer created by a student for an upcoming rally to promote literacy in developing countries. In only a few short words, the student needs to:

1. Grab the reader's attention.
2. Call the reader to action.
3. Provide reasons that encourage action.
4. Acknowledge potential objections and provide factual, compelling answers.
5. Impact the reader with a powerful statement.

Turn to the back of the book. Tear out the last page to review the flyer.

The flyer incorporates many of the communication techniques discussed in this chapter, while also being persuasive. Let's break it down into the necessary steps listed earlier.

- Engage the reader. Big, bold letters immediately attract the reader's attention. A strong fact right up front helps appeal to the reader's emotions.

- Provide convincing reasons. Hard facts from a reputable source (UNESCO) support the need for the rally.

- Call the reader to action. The simple phrase, "They need YOUR help!" in bold letters immediately grabs the reader.

- Predict obstacles and questions. The second half of the flyer is devoted to countering arguments against attending the rally. Each argument is posed in the form of a question and answered effectively, addressing objections the reader might have.

- Leave them wanting more. The final line of the flyer once again relies on large, bold letters to make a powerful statement that serves as an exclamation point for your entire message.

No one ever said writing has to be drudgery. Have fun. Make it come alive. The best leaders know how to use words in a compelling way to acquire followers, foster respect, and earn credibility. Whether it's a flyer for an event, an article for the newspaper, or a letter asking followers to support your cause, your leadership can shine through your words and generate action and support from your readers.

Using Writing to Lead

When it comes to convincing others to do the right thing, few have used words so eloquently as ecologist, Rachel Carson. Born with a natural interest in both nature and writing, Carson spent most of her childhood outside her Pennsylvania home studying the environment and writing short stories about the world around her. After college, she began to write articles and pamphlets on conservation and natural resources for the government.

After World War II, Carson's path took a dramatic turn. Concerned about the effects of chemicals on the environment that were developed during the war, Carson tried to warn people. Using her talent for the written word, Carson put passion on paper in a powerful plea for the natural world. In 1963, her controversial book *Silent Spring* was published. The book challenged the traditional views of agriculturists and demanded that humans change the arrogant way they viewed the resources of Earth. The chemical industry attacked Carson for her beliefs, singling her out as an extremist. Ignoring their warnings, Carson proceeded to testify before Congress about the need for new agricultural policies to protect both the health of humans and of the environment.

Though she died from breast cancer before seeing the fruits of her labor, Carson's work made a lasting impact. In 1970, the Environmental Protection Agency was established and took on several of the issues highlighted in Carson's writings. In 1972, directly influenced by Carson's work, the government banned the use of the harmful pesticide DDT almost entirely.[7] Today, her words live on in one of history's most influential pieces for the protection of the planet.

ENDURING leaders

CONNECTING YESTERDAY TO TOMORROW

JANE GOODALL (1934–Present)

When you were a young child, did you dream of exploring exotic places, hacking through jungles, and befriending unusual animals? If you did, you're not alone. Jane Goodall, world-renowned ethnologist, primatologist, and anthropologist, did just the same. She dreamed of visiting the jungles of Africa and learning about all sorts of animals.

As she grew, Goodall's love of animals continued to evolve. After finishing school in 1952 and traveling for the first time to Africa, Goodall met anthropologist, Louis Leakey. Leakey invited Goodall on archaeological digs and eventually hired her as an assistant. Leakey saw promise in Goodall's enthusiasm and temperament and encouraged her to research the behavior of chimpanzees. Goodall traveled to Lake Tanganyika in the Gombe Stream Reserve to do just this.

For the next twenty-five years, Goodall lived and worked among these animals. Her research led to important discoveries that changed the way the rest of the world thought about the animal kingdom. By studying the nonverbal communication of chimps, Goodall was able to categorize specific and previously unknown animal behavior patterns. Among other discoveries, Goodall witnessed chimps eating meat and making and using tools—a trait thought to be unique to humans.

Her period of observation also led to revelations in the field of animal language. By listening intently to the chimps, Goodall identified a repertoire of nearly twenty distinct sounds chimpanzees use to communicate emotions and situations.[8] Before her research, these aspects of primate life were largely unknown.

During these years of research, Goodall married, had a son, and began the process of revealing her findings to the world. Goodall utilized powerful language to write persuasive papers documenting the fascinating new claims. Beyond the factual evidence she presented, Goodall's writing also illustrated a world that was, for many, unlike anything they had ever known. She wrote about the humor, the danger, the love, and the passion her chimps demonstrated in their world. The impact of her words was felt immediately in universities around the world: She was awarded a multitude of medals for her leadership in the field and earned a Ph.D. in etiology from Cambridge University.

In the years since her time with the chimps of the Gombe River Reserve, Goodall has become an advocate speaking on behalf of animals everywhere. Her efforts have led to partnering with African governments to develop nature-friendly tourism programs that both support the economy and preserve and protect the habitats of the animals. She has made moving speeches to encourage humane treatment of animals in laboratory settings and has pushed for finding alternative methods for product testing that do not involve animals. Her dedication to spreading the word of conservation also led to the founding of the Jane Goodall Institute in 1977, dedicated to improving global understanding of apes and their habitats.[9]

Today, Jane Goodall spends her time writing about her experiences and the need for more research. She also speaks to young people all over the world about appreciating animals and continuing the cycle of knowledge.

Jane Goodall is a master communicator and has used these skills to become a global leader in her field. If you can begin to develop your communication skills today, you will be better positioned to lead no matter what line of work you pursue.

PIONEERING young leaders

SHADRACH MESHACH

The day Jane Goodall came to speak to Shadrach Meshach's class was a turning point in the young man's life. Growing up in Tanzania, Meshach had witnessed the struggles of people around him. After hearing Goodall's message, Meshach was inspired to make a difference.

For the next several years, Meshach volunteered in his community and worked with refugees. During that time, he became a member of Jane Goodall's youth program, Roots & Shoots, which aims to connect young people from around the world to solve problems of communities, the environment, and animals. Meshach took the knowledge he gained from the program back to the refugees and the communities he was helping:

"I have since learned that many Roots & Shoots participants I worked with in the Lugufu camp have returned to the Democratic Republic of Congo and are now working on R&S self-help initiatives," Meshach says. "It gives me great joy to think that my efforts have helped produce

many other volunteer leaders now facilitating R&S activities in DRC and Tanzania."[10]

Meshach's leadership didn't stop there. In 2008, he was one of one hundred young people worldwide chosen to attend the first Jane Goodall Global Youth Summit. Traveling for the first time outside of Africa, Meshach says he was finally able to see the differences between his people and the rest of the world. One startling difference he noticed was the limited opportunities for women in his native Tanzania compared to those offered to women elsewhere. When he met another Roots & Shoots member at the summit, Julia Coburn from Canada, the two began talking about the problem and promptly decided to do something about it. They formed a partnership, and the ACACIA Female Leadership Initiative was born.

The purpose of the initiative is to raise money for scholarships for young leaders and increase opportunities for young men and women to meet and exchange ideas. More than anything, Meshach says, "Our vision is to rethink and reform how leadership operates today to develop leaders that are better adapted to our extremely dynamic and interconnected world."[11]

Meshach's ability to communicate his vision paid off: In 2009, he was the recipient of the Jane Goodall Youth Leadership Award and, more importantly, his work around the world is still going strong.

SUMMARY

I n this chapter you learned how strong communication skills can enhance your leadership. When speaking and writing, it is important to use powerful words and strive for clarity. When listening and observing, give your full attention and take special note of nonverbal cues. The ability to convey your vision and receive valuable feedback depends on these critical leadership skills.

building leadership skills

FOR THE TWENTY-FIRST CENTURY

Success and Failure

ANALYZING LEADERSHIP IN ACTION

Look at your school announcements, a church bulletin, or on-line postings of upcoming events. Choose one event and create a flyer to persuade others to attend or join the cause. You can use the example included in the chapter or develop your own design. Follow the steps of persuasive writing to keep your intent clear and your message concise. When finished with your flyer present it to the class. After everyone has made their presentations, discuss if and why these flyers are more successful at communicating a message than a simple notice on a bulletin board or online posting. Finally, vote on which flyer is most influential and discuss why.

Leading in Your Own Life

COMMUNICATING WITH PASSION

Choose an issue that stirs up strong feelings for you. It can be a school, community, or global issue. Perhaps your principal changed a policy so that you no longer have an open campus and must remain on school grounds for lunch. Or maybe bike paths that you relied on to get to school have been removed to accommodate for additional car lanes. You might decide to focus on new policies states are adopting to deal with immigration issues.

Once you select your issue, develop a two- to three-minute speech or write a one-page letter to the editor to communicate your position. If necessary, do some research to find supporting facts and reasoning to help you make your case.

As you work on the assignment, ask yourself:

- Am I creating with passion and conviction?

- Am I sending a message that is clear and concise?

- Am I invoking emotion?

- Am I using powerful language that incites action?

When you are finished, deliver your speech to your classmates or post your letter to the editor for other students to read.

Teamwork for Effective Leadership

COMMUNICATING THE VISION

Get together with your leadership team. List all the people you'll need to communicate with as you execute your vision. Will you need to talk with your school principal or certain faculty members? Will you need to create posters or flyers to advertise an event? Will you be writing articles to be published in your school newspaper or sending press releases to your local newspaper?

Think through each step you will take to make your vision a reality. Next to each step, list all the communication that will need to take place. Then, look to your team. Who excels at public speaking? Who is your strongest writer? Who can create graphics on the computer? Who should attend certain meetings because of the ability to listen and process information?

Now make a communication plan.

PLANNING

What communication needs to take place as we plan to implement our vision? Who will be in charge of each of these tasks?

1. _____

2. _____

3. _____

4. _____

EXECUTION

What communication needs to take place as we execute our vision?

1. _____
   _____

2. _____
   _____

3. _____
   _____

4. _____
   _____

FOLLOW UP

What communication needs to take place as we follow up once our plan has been executed?

1. _____
   _____

2. _____
   _____

3. _____
   _____

4. _____
   _____

RIPKEN, JR.

Cal . . . never let his team down by playing 2,632 consecutive games over 17 seasons.

- What team opportunities exist in your school, neighborhood, and community?
- How can you be your best for your team?

Chapter 6

BECOMING

. . . an Effective Mobilizer

How can you direct teams that work?

When Time Warner wanted to improve its approach for giving grant money to local charities and community organizations, the company created a teen advisory board to offer guidance and fresh perspectives on where to best spend resources.

Eight teenagers from around the country came together to help Time Warner identify needs in the community and decide which organizations would receive grant money from the company. These were big challenges considering that the teens came from all walks of life, representing a wide range of interests, education levels, and cultural backgrounds. What was an important cause to one team member was not necessarily important to the others.

For Christine Mendoza, one of the eight members, it was a life-changing experience.[1] One of three children raised by a single mother on welfare, Christine had dropped out of high school for a period of time. She knew first-hand the impact these community programs have on struggling citizens. As a result, she, along with the rest of the teen board, took the responsibility of reviewing over one hundred applications and selecting twenty to receive grants from Time Warner seriously.

To be successful, the teen board had to learn to lead as a team. This meant ensuring that everyone

expressed their ideas, held each other accountable for participating and following through with commitments, and managed conflicts that came up during the decision-making process. "I realized during the meetings how important it is to be patient and listen to everyone before moving to a conclusion," said Mendoza.[2]

The experiment was a win-win for all. The teens learned how to lead as a team and weigh in on important decisions that directly affect their community, while one of the largest corporations in America gained fresh insight on issues relevant to the people it is trying to serve.

Teen advisory boards are being formed all around the country. From corporations to local governments, from marketing research institutes to teen literary journals, teams of teenagers have a voice and a chance to influence the work being done in their communities. That is power.

To lead effectively requires more than having a vision, earning respect, and communicating ideas. It involves gathering people together, uniting them behind a vision, and leading them as a team through successful ventures despite inevitable obstacles. Even the best leaders have strengths and weaknesses, but the true measure of their skills is how they recruit and interact with their teams.

Before we launch into this chapter, take a minute to review your responses regarding teamwork from the leadership assessment in the first chapter. How did you answer the following questions?

- Do you enjoy working with others?
- Do you know how to build relationships and alliances?
- Do you hold yourself and others accountable for commitments made?
- Do you solicit ideas and input from others?
- Do you feel comfortable managing group conflict?
- Do you applaud others for a job well-done?

Look at your strengths. How can you use these strengths to motivate teammates to do their best and contribute at their highest level? If you have noticeable weaknesses when it comes to teamwork, keep these in mind as you read for pointers on how you can improve these skills. If you tend to be a "lone ranger," connecting with others on a team might be difficult. If you are extremely social, being easily distracted when working with others might be an issue.

In other words, teamwork can be challenging regardless of your personality type. Yet the rewards of being able to work well with teams will be a huge asset for your leadership.

Whether you're aware of it or not, you engage in teamwork every day. Athletic teams and student council are obvious examples. What other group activities require some type of teamwork? A server at a restaurant must work with fellow waiters, cooks, and hostesses to make sure the patrons are served in a timely fashion. A group of friends must make a collective decision as to what they'll do on Saturday night. Partners playing Pictionary must work together to act out and guess the words written on the cards. These are all examples of people joining efforts as a team.

Think about school for a minute. How many of your classes involve lab work, group work, study teams, or outside study groups? If you haven't taken the chance to step up to the plate to be a valuable team member through your class work, do so now. Can you generate more ideas for the group? Can you volunteer to take notes and summarize progress? Can you encourage others to speak up with their opinions? Can you help your teacher by summarizing the findings of your team and by going further with the learning?

Reflect on the teams with which you are currently involved. List anything from your group project in art class, to the speech and debate team, to your social group participating together in an activity. Next to each example, write down one thing that works well on your team, and one thing with which the group struggles.

TEAM:_____

Something that works well . . .

_____

Something that doesn't work well . . .

_____

TEAM:_____

Something that works well . . .

_____

Something that doesn't work well . . .

_____

TEAM:_____

Something that works well . . .

_____

Something that doesn't work well . . .

_____

TEAM:_____

Something that works well . . .

_____

Something that doesn't work well . . .

_____

When people work well together, they can accomplish far more than they can on their own. The New Orleans Saints, the 2010 Super Bowl champions, are a great example of solid teamwork. There was no one single superstar on the championship team. Instead, there were many great players who together took the field by storm. By reading this chapter, you'll learn ways to become a star team player. And when it comes to leadership, you'll learn how to sharpen these teamwork skills so that you can help others become star team players.

What other teams do you notice around you beyond the obvious sports teams? Your principal, teachers, janitors, and parents all belong to a team working to make your school successful. The U.S. President, the cabinet, senators, and representatives all belong to a team to manage our country. Every time you open a Coke or Pepsi to drink, know that teams of dedicated business professionals worked together to bring their product to you. Much of what is accomplished in our world today results from teams in the business and political sectors. Let's look at examples from these fields to see how teams are effectively led by comparing our ancient leader, Cyrus the Great, with the former CEO of Xerox, Anne Mulcahy, to see how they used teamwork to achieve success.

LEADERSHIP *then & now*

CYRUS THE GREAT (ca. 580–529 B.C.) and **ANNE MULCAHY** (1952–present)

When Cyrus the Great began his quest to stop the Assyrians from overtaking Persia and Medes, his army was small. However, with each victory along the way, he folded the enemy soldiers into his own army. To keep these new soldiers from turning on him, he worked hard to build alliances with them and to make certain they felt as if they now were a part of his team. In the evenings, he'd invite soldiers of all ranks to join him in his tent for their meal. Cyrus knew the unquestionable value of having fun and relaxing with his men. He believed that as long as everyone did their duty each day, they should be celebrated and treated as equals, sharing the same fine food and wine.

To make sure that everyone on his team felt worthy, he divided his time equally among the different ranks to honor them all and minimize any feelings of superiority or inferiority. When rivalries did erupt, he quickly reminded the soldiers of their common goal and directed their anger and frustration toward their opponents who threatened to overtake them.

After a successful battle where they conquered a populated region, Cyrus needed to decide whether or not to free the prisoners. Instead of making the decision alone, he consulted his team. Together they chose to free the prisoners and allow them to resume their lives and farm their land, keeping the region prosperous under Cyrus's new rule. Cyrus believed that by sharing his power to make such decisions, he'd both increase his soldiers' loyalty and keep his own ego in check.

Most importantly, Cyrus took time to listen to his subordinates and ask for their suggestions. He understood that his soldiers would feel more appreciated and committed to his cause if they could express their opinions. And he took the time to solicit suggestions from men of all ranks, not wanting to miss out on untapped ideas. Now let's take a look at a contemporary leader using many of the same tactics.

Anne Mulcahy, former CEO of Xerox, joined the company right out of college as a sales representative. Over the years, she climbed the corporate ladder but did not feel prepared when she was appointed as the chief executive officer of the company in 2001. At that time, Xerox was in serious financial trouble with $7 billion in debt and on the verge of bankruptcy.[3] Many people thought an outside leader should have been brought in to cut certain divisions and fire unnecessary employees. But Mulcahy proved them wrong. She rolled up her sleeves and got to work. She knew she needed a bold, comprehensive plan to help her company recover, so she met with teams of employees around the world to gather their input and ensure their commitment to a unified vision. Mulcahy was known for being tough and frank. She asked her team to commit to the company and help to turn it around or look for a job elsewhere. She didn't want anyone involved who wasn't behind her one hundred percent.

Difficult choices had to be made. Divisions were closed and sales and administrative expenses were cut by thirty percent. Mulcahy always delivered the negative news herself and explained her reasoning, believing that team morale could only be kept strong if honest and transparent communication occurred.

She said her years working to turn Xerox around made her a better listener. When she met with her employees, she'd take valuable time to ask them about their families, their new babies, or sick parents. It was important to her that everyone felt like they belonged on the team and that they were recognized as human beings with lives both at work and at home. As Xerox emerged from near ruin to become a thriving company once again, she became a celebrated corporate leader, known for getting her people to pull together in one direction. In turn, she credits the company's success to the long hours and hard work delivered by her team members, acknowledging them as the true champions responsible for Xerox's success.[4]

After reading these two very different examples of leaders guiding teams, what did they do in common to be successful?

_____

_____

_____

_____

_____

Compare your response to what we believe to be the cornerstones of effective teamwork. Use these cornerstones to gauge your actions on the teams you're on now:

1. Building alliances, developing camaraderie and community.
2. Holding yourself and teammates accountable.
3. Acknowledging and rewarding good performance.
4. Managing conflict.

Mastering all four of these skills will put you in a strong position to lead and participate effectively on a team, whether you are on a sports team, in a school club, negotiating your peer group, or working at a summer job. Let's begin with the top of this list.

BUILDING ALLIANCES, DEVELOPING CAMARADERIE AND COMMUNITY

I magine it is summertime and you've been hired to help open an Apple store in your town. When you meet up with the rest of the staff to paint the store and unload the newest version of the iPhone, you notice the culture—the way they interact with one another. Which of the following two situations would make you feel most comfortable?

You arrive and meet the other workers. Immediately, you notice they seem genuinely excited to be there. You share stories, tell jokes, and brainstorm ideas. When something isn't working, you collaborate and come up with creative solutions. By the end of the day, you look around and realize how much you and your team have accomplished. Strange, but it never even felt like you were working!

You arrive and meet the other workers. Some of them are texting on their cell phones, while others are flipping through the unpacked boxes. No one stops to talk to you and you suddenly feel too self-conscious to break the silence. The day passes slowly and you find yourself constantly checking the time. You complete the required tasks, but you feel exhausted, lonely, and unappreciated—and it's only the first day!

What might be a reason for the differences in these two scenarios? If you answered a skilled and effective leader, you're right. The leader who knows how to engage people in conversation so that they get to know one another, how to get team members actively involved in problem-solving, and how to make people feel comfortable while working will be more successful at keeping team members onboard and ultimately getting the job done successfully. Read on to see how you can create this type of supportive community.

The truth is, not every situation you work in will have someone who has the time or ability to lead the group well. Sometimes, your team leader or manager might be distracted by having to do two jobs at once, he or she might be on vacation, or perhaps he or she simply lacks leadership skills. You can make a difference by acting in the most helpful ways as if you are a team leader—by supporting others, having firm boundaries around negative individuals, and by asking naysayers what their solutions are for making improvements. If you learn to do this when you don't have effective leadership on a team, you will be able to lead more effectively when you have the formal title of president of the senior class or as team leader or manager at work.

The motto of a successful team: Work hard, play hard.

Once you bring people together around a vision or goal, find ways to have fun with your teammates and encourage them to have fun as well, all while maintaining respect for the work that needs to be accomplished. There are many ways to have fun while working, ranging from an informal ice breaker at your first meeting, to planning social events after working hours, to hosting friendly competitions within your team.

An example of a quick and easy ice breaker is Two Truths and a Lie. Gather your teammates in a circle. Each person states two truths and a lie about themselves. Each group member then guesses which statement of the three is the lie. This quick activity offers a chance for people to learn a few things about each other while having a good time.

Make sure you partake in the fun as well. Make yourself accessible and be a part of the team, not just someone who stands up in front. Investing time in the beginning to get to know one another helps to build the bonds that make great teams work.

James Cameron, director of the Academy Award winning films *Titanic* and *Avatar*, is an expert team builder. He says that the bonds he has with his crew

JAMES CAMERON

while making films is certainly critical for his success, but that the rewards he reaps from working with these tight-knit teams is more satisfying than all the accolades he's received for his movies.[5]

When have you most enjoyed working on a team? What set it apart from other team experiences? How could you recreate this type of experience on other teams?

_____

_____

_____

_____

_____

Different voices offer different strengths.

Effective teams require more than the voice of a single person. Perhaps you've worked with a group where one person made all the decisions and everyone else followed along. This situation can be frustrating for the team members who might feel that their opinions don't count. It can also be a burden on the person offering up the ideas who might feel that no one else is willing to contribute. The main problem, however, is that the opportunity for any exchange of ideas is lost.

The best way to address this problem is to solicit comments and suggestions from those who tend to be quiet. If you are working on a group project in history and several of your teammates sit back and never say a word, step up to the plate. Be the leader. Ask them what they think. Invite them to share their suggestions.

If you have the chance to choose your own team, push yourself to work with people different from you. Weak leaders surround themselves with people just like themselves, but strong leaders value diverse strengths and opinions and are able to make the most of opposing views. Steve Case, who started his first business selling seeds and greeting cards to neighbors when he was only six years old and later founded the multi-billion dollar company America Online, warns against surrounding yourself with too many people who have similar ideas to yours. "You have to force yourself out of a comfort zone and try to figure out the key ingredients, the key skill-sets, and the key perspectives that are necessary [to get a job done], and then figure out a way to attract the very best people to fill those particular roles."[6]

> ## Keys for Leadership
>
> **ADAPTABILITY:** Teams are fluid and ever-changing. To lead, you must adapt to situations and work with people who bring different strengths and needs to the table. While you must keep your eyes on your vision, you need to be flexible and creative in your approach.

Think about a team with which you are currently involved and reflect on the following questions.

Who on the team offers a different perspective?

_____

_____

_____

What different ideas are you willing to share with the group?

_____

_____

_____

_____

If you could add one additional person to the team, who would it be and why?

_____

_____

_____

Recognize and bring out the unique talents of those around you.

Have you heard the saying, a team is only as strong as its weakest link? What does this mean to you? Perhaps you've been a part of a group that has had one or two less-than-helpful members that pulled the team down. Maybe they never came to meetings or didn't follow through with their part of a project. Being on a team with a weak link can be irritating, and it can prevent your success. You might even feel resentful. This is where your leadership skills need to kick into gear.

In the working world, you might be able to fire your weak links. Anne Mulcahy told those at Xerox who weren't willing to give one hundred percent to look for jobs elsewhere. But as a student, you're often assigned to a team and many times a slacker will be involved. You can complain to the teacher, or you can step up as a leader and guide the team. Ask yourself the following questions to deal with the challenging teammate in a positive, proactive way.

- What strengths could make this person a valuable asset to the team?

- How can I inspire this person to contribute rather than detract from the team?

- What types of experiences might help this person connect with the project and the other team members?

- What might be causing this person to feel alienated or uncomfortable with the group?

- How can I bring out his or her unique strengths and make the most of them?

- How can I use my influence to inspire others to participate and make a difference?

Answering these questions can help you tap into your problem-solving skills so that you and your team can work toward a solution rather than dwell on the problem. We'll spend more time dealing with conflict resolution later in the chapter. For now, let's look to how our Pioneering Young Leader built alliances and developed a strong sense of community by uniting others behind his vision.

PIONEERING young leaders

NICK GRAHAM

At seventeen years old, Truman, Minnesota resident, Nick Graham, rallied the support of community and business leaders alike. He never set out to be a community leader, or the country's youngest grocer, but when he saw the grocery store for sale in his small hometown, he simply thought it would be a neat way to make money. "It was a buyer's market and I pretty much got to name my price," he said.[7]

But Graham could also see how beneficial the enterprise would be for local citizens and the community. At the time, the nearest grocery store was fourteen miles away—too far for many of the city's aging citizens and an inconvenience for those who needed to pick up one or two items.

When Graham approached Truman Development Corporation for the $22,000 loan needed to buy the store and fix it up, he was shocked by the outpouring of support. Although he was too young to legally buy property, the group leased him the building until his eighteenth birthday. To Graham's great surprise, they were thrilled by the prospect and were determined to help out in any way. Suddenly, a team was born.

The support was instantaneous and practically infectious. "People would walk in and mop the floor," said Graham.[8] Residents got in on the action, too, helping to stock shelves and clean. Members from the investment group were among the teammates that showed up to work, something generally unheard of in the business. Because of Graham's young, pioneering spirit, these town members rallied behind him, helping him succeed with his vision.

Today, Graham's renovated store, Main Street Market, is a focal point of community involvement, activism, and teamwork in the small

city. For the residents, Graham represents a time of long-lost civility: He is well-known for making free deliveries to retirement communities, putting groceries away if needed, and remembering the names of his customers. They are grateful for his leadership and contributions to their community.

HOLDING YOURSELF AND
TEAMMATES ACCOUNTABLE

T he second rule for leading a team effectively is holding yourself and teammates accountable. What does it mean to be accountable? It means to do what you say you'll do, to follow through with your commitments, to show up for meetings on time and prepared, and to commit to working toward the goals defined by the team.

As the leader, you set the tone. If you arrive for practice or meetings late, it sends the message that you aren't wholeheartedly committed, and that the work you are doing together isn't a priority. Remember that team members often model the leader's behavior. So make sure your actions set the best example possible. If you do make a mistake, like failing to follow through with a commitment or arriving to a meeting unprepared, acknowledge it in front of the group. Apologize for not upholding the expectations the team needs to have for each other. Then, do your best not to let it happen again.

Along with holding yourself accountable, you'll need to hold other team members accountable for their participation. Doing this can be challenging, especially when your teammates are your peers. You've probably experienced the team member in science class who forgets (on a regular basis) to bring his or her share of the project to school. Or the teammate that shows up just minutes before the competition, having made the rest of the team a nervous wreck over whether or not he or she would even make it to the event. Here are some steps to help you manage this accountability issue.

- **Make sure everyone is clear about the goal the team is pursuing.** Usually a team forms to perform a task. This task can be as far-reaching as raising money to cure cancer to making a float for the homecoming parade. Keeping the team focused on the purpose of working together will help members know what's expected and stay on track.

- **Define the desired outcomes.** Early in your working process, take time to discuss the team's specific goals to help everyone be accountable. Whether it is finishing posters to advertise your event, or winning five out of the last seven games to claim the city championship, knowing what you want the end result to be can help you stay focused.

- **Define clear expectations for participation.** Create an atmosphere where the members feel comfortable and willing to participate. It helps to talk about some of the following things to set a standard for how the team will interact.

- Agree to listen to everyone's ideas.
- Commit to treating each other with respect.
- Refrain from talking negatively about one another.
- Acknowledge everyone's input.
- Agree to work through conflict.

■ **Create well-defined action steps and timeframes for completion.** Each meeting should end with every team member knowing exactly what they need to accomplish before they meet again. It doesn't hurt to go around the room and write down what each person has promised to do and when the task will be completed. Perhaps you are in a band and practicing for an upcoming performance. The group will be in a much better position if each player knows exactly what songs he or she needs to practice individually, and when they need to have the new material mastered. This process is a great way to summarize a session, ensuring that all members are in agreement before the meeting adjourns.

Let's take a moment to elaborate on how to set goals when working with a team. It helps to establish smaller goals as steps for fulfilling your ultimate vision. One way to do this is by using a system called SMART. The SMART method helps you define small, attainable steps with specific, measurable outcomes. Here's how it works:

Review your overall vision and then identify the best action to take now to help you move toward this objective. Answer the questions in the following list to fine-tune this goal:

Specific. How exactly will you achieve this goal?

Measurable. How will progress over time be measured?

Attainable. Is the goal challenging, yet reasonable?

Relevant. Will the goal move you closer to the ultimate vision?

Timely. What timeframe is needed to achieve this goal?

Let's return to the band example. Imagine you're in a band and your vision includes paid gigs at clubs and other venues in your city. The band's specific goal might then be playing for an upcoming graduation party. You can ask yourself the following questions to help your band achieve this goal:

1. *How exactly will you achieve this goal?*

   By meeting with the hosts of the graduation party to confirm the date, time, location, and expectations for the performance.

2. *How will progress over time be measured?*

   By holding weekly rehearsals for three months to ensure that all songs on the playlist are polished and ready for the show.

3. *Is the goal challenging, yet reasonable?*

   Yes, the group has performed for others but has yet to entertain a crowd for an entire evening. The goal will stretch the band. However, we are ready to take on this challenge.

4. *Will the goal move you closer to the ultimate vision?*

   Yes, it will give us practice for professional appearances, and if we do a good job, we'll have references for future bookings.

5. *What timeframe is needed to achieve this goal?*

   The graduation party is May 27th, so rehearsals must begin by February 1st. The first month will be spent reviewing songs from our playlist. The second month, we will learn one new original song and continue practicing songs from the playlist. In the third month, we will fine-tune the pieces, set an order for the playlist, and invite people to the rehearsal for their feedback.

For this band, working through this specific goal will help them develop their team efforts and prepare them for achieving their ultimate vision.

Former President, Franklin Delano Roosevelt (FDR), worked with teams in a similar manner to set and achieve goals for the United States. Following the crash of the stock market in 1929, the nation was under considerable strain to create jobs and return the country to economic stability. Knowing he needed to act quickly when he took office in 1932, FDR assembled some of the greatest minds of his time to face the challenges ahead. The group, which came to be known as The Brain Trust, was instrumental in developing the framework for what became known as The New Deal.

Together, this team had a vision: to get America back on track. To do this, they set specific goals by designing an economic plan that included rules for regulating bank and stock activity, large-scale relief efforts for people in need, and public works programs for the unemployed. After their first one hundred days in office—an important timeframe they had to work within—The Brain Trust helped FDR enact fifteen major laws, including the Banking Act of 1933, which resolved much of the banking panic.

Even as one of history's most recognized leaders, FDR knew he alone could not solve America's economic crisis. By turning to a team of diverse thinkers, he was able to fulfill his vision in a timely and creative manner. In the end, the group identified specific, measurable goals and was able to overcome the obstacles keeping the country from moving ahead.

Think about a successful team with which you've been involved and reflect on the following questions. What were the specific goals for the team? How did the members treat one another? How were expectations communicated to and understood by each member? Who assumed a role of leadership in the group? How effective was this leadership and why?

_____

_____

_____

_____

_____

_____

Learn how to confront courageously

Once the team is organized with specific goals and clear expectations, it is positioned for success. But what happens when one member of a team fails to meet these expectations? How can a leader confront this person before he or she derails the team?

The best action normally involves mustering the courage to have a conversation with the person to get things moving in the right direction as soon as possible. To begin, make sure the purpose for your communication is clear for both you and the team member you are confronting. A simple opening like, "Can we talk about the last two deadlines?" is direct but avoids attacking the person.

Consider these other tips for communicating in these types of situations:

- Always try to have the conversation face-to-face so you can maintain eye contact and read body language. Avoid confronting your teammates using email, voice mail, and text messages.
- Concentrate on hearing what is being said by the other person, even if you don't agree with him or her.
- Ask questions if you don't understand what's being said.
- Use open-ended questions to get the other person talking if necessary.
- Don't let your mind race ahead to what you want to say next. Instead, stay in the moment and listen to what the other person is saying.
- If the message is confusing, repeat what was said to confirm what you heard was correct.
- If the conversation is emotionally charged, take a breath before you respond so that you don't overreact. Don't raise your voice. Maintain a calm tone.

One last suggestion: Tough conversations can be made easier using a feedback sandwich. When you offer criticism, sandwich it between two pieces of positive feedback. For example, a head cheerleader might confront one of her teammates for not knowing the new cheers well enough by saying, "Meisha, your enthusiasm at the games is great, but it is important that you have all the cheers memorized and perfected for our squad to look its best. If we all look good, your tumbling at the end will really stand out." The head cheerleader might go on to ask, "How can we help you practice these cheers so they are really polished?"

When using the sandwich strategy, make sure your positive comments are sincere. Otherwise, the person may dismiss everything you are saying.

Write about a time when you witnessed a leader on a team have a courageous conversation. How did he or she handle it? What was the outcome? Would you have handled it the same? What might you have done differently?

_____

_____

_____

_____

_____

ACKNOWLEDGING AND REWARDING OUTSTANDING PERFORMANCE

A s mentioned earlier, motivation is an important tool for leadership. For many people, being acknowledged for a job well-done is a strong motivator. Take every opportunity to let people on your team know when they are doing well, whether it involves sharing with the yearbook staff an excellent cover design that a teammate created, or giving a high-five to your fellow player on the basketball court for scoring a free throw. Pointing out a great performance goes a long way in leadership. It helps to build respect and trust.

There's nothing worse than a leader who basks in his or her own glory and ignores the contributions of others. When LeBron James was awarded the NBA MVP in 2010, he credited his high school coaches, his mother, and his best friends. Then, he asked all of his current teammates to join him at the podium. He told the packed audience, "My name may be put on the front of the trophy, but these guys have a lot do with it."[9]

Even the famed mathematician and scientist, Isaac Newton, who worked alone for most of his career to make groundbreaking discoveries regarding motion and gravity, said, "If I have seen further, it is only by standing on the shoulders of giants."

You've all seen it: the leader who takes full credit for a team's success and blames others for a failure. Yet the leader who praises others almost always finds that his or her teammates work harder and contribute more when they feel appreciated. You can show this appreciation in many ways, including a personal thank you, a public statement, a handwritten card or an informal handshake. Some teams even conduct acknowledgement circles where one person starts out by acknowledging a positive contribution made by a team member. This member then acknowledges someone else and so on, until every teammate has both been acknowledged and has acknowledged someone else.

The bottom line: It's about giving credit where credit is due. What type of leader do you want to be? How can you acknowledge the performance of others?

MANAGING AND RESOLVING CONFLICT

onflict is inevitable. It's part of the process. The trick is to know how to effectively manage it. Let's look at why conflict arises and, if ignored, why some teams break down.

- **Conflicts of interest.** Team members can get caught up in their own goals and lose sight of the team's overall goal. Think about the soccer player who never passes the ball and instead always takes the shot.
  - How to combat: Consistently remind teammates about the overall goal and how their roles fit into the broader mission.

- **Lack of clarity about roles.** Teammates can experience conflict when their roles aren't clearly defined. Imagine a student director and assistant director of the school play tripping over one another as they work with the cast.
  - How to combat: Clarify what each member is expected to deliver for the team. Help people feel good about their roles and their contributions.

- **Power struggles.** A need to control a project or process can often cause conflict. Consider two straight-A students conducting a science lab together, each with a unique vision for approaching the problem.

  - How to combat: Encourage team members to communicate and practice being flexible with one another.

- **Personality differences.** Differences in personalities can result in conflict due to differing approaches and work styles. Have you ever worked on a group project where some students think and work methodically in a linear fashion, while others like to experiment and mix up the process?

  - How to combat: Start by understanding your own personality and working style. Take time to discuss with your team members how to accommodate people with various personalities.

Write about a time when you had to work with someone whose work style and approach differed from yours. How was the process? If there were conflicts, how did you resolve them? If not, how did your differences enhance your process?

_____

_____

_____

_____

_____

_____

The best leaders turn conflict into opportunity. The next time your team breaks down, follow these suggestions.

1. Stay calm. Take a deep breath. Refrain from raising your voice.

2. Restore order by taking a group timeout. If needed, have the parties involved take a walk or get some fresh air.

3. Hear stories from both sides of the argument.

4. Listen carefully. Make eye contact and don't interrupt. Make sure everyone feels like they are being heard.

5. Ask the people involved, "How might we resolve this?" This moves the discussion from problem mode to solution mode.

6. Agree on a solution. Ask team members, "Will this work for you?" This step is an essential move from conflict to resolution.

7. Test the solution to see if it works for the group.

8. If necessary, agree to disagree for the time being. By temporarily tabling the discussion, other solutions might emerge.

Successful business leaders must be adept at managing conflict ranging from disputes between employees, conflicts between divisions within the company, and large-scale conflicts between the company and the consumers it serves. When conflicts arise, decisive action must be taken to protect employees, consumers, and the company's reputation.

In 1982, Johnson & Johnson faced a serious crisis when several deaths were linked to one of its top-performing products, Extra-Strength Tylenol capsules. Conflict over how to manage the crisis ensued. However, under the guidance of well-trained leaders, Johnson & Johnson came together and took swift action that saved the company's good reputation. Business and leadership professionals now look to this example as a hallmark case study for successful leadership and crisis management.

When the deaths were first reported, Johnson & Johnson executives took action. Initially, no one knew why the deaths had occurred. Instead of waiting to find out, they quickly recalled 31 million bottles of Tylenol, costing the company approximately $100 million. The leaders directed their advertising team to come up with TV commercials and newspaper ads warning consumers not to take the capsules and to throw away any bottles they had at home.

It was soon discovered that lethal capsules were tampered with after leaving the manufacturing plants, and that someone had taken bottles of the medicine from stores, replaced the capsules with deadly cyanide poisoning, and returned them to the store shelves. Johnson & Johnson was cleared of any wrongdoing. However, the company continued to respond to the crisis in solution-oriented ways.

The leaders called on their marketing team to suspend all regular product advertising and replace it with messages explaining how they would exchange consumers' capsules for tablets not vulnerable to tampering. Their communications team sent direct messages to doctors, hospitals, pharmacies, and distributors to clarify the situation and outline actions being taken. They then instructed their design team to create tamper-proof packaging to better protect consumers.

By managing its teams effectively and keeping the communication channels open, Johnson & Johnson was able to take corrective actions despite enormous costs to the company. Johnson & Johnson demonstrated genuine concern for its consumers and made a positive impact that helped the company weather the crisis.[10]

In the business world, teamwork is essential for getting the job done. However, for some cultures, teamwork is at the heart of their survival.

CULTURAL SURVIVAL THROUGH TEAMWORK

Y ou've read numerous examples in this chapter of how teams work and how leaders use them to make businesses and organizations successful. But for the Maasai tribe in Africa, teamwork is essential for their very survival. The Maasai (also spelled Masai) are a nomadic people who roam the land of Kenya. Their wealth is determined by the number of cattle they own, and they are considered by some to be the most mentally tough warriors on the planet. Much of this toughness stems from the bonds they form as a tribal team.

The Maasai practice communal living where they set up temporary camps, called enkangitie, that consist of huts for the people and corrals for the cattle. This sense of living together and protecting one another creates a team-like bond and is rooted deeply in their traditions and practices.

The tribe is also organized in a way that fosters a sense of team unity, especially for the males. Males ranging in age from fifteen to thirty are gathered together and initiated as warriors who then become the team responsible for protecting the people and their herds of cattle. During the initiation process, the young men bond as they endure pain and suffering. For example, the young men share the experience of circumcision without any anesthetic as a way to develop their mental toughness.

During these first fifteen years, the young men remain solely focused as warriors and are not allowed to marry. They don't live with their families in the huts but remain on the periphery of the site to protect the tribe and cattle. These young men then continue to move through the tribal ranks as a team in fifteen-year cycles. During the next fifteen-year interval, they become senior warriors where they are allowed to live with the rest of the Maasai tribe and marry. The following fifteen-year cycle elevates the men to junior elders, and after that they progress to senior elders, making decisions for the tribe.

Their bonds as tribal men are created during initiation and continue to cement as they pass through the various stages in their lives.

The Maasai have a rich oral history and their stories are passed down from the elders to the children. Today they face the pressures of modern society pulling them from their rich traditions. However, part of the reason they've been able to survive and maintain their culture to any extent is because of their tightly woven ability to work and live together as a team.

As you can see, teamwork can take many different forms, and teams appear in a variety of situations, from sports and social clubs to businesses and entire cultures. Teams are not strictly defined, and the best ones include a variety of people with different experiences, mindsets, abilities, and contributions from which to draw. Your effectiveness as a leader will be determined by your ability to gather people together in different situations and guide them successfully toward fulfilling a vision. These abilities can be developed with practice. Get involved. Join teams. Practice being the star team player. Assume leadership positions. There's no substitute for experience, and you will learn the most by putting yourself out there.

ENDURING leaders

CONNECTING YESTERDAY TO TOMORROW

HENRY FORD (1863–1947)

Coming together is a beginning; keeping together is progress; working together is success.

HENRY FORD

For Henry Ford, the father of the modern automotive industry, life was a series of opportunities to experiment. Innovation was a constant motivator for the tycoon and the driving force behind his many accomplishments. At the same time, Ford knew that innovation was useless without a team to put the ideas into practice.

As a young man growing up on a farm, Ford put his engineering talents to work in the cornfields. When he was sixteen, he built his first self-propelled machine: The locomotive was essentially a tractor made with a mower's chassis powered by a homemade steam engine.

Soon after, Ford went searching for work in nearby Detroit. With his engineering skills, he was quickly hired by the Detroit Edison Company as chief engineer. His job required that he be on call twenty-four hours a day, resulting in plenty of time to experiment with new forms of locomotion in the company's labs. Eventually, Ford invented the quadricycle—a four-horsepower vehicle mounted on the chassis of a buggy with four bicycle wheels attached. Ford's best idea came shortly after: the Model T. Convinced that current automotive companies had it wrong with their creations geared toward the small upper-class, Ford created his car for the common people, proclaiming, "I will build a motor car for the great multitude."11

Sure enough, Ford's Model T was a success—but it didn't happen overnight, and it certainly didn't happen without the assistance of many dedicated teammates. Working with several close advisors, Ford devised a new system to speed up the manufacturing process as efficiently as possible while making the most out of every worker involved. The result became a globally recognized production model for the next fifty years: the assembly line.

By utilizing the strengths of each of his workers and streamlining the process, Ford realized that he could build a car quickly and cheaply—two qualities that would result in profits and help make cars accessible for the masses.

As an employer, Ford knew the benefits of motivating his staff. With the increased demand for the Model T, he knew he needed to attract the very best teammates to get the job done. Rather than paying the average industry hourly wage of $2.34, Ford enticed prospective employees with an astonishing $5 per hour—unheard of in the early 1900s. Additionally, Ford cut the standard work day from nine hours to eight, resulting in improved productivity and lower turnover rates. The money not spent on hiring and training new employees could be spent on his high-performing teams.

The new assembly line system did its job. Production time for a Model T went from 728 minutes to merely ninety-three minutes. At its peak, one Model T was produced by the team every twenty-four seconds.[12]

Ford was both a brilliant businessperson and an incredible leader. He won respect and encouraged loyalty from his teammates. His concept of the assembly line revolutionized manufacturing around the world and brought teamwork into the forefront of every major company for years to come.

SUMMARY

I n this chapter, you've learned the four keys to successful team-work: building alliances, holding yourself and your team accountable, acknowledging strong performance, and managing conflict. You've gained self-awareness as you've measured your leadership potential against other great leaders. And, you've been able to set some goals for the ways in which your team participation can be the hallmark of your leadership.

building leadership skills
FOR   THE   TWENTY-FIRST   CENTURY

Success and Failure

ANALYZING LEADERSHIP IN ACTION

Think of two teams that have worked toward achieving a similar vision where one team experienced success and the other failure. If you love sports, you might pick the Yankees' winning season in 2009 vs. their losing season in 1992. If you enjoy politics, you might think about President Barack Obama's campaign team vs. Senator John McCain's team in 2008. Or, you may select two teams you saw in either the summer or winter Olympics. Feel free to choose two teams that you've been on at school.

List the two teams you will compare and contrast:

_____

_____

Now answer the following questions:
What strengths did each of these teams demonstrate?

_____

_____

_____

What weaknesses affected these teams?

_____

_____

_____

Who emerged as leaders on these teams?

_____

_____

_____

What skills did these leaders have?

_____

_____

_____

What skills were lacking?

_____

_____

_____

How did these teams differ?

_____

_____

_____

What contributed to the success of one team?

_____

_____

_____

What led to the failure of the other team?

_____

_____

_____

What can you learn from these two teams that you can apply to teams you are involved with today?

Name one goal you have as a team leader.

What specific actions will you take to ensure that this goal happens?

Leading in Your Own Life

EMERGING AS A TEAM LEADER

Who are you as a team leader? What do you bring to the groups with which you work? Are you someone who listens well to help a team come together? Do you have a fiery spirit that motivates and incites action? To be a better team leader, what do you need to do? Do you tend to take over the group, or are you likely to let someone else assume responsibility? In the space below, answer this question as honestly as you can. Remember, we are all human, and your ability to admit your growth areas is a big step toward becoming a strong leader.

List three things you will commit to doing on the teams with which you are currently involved. These might include offering more suggestions, making an extra effort to listen to others' viewpoints, or asking someone with unique qualities to join your group.

1. _____

2. _____

3. _____

Teamwork for Effective Leadership

WORKING TOGETHER TO MAKE A DIFFERENCE

Meet with your leadership team. Now is the time to pull together the best teams possible to help you fulfill the vision you've been working on for making a difference at school.

Begin by assessing your immediate team. Answer the following questions.

What are our strengths as a team?

_____
_____
_____

What are our weaknesses?

_____
_____
_____

What do we need to do as a team to ensure we work together to achieve the best results?

_____
_____
_____
_____

Now reflect on these additional questions.

Do we need to include others on our team?

_____

_____

If so, who are they and what purpose will they serve? Perhaps we need to include a faculty member, someone from the administration, an upperclassman, etc.

_____

_____

_____

_____

_____

_____

Do we need to form additional teams to achieve smaller, more specific goals?

_____

_____

Would a group in charge of publicity, decorations, or donations be helpful?

_____

_____

Where do we see holes in our team that could be filled by others we know?

_____

_____

_____

_____

_____

_____

Do we need to include someone who can help us reach out to other students we don't know well, etc.?

_____

_____

List three actions your team is ready to take to move your vision forward.

1. _____

   _____

   _____

   _____

2. _____

   _____

   _____

   _____

3. _____

   _____

   _____

   _____

SOTOMAYOR

Sonia

. . . grew up in a South Bronx housing project and became the first Hispanic justice to serve on the U. S. Supreme Court.

- What ethical issues interest you?
- What influences your ethics and behaviors?

Chapter 7

BECOMING

. . . a Person of Integrity

How can you set an ethical standard?

tudents at Glendale High School filed into the auditorium for the much-anticipated debate forum—a favorite biannual event for many students. Three seniors came up with the idea after having a heated discussion about recently passed immigration laws. They asked, "Why not invite people who are knowledgeable about these issues to come and debate in front of us?" Their principal loved their idea and agreed to give the students money to pay panelists an honorarium for participating.

The students invited professors of psychology, theology, philosophy, and business administration to sit on a panel and debate issues raised by the students. To prepare for the forum, students researched various issues and held in-class debates during their advisory periods to become familiar with the questions they hoped to raise.

On the day of the event, students passed around a microphone and asked the experts to debate such topics as:

- Should taxpayers pay for the same medical coverage for smokers and nonsmokers alike?
- Is it ethical to control population growth by limiting the number of children a person can have?
- If students don't like to study in high school but end up going on to a public college, should taxpayers be obliged to help them get caught up and take remedial classes?

- Should wealthier nations be obliged to help other nations and governments with both humanitarian and military aid?

- Should capital punishment be allowed?

- Should nations intervene when other governments condone massive human rights abuses?

- Should students advance to the next grade level (social promotion) even if they don't meet the satisfactory requirements?

- Should people belonging to groups considered "disadvantaged" be given priority when applying for jobs?

Students came away both inspired and enlightened by the different opinions and points of view. They learned about the complexities of these contemporary ethical issues and gained insight into the challenges leaders face when making difficult decisions.

To make decisions about such complex dilemmas as these requires you to question your values. Because these issues aren't black and white, you must wrestle with what you believe to be true. You might find yourself asking, What is fair? What is reasonable? How much is enough? What is right and what is wrong? For leaders determining policies and laws, they must look to their own values and sense of ethics, as well as to the values of the people they represent, to guide them with such decisions.

In our society, most of us share the following basic values: One shouldn't lie, cheat, steal, or kill. We expect our leaders to uphold these values but you only have to read the newspaper to see how difficult this challenge can be. Every week, headlines feature stories about leaders in politics, business, and other fields falling short of these standards.

For example, in 2001, executives of the corporate giant, Enron, filed for bankruptcy. It soon became apparent that for years they had lied on the company's financial statements, hiding debts that made Enron appear to be far more profitable than it actually was. The company collapsed, and as a result of these false statements, employees and investors lost billions of dollars in what became the largest U.S. corporate bankruptcy at the time.[1]

Leaders from China's dairy industry were recently sentenced to prison for falsely representing the ingredients in the milk they sold to the public. They were charged with adding melamine, a chemical used in wood adhesives, ceiling tiles, and flame retardants, to various milk products to make them appear to have higher protein content. The toxic chemical was responsible for killing six infants and making over 300,000 others sick.[2]

Such lack of honesty in leadership is not limited to business or politics but can be witnessed in every realm of human life. Take, for instance, Marilee Jones, the former dean of admissions for the Massachusetts Institute of Technology (MIT), who claimed on her résumé to have degrees from three institutions, none from which she graduated. The very successful professional woman had felt so much pressure to stand out early in her career that she fabricated the facts.[3] Nearly thirty years later, when they were discovered not to be true, her career was brought to an abrupt end.

Perhaps you heard about the valedictorian from Ohio's Circleville High School in 2008 who plagiarized the commencement speech he gave at graduation. The young man later admitted he pulled two-thirds of his speech from a YouTube video and stated that he had been "lazy and inconsiderate in choosing the easy way out."[4] The mistake cost him the valedictorian title he had worked so hard to obtain.

Whether you become a leader of a multinational corporation or a student leader in your class, temptations will challenge your honesty and integrity. As you can see from the previous examples, how you choose to respond to such temptations, and whether or not you act according to your values, makes all the difference.

ETHICS AND INTEGRITY

T he fourteenth century German philosopher, Henrich Seuse, believed that quality of life is closely linked to your ethics in life. In other words, when you make ethically sound decisions and act with integrity, you are happier.

What exactly does it mean to act with integrity or to make ethically sound decisions? These terms are often used loosely and may mean different things to different people. Let's take a look at their definitions and establish a common understanding to guide the rest of this chapter's discussions. *Webster's II New Riverside Dictionary* offers the following definitions:

Ethics: 1. A principle of right or good conduct
2. A system of moral values
3. The branch of philosophy dealing with the rules of right conduct

Integrity: 1. Strict adherence to a standard of value or conduct
2. Personal honesty and independence
3. Soundness

In general, ethics are the what—the principles of expected conduct or moral values, while integrity is the how—the behavior that aligns, or fails to align, with the principles of expected conduct.

The question of who decides what is good conduct or standard ethical behavior is a difficult one. What is morally upright in one instance, may not be in another. Consider a teenager from the United States dressed in a miniskirt and tank top. Her outfit would not be questioned if she was shopping in a US mall. However, this same young woman's dress would be objectionable if she entered a marketplace in a Muslim country where women are expected to cover their skin in public; the standard of conduct is very different between the two countries.

Think about the ethics of war. One nation might believe that women and children off the battlefield should be spared from warfare, while another country might believe all human beings are fair game and that launching bombs into villages where civilians reside is acceptable. Wars have been won and lost by enemies having different perceptions on such ethics. Terrorists do not abide by the Geneva Conventions, nor do they wear soldiers' uniforms, making warfare today even more complicated.

Look at your own life. What you and your family might value as being acceptable behavior and ethical conduct may differ from your next door neighbor's. Perhaps your parents believe you should pay taxes on the $1,000 you earned in cash last summer for mowing lawns, while your friend's parents feel that it isn't important for him to file a tax report with the Internal Revenue Service since there is no formal record of the income.

These examples illustrate how different cultures, countries, and families can have varying ethical standards. The question then becomes: How do leaders uphold ethical standards when they vary from person to person and culture to culture?

To begin, leaders must clearly define their personal values. They need to know what they stand for, openly express these values, and then, most importantly, act in accordance to these values. The process of behaving in a way that reflects one's ethical standards is acting with integrity.

At the same time, a leader who works for a large corporation must act on behalf of the company's values and follow the rules of conduct and the laws that govern the company. The earlier example of Enron clearly illustrates leaders who failed to behave in ways that were expected of them, as well as in a manner that was legal. As a student, you are expected to uphold the values of your school and other organizations with which you're involved. Perhaps your school has an anti-bullying policy. Being a student leader, you are expected to treat all fellow students with honor and respect, and stand up to those susceptible to falling into such destructive behavior.

But let's say you are caught in the heat of the moment. You have a chance to sneak a look at the answer key for an upcoming history test; a friend offers you his homework to copy; a person is being bullied in the cafeteria just as you walk by. How do you act?

A great rule of thumb is to ask, "How would I feel if everyone could see my action right now?" If you feel good about your behavior being exposed, you're probably acting with integrity. If you feel that you'd rather have no one know what you are doing, you might want to stop and think about your choice.

For now, the most important thing you can do to ensure you are leading with integrity is to spend time reflecting on your values and what your actions say about you. Let's take a moment and review your responses to the ethics questions from the leadership assessment in chapter one.

- How honest are you with yourself and with others?
- Is it easy for you to acknowledge when you've done something wrong?
- Do you allow others to see and learn from your mistakes?
- Do you treat yourself and others with respect and dignity?
- Are you aware of how your actions affect others?
- How willing are you to do the right thing in the face of adversity?

As you move into leadership positions, it might be easy to say that you'll be honest with yourself and others, that you will make choices that are ethical, and that you will commit to taking the high road. But there will be times in life where you'll feel like you are in a pressure cooker, when acting with integrity can be challenging, to say the least.

In chapter nine, you will have several opportunities to identify and define your core values and shape leadership goals that stem from these ideas. But for now, the following activity gives you a chance to assess choices you might make if you found yourself in challenging situations.

Ethical Values: Taking a Stand

1. You sign a contract pledging you will refrain from alcohol and drugs while you are a member of the speech and debate team. You show up at a party at one of your fellow teammate's houses. The teammate's parents have purchased beer for you all to drink. Do you go along with the other teammates and drink the beer or honor your contract, even if you are the only one doing so?

2. You work at a fast-food restaurant and, in the middle of the dinner rush, you make a mistake and short-change a customer. At the end of the night you count your cash drawer and you have $20 more than the cash register printout shows you should

have. Do you put the $20 in your pocket and give your manager a perfectly balanced cash drawer, or do you explain to your manager the mistake you made and give her the extra $20?

3. You show up for your study group to prepare for tomorrow's biology final. Someone from your group purchased a copy of the final from a classmate who stole the exam from the teacher's computer. You don't ask to see the test, but your friend is giving you hints as to what to study to ace it. Do you stay and continue to study with this advantage?

4. Your teacher singles you out and praises you for work done on a recent team assignment. However, you had missed the majority of the meetings and contributed little to the end product. A teammate from another class actually deserves the credit. Do you accept the praise, knowing that your teammate won't know that you received this personal recognition, or do you explain that your teammate is actually responsible for the fine work?

5. You make over $550 from one family each year for your lawn mowing services. The law requires citizens to pay taxes on income over $500 from one source. Do you report this income to the IRS and pay taxes on it even though no one is reporting your income to the government?

6. You are scheduled to work at your part-time job at a restaurant, but you have several exams the following day and you desperately need to study. You can't find anyone to take your shift at work. You know the restaurant will be busy and, if you aren't there, short-handed. However, these exams will affect your final grades and you are worried about your transcripts for college. Do you call in sick so that you can study?

Making choices according to ethical standards is a challenge all people face throughout life and is a major step toward leadership. If you practice making decisions that reflect your core values, you will be on your way to becoming an authentic, genuine leader. Let's look at how Cyrus the Great led with integrity and how, centuries later, former U.S. Supreme Court justice, Sandra Day O'Connor, followed similar practices while serving on the nation's highest court.

LEADERSHIP *then & now*

CYRUS THE GREAT (ca. 580–529 B.C.) and **SANDRA DAY O'CONNOR** (1930–present)

Cyrus the Great understood that being a man of honor would contribute more to his legacy than all the land and riches in his kingdom. Before he set out on his first quest, his father reminded the young Cyrus that leaders must always set the highest standard, endure their share of the hard labor, and most importantly, make every effort to share the glory they receive. These words guided Cyrus through his many battles against the Assyrians.

After a particularly long, yet successful day at battle, he said to his army, "Success always calls for greater generosity—though most people, lost in the darkness of their own egos, treat it as an occasion for greater greed."[5] He then convinced his army to prepare the finest meals with the most expensive wines for their allies, and allow the allies to eat and enjoy themselves first, before they did.

When Cyrus the Great made a mistake, he was quick to admit his wrongdoing and humble himself in front of others so that they could witness his actions. After Cyrus succeeded in his quest against the Assyrians, largely because of troops his uncle lent him, he returned to visit his uncle. The uncle was angry with his nephew who, from his perspective, had taken over his troops and stolen the thunder and glory away from him. His uncle was humiliated that Cyrus had achieved great victory while he had been left behind in the background. Cyrus begged for forgiveness, acknowledging that his ego and pride had gotten the best of him. He promised never to act with such arrogance again, and deferred to his uncle as the senior partner in their efforts to make the land safe for the Persians and Medes.

Once Cyrus conquered Babylon and began ruling over the Persian Empire, he put other leaders in charge of various duties and territories throughout the land. He encouraged them to lead by example, commanding them to be a living law, as he'd witnessed his own followers learning more from his example than any written law. He also believed that by living according to these high standards, leaders could then become wise judges, serving people honestly and justly.

Today, former U.S. Supreme Court justice, Sandra Day O'Connor, is a contemporary example of a leader living according to high ethical standards, who serves honestly and justly. In fact, Justice O'Connor, who happened to be the first woman appointed to the U.S. Supreme Court, was recently honored with the Paul H. Douglas

Award for Ethics in Government for her integrity and display of ethics while serving the people of the United States from 1981 to 2006.

Justice O'Connor has been hailed for her wisdom and pragmatic thinking. During her tenure on the Supreme Court, she made difficult decisions in favor of people's privacy, the rights for people with disabilities, preserving the federal government's ability to protect the environment, forbidding the execution of children for crimes they commit, and upholding America's efforts to separate church and state.[6]

Not easily swayed, Justice O'Connor held to her values and made decisions accordingly, even if they were not popular with her fellow justices or the public at large. President Obama awarded her with the Presidential Medal of Freedom, the highest civilian honor, in 2009.

LEADING WITHOUT INTEGRITY

The example of Cyrus the Great shows how leading with integrity can enhance one's ability to mobilize followers and achieve victory. However, some of the most renowned leaders from history were incredibly successful at attracting followers, yet they failed to uphold basic ethical standards.

Think of Adolf Hitler, the Nazi German dictator who ordered the deaths of six million Jews, along with millions of gypsies, homosexuals, and disabled people. Or Idi Amin, sometimes referred to as the "Butcher of Uganda," who served as president and military dictator of Uganda from 1971–1979 and was responsible for human rights abuse and ethnic persecution that killed approximately 300,000 of his countrymen. Pol Pot, the ruler of Cambodia during the mid-to-late 1970s and head of the Khmer Rouge movement, led one of the most lethal regimes of the twentieth century. Under his leadership, approximately 1.7 million people were killed by execution, starvation, and forced labor.

These leaders were masters at using intimidation to further their causes. They united followers by stirring up fear and hatred. They preyed on their followers' vulnerabilities and inability to take a stand against them.

Were they leaders? Absolutely. These men had visions for their countries, they were strategic and masterful problem-solvers, they generated respect amongst many followers, they communicated their ideas and action plans with power and clarity, and they created successful teams. What they didn't do was act according to an ethical standard most human beings expect for great leadership.

It is interesting to note that, for centuries, doctors have pledged the Hippocratic Oath before they begin their medical practice. This oath of Greek origin bound them to make ethically sound decisions for their patients. While the Hippocratic Oath has been modified over the years, its basic intent—*to do no harm*—is still considered the ultimate ethical standard for medical professionals today.

Such an oath could be beneficial for leaders from all walks of life to consider. Of course, there are times when leaders must make decisions that cause harm on some level. If a political leader makes the decision to take his or her country to war, people will be harmed. The question then becomes: Will the benefits of such a decision outweigh the costs? The greatest leaders wrestle to make choices that serve their people while causing the least amount of damage.

But how does this relate to you making decisions that affect your life, your family, your peers, your school, and community? If you can take time to reflect and ask yourself, **"Will my actions cause harm?"** you will be on the road to ethical leadership. Once you think through the consequences your actions will create, you can decide whether the benefits of such actions will outweigh the harm. By making this process a habit, you will develop the skills to match your actions with your values and maintain integrity as a leader.

REFLECTING ON YOUR ACTIONS

Describe a time when you took action and your actions caused harm.

_____

_____

_____

How might things have happened differently if you had taken a moment to reflect before acting? What might you have done differently?

_____

_____

_____

Describe a dilemma you currently face where an action seems neces-
sary but might cause harm. Write down the benefits vs. costs of such
action. What do your instincts tell you to do?

_____

_____

_____

Great Leaders Match Their Actions to Their Values

It takes courage to act according to your values when others feel differently than you do about a situation. Imagine sitting around the lunch table and listening to your friends make fun of someone behind his or her back. This type of discussion might go against your values of treating others with respect and kindness; however, putting a stop to the conversation or walking away from the table can be challenging. And while you might not consider ending the conversation or walking away from the table a great deed, it is an action that is at the very heart of leadership.

To take action in a situation and move things in a different direction has the power to change the world. The work of Sister Helen Prejean is a perfect example.

Sister Prejean, a Roman Catholic nun, spent her early years serving the poor. In 1981, she began a pen-pal relationship with a prisoner on death row. She visited him several times and, after observing the execution process, she committed to work tirelessly to end the death penalty.

Sister Prejean believes that some "human rights are non-negotiable, even for those who commit the most heinous crimes."[7] In fact, two of these basic human rights are highlighted in the Universal Declaration of Human Rights by the United Nations. The first is the right not to be tortured, and the second is the right not to be killed. Believing in this right not to be killed is a core value for Sister Prejean, and she's based her life's work on upholding this value, becoming one of the leading opponents of the death penalty.

You may have heard of the movie adapted from her book *Dead Man Walking: An Eyewitness Account of the Death Penalty in the United States*. The book was on *The New York Times* bestseller list

and the movie adaptation, which starred Susan Sarandon and Sean Penn, won numerous Academy Awards. The story raised public awareness of the many difficult issues surrounding capital punishment and has helped lead the movement to put an end to the death penalty.

However, many people today remain strong proponents of capital punishment. Fear of criminals' repeated offenses and the need for justice are just two of the reasons citizens continue to support it. The point here isn't to make a case for or against the death penalty, but rather to illustrate the power a leader can have by taking action in support of his or her core values.

Our Enduring Leader for this chapter also illustrates this concept of aligning actions to values, helping influence the course of a nation.

ENDURING leaders
CONNECTING YESTERDAY TO TOMORROW

NELSON MANDELA (1918–present)

Peace Activist, Nobel Peace Prize Winner, and Former President of South Africa

In the 1960s, Nelson Mandela was a well-known anti-segregation activist who was imprisoned for twenty-seven years in the Republic of South Africa on charges of sabotage. But his difficult years in prison shaped the leader he was to become. In 1993, he was awarded the Nobel Peace Price for his political activism.

After he completed his prison sentence and apartheid (segregation) had been dismantled in South Africa, Mandela ran for president in the country's first multiracial election. In 1994, he won the election and became the country's first black president, having received sixty-two percent of the votes.

Mandela emerged from his years in prison with the core values of forgiveness over retribution and of unity over division. These core values shaped how he governed South Africa, affecting everything from his process of choosing who he would work with to lead his country, to his treatment of South Africa's beloved national rugby team, the all-white Springboks.

A year after Mandela was elected, South Africa was appointed to host the 1995 Rugby World Cup. Up until that point, the country's national team, the Springboks, were disliked by the majority of black South Africans, and racial tensions between blacks and whites were running high. Realizing the opportunity, Mandela knew the event had the power to unite the divided citizens of his country. He encouraged black South Africans to rally behind the Springboks, a decision that was at first unpopular. The black South Africans had viewed this as an opportunity to pay back the white South Africans by changing the name and nature of the team. But Mandela stood up to his fellow black South Africans and claimed that he believed in forgiveness over retribution. He convinced these people that supporting the Springboks as they were could create unity for their torn country. The approach worked: The Springboks narrowly beat the rival team from New Zealand—a victory that elated the downtrodden citizens and launched the national team to legendary status.[8]

When Mandela presented the trophy to the Springboks's captain, Francois Pienaar, an Afrikaner (Caucasian South African), he wore a Springboks jersey with Pienaar's number on the back. This gesture alone was seen as a monumental step toward the reconciliation between the blacks and whites of South Africa. The Springboks eventually went on to win every title possible in professional rugby, all with the dedicated support of their countrymen, regardless of race.

Nelson Mandela's ability to bring people together over a single cause resulted in the uniting of a nation. By standing up and acting decisively to create unity over division, Mandela created an invaluable opportunity for people to look past their differences and toward a brighter, stronger future as a united front.

We've seen how leaders such as Nelson Mandela and Sister Prejean act to support their core values. Now, let's reflect on the following leaders and how their actions stem from what they believe to be important.

For each of the names listed below, do a little research to find out some of the actions they've taken as leaders. Record this information along with the core values you think these actions reflect. In the last few spaces, list leaders you personally know, the actions they've taken, and the core values represented. These leaders can be contemporary or historical. They can be leaders from any walk of life. You may even want to consider leadership you've witnessed in your neighborhood, in your school hallways, or in your family.

DESMOND TUTU

Actions: _____

Core Values: _____

BELLA ABZUG

Actions: _____

Core Values: _____

MAHATMA GANDHI

Actions: _____

Core Values: _____

ELIZABETH CADY STANTON

Actions: _____

Core Values: _____

MARGARET SANGER

Actions: _____

Core Values: _____

GREAT LEADERS KNOW
HOW TO ADMIT MISTAKES

One of the key components to acting with integrity is openly admitting when something goes wrong. But doing this can be tricky, even for the best leaders. Mistakes can cause followers to lose confidence and doubt the leadership. However, if mistakes are made and people don't find out until much later, the trust between a leader and his or her followers can be damaged forever.

The following quote is from Stephen Covey, the popular personal success coach.

> "People will forgive mistakes, because mistakes are usually of the mind, or mistakes of judgment. But people will not easily forgive the mistakes of the heart, the ill intention, the bad motives, the prideful justifying, the cover-up of the first mistake."

So how can you as a leader admit to a mistake without jeopardizing your role? How can you acknowledge a wrongdoing without losing your influence as a leader? The following steps will help you handle mistakes, which are bound to happen in any leadership role.

1. Acknowledge any problem, wrongdoing, or mistake as soon as possible. The sooner you can publicly address the issue the easier it will be to salvage trust among your followers.

2. Communicate as clearly as possible what happened, why it happened, and most importantly, what you plan to do to fix the situation. Being able to express these points in a genuine manner is critical for helping your followers regain confidence in you. As mentioned in chapter five, these communication skills are a hallmark of great leadership.

3. Take action to fix the problem or remedy the situation. This is where followers look to see if you are true to your word.

4. Finally, don't be afraid to take risks. Mistakes happen. People will forgive you if you genuinely work to regain their trust. But if your mistakes keep you from reaching out, trying new things, and pursuing your vision, they will rob you of your leadership potential.

Just one month after President Obama was sworn into office, he spoke to millions of TV viewers and admitted to making a mistake in nominating Tom Daschle for the cabinet position of secretary of health and human services. It turned out that Daschle had failed to pay some of his taxes. "I've got to own up to my mistake," Obama said on NBC's *Nightly News*. "Ultimately, it's important for this administration to send a message that there aren't two sets of rules, you know, one for the prominent people and one for the ordinary folks who pay their taxes." [9]

While admitting to wrongdoing so early in his presidency was risky, not admitting to it could have meant political death. President Obama knew he had to preserve the trust Americans had placed in him. What could have been a serious fiasco for a new president ended up being an opportunity for him to drive home his message that lies and covered-up mistakes would not be the way he or members from his administration would lead in Washington.

Keys for Leadership

ACCOUNTABILITY: To be liable for your thinking, decisions, and actions is necessary for earning trust. Great leaders not only hold themselves responsible for doing the right thing, they encourage others on their team to take ownership of their actions as well. How do you hold yourself accountable to your family, your peers, and in your current leadership roles?

This process of accountability might seem okay for national political leaders, but how does it work for students in peer leadership roles? Here's Maya's story. Maya was voted captain of her volleyball team. In this role, she was responsible for keeping her teammates focused and motivated both on and off the court. As part of the team requirement, she and her fellow teammates signed a contract to keep all their grades at a C level or higher.

Just days before the playoff game that determined whether her team would advance to the state championship, Maya learned that her grades in several classes had fallen below the required C. Her coach confronted her and told her she would not be allowed to play in the upcoming game. Suddenly Maya found herself in the difficult position of admitting to her teammates that she had failing grades while struggling to maintain her leadership role on the team.

Maya's first step was to acknowledge her shortcomings to her teammates. She called a meeting in the locker room and explained that she had been placed on academic probation. Rather than making excuses or blaming her teachers, she accepted full responsibility and explained how she failed to make up the necessary work when the team was away at a tournament. She also acknowledged how she avoided going to a tutor for extra help once she knew her grades were suffering. Maya apologized to the team for letting them down and promised to do all she could to get things back on track before the championship. However, her promises were specific. She explained that she'd be at school early each morning to work with the math tutor and that she could be found in the library after school everyday until practice began at five o'clock. Maya then encouraged the other girls to learn from her mistakes. "Do what you need to do today to keep your grades up," she encouraged them. "Don't ignore things until it's too late like I did."

Maya then stayed true to her word and upheld her commitments to study and get her grades on track. When her teammates asked her to go out with them on Friday night, she declined and instead focused on her schoolwork. For the next two weeks, she showed up at practice and watched her teammates. At game time she sat on the sidelines and cheered for them.

In the end, Maya realized that these mistakes would help her lead in the future because they taught her how to own up to her responsibilities and take the appropriate actions. Both her team and coach acknowledged how she handled the situation; this in turn gave her confidence to take on other leadership roles in high school.

By being humble and admitting her mistakes and then doing all she could to rectify the situation, Maya emerged as a stronger leader than she was when she started.

GREAT LEADERS AVOID THE TRAPS OF POWER AND PRESTIGE

Avoiding the traps of power and prestige is a challenge for many leaders, especially when power, money, and fame come into the picture. You only have to look at the newspaper to find examples. Tiger Woods lost numerous endorsements and stepped down from the PGA tour after he was caught in several relationships with women outside of his marriage; Illinois Governor Rod Blagojevich was charged with corruption for soliciting bribes to fill President Barack Obama's vacated U.S. Senate seat. In just the last few years, several Major League Baseball stars, including Mark McGwire and Alex Rodriguez, have been accused of using illegal steroids to enhance their performance.

On the flip side, Canada's alpine, nordic, and freestyle skiing teams have made a commitment to staying drug-free, and they've been relatively successful at achieving high levels of excellence without doping. Educating athletes about the physical dangers of drugs, while driving home the fact that as world-class athletes they serve as role models to the next generation, has helped the teams collectively take a stand against steroid use.

Some people succumb to such trappings because they need to stay on top of their game at all costs and will do whatever it takes to maintain or increase their power. Others need to feed an increasing desire for fame, attention, or money. And some simply believe they are above the rules and lose touch with the standards that once defined them.

It is often said that hubris can be the greatest trap for leaders. So what is hubris? It is excessive self-confidence, or arrogance. It can make people lose sight of reality and feel they are untouchable. It strips them of humility.

The Greek myth of Icarus is one of the most renowned stories of hubris. According to Greek mythology, Icarus and his father were imprisoned by King Minos. To escape, his father made two pairs of wings out of wax, feathers, and reeds so that they could fly away. Before they took off, the father warned Icarus not to fly too close to the water or the wings would become dampened. He also warned Icarus not to fly too close to the sun or the wax on his wings would melt. Once they took off and were flying, Icarus soared high in the sky. Thrilled by his wings and freedom in the air, he climbed higher and higher, ignoring the warnings of his father. But soon the wax melted and Icarus tumbled into the sea below and drowned.

Much like Icarus, many leaders get caught up in the glory and prestige that often accompany leadership roles. They fly higher and higher, and eventually ignore warnings or deny what was previously important to them. It doesn't just happen to leaders in national politics or major league sports teams. It can happen to student leaders as well.

Have you had a friend move into a new role and suddenly have no time for you? You may have even felt like the glory of the role went to his or her head. Or perhaps you've been chosen for a prominent leadership position or selected for a new team. Did you experience struggles with balancing the demands of your new role and the expectations friends and others had of you before you took on the new challenge? Taking on leadership responsibilities can put you in a position where you might be rewarded with privileges and prestige, yet expected to maintain humility and the sense of character that you had before being granted the new role.

Bono, the singer from the rock-and-roll group U2, has been a champion of balancing such prestige and humility and of dealing with stardom while pursuing an earnest calling to help humanity. Today, Bono is known worldwide, not just for attaching his picture or fame to humanitarian causes, but for working tirelessly in the trenches to make the world a better place. Since 1983, he has spearheaded efforts to combat AIDS, poverty, and third-world debt. He co-founded DATA—Debt, AIDS, and Trade in Africa—to fight the destruction facing the continent of Africa.

Using his star power and his extensive knowledge of the issues, he has mobilized such leaders as former President Clinton, Microsoft founder Bill Gates, Ghanian diplomat and former Secretary General of the United Nations Kofi Annan, and the Pope to take action on these issues. Not the typical company of rock-and-roll stars. In 2005, Bono received *Time* magazine's Person of the Year award. He once said, "You can't make a movement, you grow one."[10] He has been a true leader, using his gifts and talents to nurture social movement that improves the quality of life for many living in developing countries.

Like Bono, great leaders know how to share their gifts and privileges with others, and as a result, enhance their ability to influence the world around them. Juan Pablo Romero Fuentes, our Pioneering Young Leader for this chapter, is doing just this, and positively affecting the lives of hundreds of Guatemalan children.

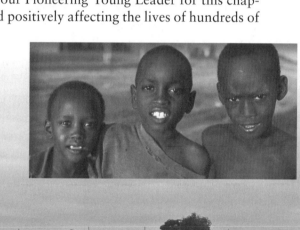

PIONEERING young leaders

JUAN PABLO ROMERO FUENTES, FOUNDER OF LOS PATAJOS

Juan Pablo Romero Fuentes grew up in the impoverished city of Jocotenango, Guatemala. In a place where drug trafficking, violence, and corruption were a part of daily life, his family's survival and safety were his main concerns.

As a young man, Fuentes got a job working for an English-speaking man. Like many others in his country, Fuentes was frustrated by the effects of globalization in his daily life: English speakers were known to come and take jobs away from natives simply because they could converse with English-speaking employers. His anger grew as Fuentes's job revealed injustices of its own. Unable to speak up for himself against the way he was being treated, Fuentes made a vow to learn English at whatever cost.

Fuentes scrubbed dishes and scraped together what money he could to pay for the education. When his teachers saw how hard he was working, they helped him get scholarships.

His dedication paid off when he graduated with a degree in psychology. Upon returning to his village, Fuentes realized the impact learning English had had on his life. Inspired to help those around him, Fuentes began the Los Patojos School out of his parents' house. Very shortly, the house was overflowing with students learning English. Fuentes gave up his own bedroom to make space, and his parents eventually donated the entire home to the cause.

Several helpful donations and more than one hundred pupils later, Fuentes's Los Patojos school is thriving. Beyond teaching English, the school specializes in creating community awareness through education, art, music, dance, and theater. Some of the newest additions to the project are a women's cooperative that teaches valuable life skills to women of the community, a kitchen which provides one thousand free lunches to children every day, and a free clinic to provide healthcare to children and their families.[11]

Fuentes's desire to communicate stemmed from adversity. He worked diligently to develop language skills to help him throughout his life. His true talent can be seen in his ability to unite and inspire those around him into action. Through his work and commitment to bring learning to others, he is giving those in his community the chance of a lifetime.

GREAT LEADERS FOLLOW
AN INTERNAL COMPASS

T o successfully lead with integrity—to match actions with values, acknowledge shortcomings, and avoid the trappings of power and prestige—requires a strong internal compass. Leaders must develop an inner life where they take time to define and reflect upon their ethical standards. Then, they must commit to honoring these standards, using them as a compass for all decision-making. This reflective process is important for great leadership, and critical for students like you who are now developing your leadership goals.

One of the greatest examples of someone developing an inner, reflective life that then guided his leadership is Victor Frankl, a Viennese neurologist, psychiatrist, and Holocaust survivor. During his years imprisoned in concentration camps, Frankl developed his theory that people's thoughts and beliefs hold the power to shape and save them when facing the cruelest of circumstances.

In his book, *Man's Search for Meaning*, he writes that it wasn't necessarily the strongest, most-fit prisoners who survived the concentration camps, but rather the ones who could go inside and find a strength of the mind and spirit, the ones who possessed faith despite the sufferings they endured, the people who could find meaning in life amidst cruelty.[12] His experiences gave him the insight that your possessions, your family, and all of your belongings can be stripped from you, but no one can take away your attitudes or manner of looking at things. It is the one thing that solely belongs to you. Released from the prison camps in 1945, Frankl went on to become a leader in the field of psychiatry, helping people from all walks of life find meaning and purpose in their lives and struggles.

It is this same strong mind and spirit that Frankl talks about that helps one endure the tests, trials, and tribulations faced on this road to leadership. Those who develop a strong inner life have the clarity and focus to stay true to what they believe. By using their own internal compass to make ethical decisions, leading with integrity becomes a habit, not something done only when easy or convenient or when others are watching.

The final chapter of this book provides opportunities for you to reflect and think deeply about your own personal values. From these values you can create an internal compass to help you effectively lead in the face of peer pressure, media influence, and other challenging situations. The work you will do here can become the building blocks of your leadership for years to come.

SUMMARY

C hapter seven discussed how you can lead with integrity by acting in ways that reflect your values. You learned about the importance of standing up for what you believe and admitting to mistakes when they happen. By developing a strong moral compass for yourself, you'll be able to set an ethical standard to guide you as a leader.

building leadership skills

FOR THE TWENTY-FIRST CENTURY

Success and Failure

ANALYZING LEADERSHIP IN ACTION

In this chapter, you read about Alex Rodriguez and Mark McGwire accused of taking steroids to enhance their athletic performance. You also read about members of the Canadian ski teams who made different choices.

Perhaps you've known a student who has labored over a speech, spending hours coming up with the exact words. On the other hand, the valedictorian you read about in this chapter took a shortcut and pulled his speech off the Internet.

Come up with an example of two people approaching a similar task. One who upheld ethical standards that you value, and one who did not.

List the two people you will compare and contrast:

_____

_____

Answer the following questions:

What was gained and what was lost by these two different sets of choices?

_____

_____

_____

What were the costs of failing to uphold a certain ethical standard?

_____

_____

_____

What do you think influenced each of your two people?

_____

_____

_____

If you were in the same situation, what would you have done?

_____

_____

_____

What would have challenged you in the situation?

_____

_____

_____

Have you ever faced a similar dilemma?

_____

_____

_____

How did you handle it?

_____

_____

_____

Would you do things differently if you were to face the same situation again?

_____

_____

_____

Leading in Your Own Life

UNDERSTANDING YOUR MORAL COMPASS

Describe the greatest moral dilemma you have personally faced.

_____

_____

_____

_____

What was at the heart of the conflict?

_____

_____

_____

_____

What values were challenged in this conflict?

_____

_____

_____

_____

What actions did you take when you faced the dilemma?

_____

_____

_____

_____

How did these actions serve you?

_____

_____

_____

_____

How did these actions fail you?

_____

_____

_____

_____

If you were to face this dilemma again, what would you do?

_____

_____

_____

_____

_____

Teamwork for Effective Leadership

WORKING TOGETHER TO MAKE A DIFFERENCE

Meet with your leadership team. As you plan to implement your team vision, what ethical challenges might you face?
Discuss the following questions with your team:

Will you be tempted or swayed by a particular group?

_____

_____

_____

Will you be inclusive of all students? If not, how will you be equitable with what you are doing?

_____

_____

_____

_____

What standards of behavior will you set for yourselves?

_____

_____

_____

_____

What standards of behavior will you expect from those participating in your efforts?

_____

_____

_____

_____

How will you uphold these standards?

_____

_____

_____

_____

_____

_____

_____

What things might happen to challenge your integrity? How can you prepare to meet these challenges?

_____

_____

_____

_____

_____

_____

JOBS

Steve

. . . worked alongside his peers to launch Apple, Inc in 1976, which has become one of the most admired companies in the world.

- What makes peer mentorship powerful?
- How can you be a peer mentor?

Chapter 8

BECOMING
...a Peer Mentor

*How can you practice
your leadership skills today?*

S In the 1980s and 1990s in Salt Lake City, gang activity was on the rise. No one wanted to admit it. But Duane Bourdeaux witnessed the effects first-hand. While employed by the Department of Corrections, he saw floods of talented young men sentenced to prison because of the poor choices they made.

He asked himself, *What if I was able to help some of these kids before they join gangs and land in prison?*

Bourdeaux was the junior varsity basketball coach at Salt Lake's West High School, and this was where he saw his opportunity. He and a colleague worked for over a year without pay as volunteers at West High. They helped at-risk teens identify their issues and worked with them to instill protective factors to make safe and sound decisions. Their over-arching goal was to direct the youth to lead pro-social, productive lives.

They experienced first-hand this power of one-on-one guidance. Bourdeaux saw his mentoring program begin to grow, and he named it Colors of Success.

Members from the Utah House of Representatives read about the work Bourdeaux was doing with these at-risk students and gang members at West. They realized his model of adults mentoring teens, and older students mentoring younger ones, was powerful. They asked him to help write a house bill for the legislature based on his program. The bill was approved, and the Colors for Success program became the state-wide gang prevention/intervention model for Utah. It has since been adopted by many other states around the country.

Mentoring is at the very heart of Colors of Success. Principals, school counselors, and case workers monitor students' academic performance, school attendance, and behavior.[1] When problems arise, they step in and help. The caseworkers make home visits and are on-call twenty-four hours a day. Older students who've struggled with experiences that have led them astray share their stories with younger students. They hope these younger teens can learn from their stories and make different choices. The goal of each mentor is to help teens find the strength to overcome obstacles and make decisions for their lives that will carry them forward in a positive, proactive way.

T hese students in Utah learned about the power of sharing their stories, the value of helping one another deal with challenging circumstances, and the rewards of calling each other forward to do and be their best. You don't have to be a former gang member to be valuable as a mentor to another student. On the flip side, you don't have to be at-risk to benefit from having a mentor.

This leadership model of peers helping peers can be seen in all walks of life. In this chapter, you'll read about ways you can be both a mentor and mentee and put to practice the elements of leadership that have been outlined in this book. Your job is to take the initiative and seek out mentoring experiences that will help you ultimately emerge as an influential leader.

Keys for Leadership

INITIATIVE: Leadership is about taking the initiative. It's about spotting opportunities. It's about transforming ideas into action. Where can you take the initiative? How can you jump-start your leadership?

PEER MENTORSHIP: EXPERIENCING THE GIVE-AND-TAKE OF EXPERTISE

What is a peer mentor?

Peer mentorship is "a relational experience where one person empowers another to develop his or her potential by sharing various resources."[2] Generally speaking, a peer mentor is someone relatively close in age who can share knowledge and expertise. Often, a peer mentor has had recent experiences that help him or her give advice and support to others in a similar situation. Peer mentors (or peer leaders, as they will also be called throughout this chapter) are guides, allies, and advocates. Some examples of peer mentors include:

- *A senior on a sports team mentoring a new recruit.* The mentor may guide the new recruit by setting an example on the team, helping the recruit maintain good grades, and assisting the new player with managing the demands of both athletic and academic requirements.

- *A junior assigned to an incoming freshman during high school orientation.* The junior might show the freshman around the school, tell about school resources, and assist him or her in locating classes.

- *A student helping a lab partner.* A student in a science class might mentor a lab partner by breaking down the steps and explaining the procedures for a challenging lab assignment.

What types of peer mentorships are there?

The prior examples show how peer leadership takes many forms. In general, the roles of peer mentors fall into either formal or informal scenarios.

Formal. A formal peer mentor is a designated guide who helps others with less experience. Examples include:

- *Members of a Link Crew.* Link Crew is a school-sponsored leadership organization where incoming freshmen are assigned to one or two upperclassmen at the beginning of the year. The older students provide support and guidance through community involvement, academic coaching, and weekly meetings.

- *Student tutors, peer counselors, or teachers' assistants.* These peer mentors provide support for students of the same age and are monitored by the school administration and staff.

- *Tour guides.* These peer mentors give prospective students a tour of the building and answer questions about the school.

- *Community mentors.* Organizations such as Girl Scouts, Boy Scouts, Big Brothers and Sisters, and so forth match mentors from the community with members of various backgrounds and ages.

Informal. Informal peer mentorship can happen any day or any time. These are instances where leadership happens without roles being specifically designated or appointed. Here are a few examples to get you thinking:

- *Musicians in the band room.* A first-chair flutist helping out the second chair with a particularly difficult piece of music.
- *Players on the field.* A quarterback perfecting a new play with a wide receiver.
- *Actors in the theater.* A student director rehearsing lines with an actor before an audition.

These examples might strike you as situations where one student simply helps another. However, in each of these instances, one student is sharing ideas with the intent of helping another person grow, which is at the heart of peer mentorship.

If you enjoy writing, consider forming a critique group where you and your peers meet regularly to give each other feedback on your work. You'd be surprised at how many writing professionals depend on this very structure for developing their published pieces. The process works the same if you are a visual artist, musician, or filmmaker. Even your workout at the gym can benefit from having a peer mentor.

Of course, these opportunities don't end when you graduate high school, or even college for that matter. Being a peer mentor is a skill that you can take with you as you enter into the workplace.

Workplace. As a peer mentor on the job, you can use your knowledge and expertise to help solve problems, increase efficiency for others, and train new employees. Peer leadership in the workplace is often viewed as teamwork, and it is an essential ingredient for being successful on a job. Peer mentorship at work might involve:

- Training new employees on common practices and procedures of the company by showing them around, answering questions, and teaching them about their new roles and responsibilities.

- Gaining perspective from another employee with more experience than you have when you're interested in getting a promotion or trying a new position.

- Working with others on projects and presentations in anticipation of presenting the material to superiors.

Think back to a time in your life when you struggled with something. How might a peer mentor have helped you at the time? What qualities would you have looked for in this mentor?

_____

_____

_____

_____

_____

How are peer mentorships structured?

Regardless of the level of formality, every peer mentor partnership should be a two-way street with give and take. This relationship must be built on trust, respect, and honesty. It is hard to take the advice of someone you don't trust or respect. On the other hand, if you fail to uphold your commitments or act in a dishonest way, you'll loose all credibility as a peer mentor. Structuring a relationship based on trust and respect that goes both ways will help to create a positive situation for both the mentor and mentee.

However, there are limitations to these relationships. Healthy boundaries are needed. A line must be drawn as to what the mentor should and should not do to help the mentee. For example, if you are a peer mentor you should not take on the role of parent or counselor. You also should not do things on behalf of your mentee, such as talking to a teacher about an unfair grade, or fixing a situation created by poor choices. Effective peer leaders support and guide their fellow students to take control of their lives; they do not try to take control for them.

PIONEERING young leaders

DANIEL GARCIAS, COLLEGE SUMMIT PEER LEADER

For Daniel Garcia, college was something he hoped to attend someday, but not a goal he was actively pursuing. As the king at his high school's winter formal dance, Garcia was content to experience high school as a place for social interactions and not much else. "I always knew I wanted to get into Cal State or another university . . . . but nobody gave me the right tools to do it."[3]

With his senior year soon approaching, a teacher suggested Garcia apply to the leadership program, College Summit. The organization, which helps low-income students transition from secondary education to college, was looking for new members to coach and lead other teens. Garcia applied, along with 150 others, for the leadership position. From there, the selection process became more competitive. After several rounds of cuts, Garcia was finally selected as one of ten students to attend a College Summit workshop. It was then that he officially received the title: peer leader.

At first, Garcia wasn't sure what to make of the experience. But soon he became more comfortable learning the skills he would need to make college a reality and to help his peers do the same. It was at this point Garcia felt something click. "Not knowing what to expect, I thought it was going to be all work . . . but it was totally different . . . I had never seen people [workshop staff and volunteers] so passionate

about their work and helping others they had never met before in their life."[4]

When he began his senior year of high school, Garcia put his newfound knowledge to work helping other students take strides toward college. He and his fellow peer leaders assisted the senior class members achieve the five College Summit goals: fill out a college application, learn about financial aid, write a personal statement, talk to a college counselor, and become peer leaders themselves. At the same time, he successfully completed his own college applications.

Garcia began college the next year. However, his peer leadership experience had such a great impact that he decided to return to College Summit as an alumni leader working with students in summer peer

leadership programs like the one he'd attended. Looking back, Garcia reflected on the role peer leadership had on his journey and development as a person. "I always knew that if I put my mind to something I could do it; but I had never put my mind to anything significant. After the workshop, I put my mind to graduating. I graduated and now am in college." What does the future hold for Garcia? "My goal is to impact peer leaders' lives the way that mine was."[5]

Similarly, you are not expected to handle difficult or delicate situations. If a situation becomes uncomfortable or if someone's safety is at risk, refer your mentee to a qualified adult. Situations that involve drugs or violence in the home, for instance, should be passed on to someone in a position to help the victim. Remember, peer mentorship is based on sharing knowledge and expertise. As a result, peer leaders must know the limits of their position.

When might you benefit from having a peer mentor?

There is no exact science to tell you when you might need the expertise of someone who's been through what you're experiencing. Often, only you can make the call. However, here are a few situations where you might benefit from the support of a peer mentor:

1. *When you're trying something new.* Perhaps you've just joined a sports team, a band, or are trying out for the debate team for the first time. Having a mentor can help you know what to expect and how to best prepare for the challenges ahead.

2. *When you're entering a new environment.* You may have changed schools, youth groups, or have been placed in an advanced program for the gifted and talented. A mentor can answer questions, introduce you to the people you need to know, and give you background information to smooth your transition.

3. *When you are challenging yourself to move out of your comfort zone.* Perhaps you are signing up for a new internship, taking a stab at a new activity, or exploring a college campus for the first time. A mentor can reassure you as you take on new challenges, encourage you through the difficult times, and be your champion as you celebrate new personal victories.

How can you find a quality mentor?

Identifying a mentor can be a difficult task and requires you to consider your resources. Does your school offer mentorship programs? Keep an eye out for organizations like Link Crew, or look for student tutors, peer counselors, or teachers' assistants. You might find a perfect mentor through one of these channels.

Think about informal ways to find a mentor. Are there students you respect and can go to for advice? These may be peers who excel in a class or your favorite activity. Are there students among your peer group who seem to have a natural talent for listening and giving helpful advice? Potential mentors are all around you. You just have to keep your eyes and ears open and reach out for help.

Maureen, one of the co-authors of this book, found herself in a position of leading her peers without having been given a lot of instruction. As the head resident advisor of her college, Maureen was in charge of leading a staff of twelve resident advisors, each responsible for a dormitory of students. Date rape, drugs, under-age drinking, and eating disorders were just a few of the problems students faced on campus, and the resident advisers had to be equipped to assist students in the dormitories in these tough situations. In order to be successful leading her peers so that they could do the best job possible in their respective dormitories, Maureen knew she would benefit from the expertise of someone who had held the position before her. She contacted the previous head RA for guidance. During the conversation, Maureen asked her mentor the following questions:

- What were your greatest challenges with the job?
- What information do you wish you had had when you took the position?
- Who did you go to for support throughout the year?
- What advice do you have for managing the staff of RAs?
- What situations created the most difficult challenges for your team?
- How did you handle suddenly being in a position of authority over your peers?
- What from the job helped you the most when you entered the professional world?
- What lessons did you learn by the end of the year that you wished you'd known in the beginning?

Locating a mentor is important for successful leadership. People generally like to be asked for their advice, and are very willing to share their knowledge. You just need to ask. If possible, prepare a list of questions before you meet with your mentor. Having questions ready ahead of time will free you up to listen to the responses.

Think of a current situation that is challenging you. It can be a struggle in school, an issue with a parent or sibling, a doubt you have about your abilities, etc. Who can you ask to mentor you? What questions might you ask this person?

_____

_____

_____

When are you ready to be a peer mentor?

Just as you are the only person who can determine when you *need* a peer mentor, you are also the only person who can determine when you are ready to *be* a peer leader to someone else. That moment is different for everyone and is completely dependent on your skill level and the experiences you've had. For example, perhaps your parents divorced when you were young. Though you're probably not an expert on the subject, you are certainly equipped to help your friend whose parents have just separated. Your experiences and knowledge can make you a peer leader without much fuss. In that moment, you are ready to be a peer mentor.

Opportunities to be a peer mentor often arise out of situations where a good example is needed. Whether this means demonstrating a difficult move in gymnastics or being kind to a new student, you may be called on to be a peer leader with only a moment's notice. Being aware of such opportunities can help you practice your mentoring skills. Keep in mind that these moments can present themselves anywhere: in the lunchroom, on the sports field, in classes, at club meetings, and even in your own home.

Are you an exceptional listener? Do people feel comfortable confiding in you? Has a past experience given you insights that might help a peer? Perhaps you've overcome a challenge and have resources to share. What is special about you that you can offer as a peer mentor?

_____

_____

_____

There are many personal benefits to being a mentor. Eridania Brito spent three years working as a peer education leader for a teen reproductive health program in Lavapies, a poor community in the Dominican Republic. The program, sponsored by the U.S. Agency for International Development (USAID), recruits teens to help one another develop self-esteem while learning about topics including family planning, domestic violence, and reproductive health.

In her position, she worked with teens her same age to set life goals and make changes to take better care of their bodies and improve their relationships with their parents.

She was surprised that the role helped her as well. "I am less afraid to talk in public and to big groups of people, and I have accomplished my initial goal of graduating from high school."[6] Becoming a mentor changed Eridania's life. It provided her the rewarding experience of helping others and gave her the opportunity to learn what she is truly capable of doing.

There might be times where being a peer mentor will challenge you to take an unpopular stand, to be courageous, and take action even if it doesn't sit well with your friends. Remember, being a leader doesn't

Keys for Leadership

HOW TO MAKE A DIFFERENCE AS A PEER MENTOR

- Listen—actively—to both what is said and not said.
- Be trustworthy.
- Have patience.
- Show respect.
- Share ideas and resources.
- Recognize your position and act accordingly but without arrogance.
- Seek advice from others/supervisors.
- Ask questions—develop a relationship.
- Acknowledge successes.
- Help determine/work on growth areas.
- Hold your mentee accountable for his or her actions.

always mean you'll be admired and popular. For example, can you see yourself confronting a friend who is making fun of a vulnerable student? Or putting a stop to a nasty or vengeful text message that is being sent around school? To be a peer mentor won't always be easy, but it will help you develop the strength and courage to become a leader.

What if you are mentoring a younger student who skips class regularly? When he comes to you for help with his schoolwork, would you be willing to point out his poor attendance and help him see that he's sabotaging his own success? Taking such a stand is a challenging but critical part of peer mentorship. How can you courageously step into a leadership role today even if it makes you unpopular?

_____

_____

_____

When should you and your mentor/mentee part ways?

As important as it is to know when and how to find a mentor, how to work with one, and how to be one to others, it is equally important to know when to end a mentoring partnership. Due to a variety of circumstances, the timing of this step varies in each situation. As a developing leader, one of your most challenging tasks is recognizing when a relationship has lasted beyond its effectiveness. Some of the reasons a mentorship comes to a close include:

- *Natural transition times.* It might be the end of a school year or time for new people to assume specific roles. For example, a teacher's assistant position would come to a finish at the end of the school year.

- *When you or your mentee no longer need help.* Perhaps your mentee has learned enough and feels ready to help others. This moment should be considered a success for you. Likewise, when you feel you have mastered a situation and no longer need the guidance of your mentor, it is time to move on.

- *If the relationship becomes negative or if there are problems.* If you and your mentor/mentee struggle with mutual respect, honoring each other's boundaries, or achieving the goals you set out to accomplish, it might be time to look elsewhere. Not every mentoring relationship will be successful. When you see things go awry and can't get your relationship on the right track, it is better to part ways.

PEER MENTORSHIP AROUND THE GLOBE

P eer mentorship doesn't just exist in high schools and in the workplace; it thrives in cultures that span the globe. One such group that highly values the role of peer mentors is the Maori, the indigenous people of New Zealand. The Maori are of Polynesian descent and are believed to have migrated to New Zealand sometime between the ninth and thirteenth centuries.

Ngahihi O Te Ra Bidois, a modern-day Maori warrior, shares his story of reclaiming his cultural identity in his book *Ancient Wisdom, Modern Solutions*. Over the years he sought the guidance of his peers to help in this life-changing journey, which began by breaking away from Western culture, mastering the native Maori language, learning the art of Maori weaponry, and finally receiving his ta moko—the traditional tattoo that many Maori people wear on their faces. The decision to get his ta moko and reconnect with his heritage was a long and difficult one.

Ngahihi believed in the ancient Eastern proverb: *When the student is ready, the teacher appears.* And it was a peer he met while taking his own students on a field trip who became his mentor. This mentor taught him about the style of the ta moko, the important steps in the journey of receiving the ta moko, and the responsibilities of wearing a ta moko. His mentor also shared resources for where he could learn more about this tradition and what it would mean for him to keep his culture alive in this century. His peer's words, "Continue to ask the right questions and you will receive the right answers from the right people," have stayed with him to this day, and he now mentors other Maori in keeping the culture and traditions alive.[7]

Keys for Leadership

HOW CAN PEER MENTORSHIP MAKE YOU A BETTER LEADER?

It can help you learn:

- How to be of service.
- How to hold a vision and see the needs of others.
- How to develop tools for giving and earning respect.
- How to communicate and listen.
- How to help solve problems creatively.
- How to hold yourself and your mentee to a high standard.
- How to work with another person for a common goal.
- How to be patient.
- How to have the courage to stand up for values despite popularity.
- How to build consensus.
- How to work out problems with others.
- How to bring out the best in another.

LEADERSHIP *then & now*

CYRUS THE GREAT (ca. 580–529 B.C.) and **LEE KUAN YEW** (1923–present)

From his earliest years, Cyrus the Great sought mentors to teach and groom him. He learned all he could about the geography, the ruling powers, and the weapons of his day from the men who served in his father's court so that he could fulfill his destiny as a great leader. In fact, his elders referred to him as the "well of knowledge" because of his rigorous pursuit of learning.

As he moved into a prominent leadership role, he mentored his soldiers and army officials, sharing with them his wisdom about leading others. Once his Persian Empire was in place, he spent many years ruling in peace. During this time, he appointed governors to rule over various tribes, and went to great lengths to mentor these leaders. As his long life came to a close, he appointed his first-born son to take over the empire, saying, "I'm here to lend you support." He urged his son to lead as he had taught him, reminding him to " . . . treat all people with benevolence. As great men, your deeds will be known to all humankind."[8]

Cyrus the Great was both a student and a counselor of leadership. His actions and humane ways of dealing with people and inspiring the masses earned him many titles. The Iranians referred to him as the Father; the Greeks called him the Law Giver; the Babylonians, the Liberator; and the Jews, Anointed of the Lord. His teachings continue to influence business, government, and political leaders in the present century.

Today, Lee Kuan Yew models similar mentoring practices with his son. Lee Kuan Yew became the first prime minister of the Republic of Singapore in 1959 and served in the post until 1990. During his reign, he transformed Singapore from a relatively poor country into one of Asia's wealthiest economies.

Fourteen years after he retired from office, his son, Lee Hsien Long, took the helm, becoming the nation's third prime minister. In this role, Long created an official mentor post in his cabinet for his father, giving him the title "Minister Mentor," which is the first time a position of this sort has been formally recognized.[9] The goal was to ease the transition of power to new hands with the mentoring of experienced politicians. Today, Lee Kuan Yew still mentors Lee Hsien Long, helping him guide Singapore to the forefront of the global landscape.

If you were appointed to run your school, who would you want for a mentor? Why?

_____

_____

_____

_____

_____

_____

_____

If you were appointed to run your country, who would you want to mentor you? Why?

_____

_____

_____

_____

_____

_____

_____

Cyrus the Great took advantage of every opportunity to learn from mentors in his father's court and develop his leadership skills before he was called to lead. He studied. He learned. He practiced. You can do the same.

Remember that you don't have to be your class president or captain of the soccer team to be a peer mentor or leader. Start now with the situations you encounter every day and see how your unique talents and gifts can be harnessed. It can be as simple as explaining a math problem to the student sitting next to you to asking your bus driver to wait for a student who is running toward the bus. You might argue that these actions are more about having good manners or making small situations just a little better. But steps like these are at the heart of leadership. Helping someone to grasp a new concept and holding the bus for a peer are actions that make a difference. And they're actions that will help you develop your leadership muscles.

Think of a pianist who practices playing scales to develop strength and agility in his fingers so that he can master complex music. Or the athlete who spends several hours each day shooting baskets so that she can be the leading scorer. Malcolm Gladwell, the author of the book *Outliers*, presents a fascinating perspective on success. He researched professional hockey players, famous musicians, accomplished math students, and commercial pilots, and came to the same conclusion each time. Success isn't just about talent or opportunity, but about practice—ten thousand hours of practice, to be specific.[10]

It is no different with leadership. Mastery takes time. Sure, some people might seem to be natural leaders. They are charismatic, have innovative ideas, and easily win the respect of others. Yet even with such natural gifts, great leaders develop with practice. You can begin this practice today at your kitchen table, in front of your locker, in the classroom, and on the streets of your community. The more you act on leadership opportunities in your day-to-day life, the stronger your leadership muscles will become—positioning you for greatness when you assume major leadership roles.

SUMMARY

n this chapter, you've learned about the different types of peer mentorship and the advantages to having a peer mentor. You've also explored ways to be an effective peer mentor both at school and in your working life. Take the initiative and get involved. Find a mentor to help you with new goals and extend yourself as a mentor for others with less experience.

THE MOVIE BRATS

George Lucas, Steven Spielberg, Brian De Palma, Martin Scorsese (and others)

For the entertainment industry, the 1970s served as a creative springboard. Societal shifts like the counterculture movement of the 1960s, the civil rights movement, and rock and roll, combined with industry changes such as the relaxing of language restrictions and acceptance of adult content all created a fertile environment for the art of film.

For many young filmmakers, these changes meant the chance to try something new and forge their own path. Many of today's superstar directors emerged from this era including: George Lucas, Brian De Palma, Steven Spielberg, and Martin Scorsese, to name a few. Because they were contemporaries and many of them had attended film school together, they knew one another and were familiar with each other's work. They influenced and taught one another about cinematography and directing. They critiqued one another and shared perspectives about the films they were creating. They learned new approaches and became inspired by the successes of one another. More than anything, they were peers mentoring one another on craft and artistry.

The Movie Brats, as these filmmakers came to be called, produced epic films like *Star Wars, E.T.: The Extra-Terrestrial,* the *Godfather* series, *Mission to Mars, Saving Private Ryan,* and *Casino.*[11] The creative spark shared between these visionaries early in their careers fueled the development of film to become the art form it is today.

building leadership skills

FOR THE TWENTY-FIRST CENTURY

Success and Failure

ANALYZING LEADERSHIP IN ACTION

It's time to put on your creative thinking cap. Imagine a scene where a peer mentor works with a student and the situation is a disaster. It might be a scene where a new employee at McDonald's is being trained by a peer or the captain of the poms team is teaching a new squad member a routine. Create details in your mind as to what went wrong. Were boundaries ignored? Did the communication fail? Was the mentor impatient? Now write out your scene, describing in detail how and why the mentorship failed.

After you are done, rewrite the same scene, except make it a successful partnership. Include specific examples of how the two students interacted. How did they communicate and treat each other with respect? What else happened to make this scene different from the first one you wrote?

_____

_____

_____

_____

_____

_____

_____

_____

_____

_____

_____

_____

Leading in Your Own Life

List one specific way you will mentor a peer this year. It can be anything from signing up to be an after-school tutor to joining your school's freshman orientation committee. Find an opportunity that will stretch you and push you to try something new.

_____

_____

_____

If putting yourself in a position to lead your peers is uncomfortable, what can you do to help yourself step into this role more easily?

_____

_____

_____

_____

What are the biggest challenges you have with mentoring your peers? Are you intimidated? Is holding a friend accountable for a commitment difficult? Are you busy and lack the time to get involved?

_____

_____

_____

_____

_____

What do you think you will gain from being a peer mentor?

_____

_____

_____

_____

Teamwork for Effective Leadership

LAUNCHING YOUR VISION

Now is the time for you and your team to launch your vision. Whether it is hosting an event, distributing information, gathering feedback on a new school policy, or setting up an advisory council to meet with your school's administration, it's time to put your plan in place.

For the next several weeks, record the steps you're taking. Make observations about what is working well with your plan and areas where you can improve your plan. If you need to track the number of participants, this is the place to do it. If you need to keep minutes from key meetings, write them down. Feel free to track your information on additional sheets of paper if necessary. The goal here is not only to act on the vision you've been planning for the last seven chapters, but also to make careful observations about the work you are doing.

_____

_____

_____

_____

_____

_____

_____

_____

_____

_____

_____

_____

_____

YOUR NAME HERE

You . . . have the opportunity to make the world a better place. Now is the time to act!

- How can you use your interests, talents, and abilities to make a difference?

- Where can you shine and contribute as a leader?

Chapter 9

MAKING
. . . a Difference

How can you lead in your school, community, and the world?

Jonah Grant thinks big. This fourteen-year-old Chicago boy doesn't just play with the newest applications on his iPhone or iPad, he creates them. And he's gaining world-wide attention. Some of his apps that are available for purchase include: Pong, Commandments, Hot Links, and App of the Day.

This high school computer star and entrepreneur has been developing apps for the iPhone for over a year. He started working on computers at a young age, tinkering with a Windows 98 desktop PC. Soon he moved to a Mac, where he began building things before he launched into the iPhone platform. With the help of a few mentors, he taught himself code language and began developing and selling app programs of his own.[1]

His goals for the future? He wants to explore filmmaking or start his own Web-related company. You never know, he just might be the one masterminding the next MySpace or Facebook!

At fourteen, Jonah Grant merged his passion for technology with his leadership mindset. His ability to forge new paths will shape the opportunities available to him tomorrow. While you might not be generating the newest iPhone applications, you can begin leading today by combining your passions with your blossoming leadership skills. New doors will certainly open for you tomorrow.

et's begin this chapter by creating a snapshot of the personal leadership action plan that you've been developing over the course of this book.

Answer the following questions to outline specific actions you will commit to practicing today. You've addressed many of these questions earlier in the text. It's okay. Do it again. Expand your thinking. Maybe something new has come to mind. Maybe you want to reinforce ideas you came up with earlier. This is your opportunity to pull all your thoughts together.

Leadership NOW! . . . Vision

What are your personal visions for leadership? These might include the vision you committed to in chapter two, or other ideas that have struck you as you've read this book.

Can you host a fundraising event for a friend whose father just passed away? Set up a tutorial program for English language learners? Perhaps you can approach your principal and superintendent with your idea for a new school policy.

What leadership actions, big or small, can you take today?

_____

_____

_____

Leadership NOW! . . . Critical and creative thinking

How can you be a strategic problem-solver? Can you see yourself suggesting to a manager at your part-time job a more efficient way of handling a procedure? Can you envision helping your family establish a better way of sharing the household chores so that your parents aren't as overwhelmed?

How can you creatively approach current problems and develop effective solutions?

_____

_____

_____

Leadership NOW! . . . Respect

How can you present yourself in a way for both peers and adults to respect you? Do you dress in a way that shows self-respect? Can you look others in the eye and shake hands in a way that shows self-confidence? Are you dependable? Do you model excellence? Do you nurture positive relationships?

What are you willing to do each day when you walk out of your house to generate both self-respect and respect from others?

_____

_____

_____

Leadership NOW! . . . Communication

How can you communicate ideas with conviction? What opportunities exist for you to discuss an issue or problem? Can you pause to genuinely listen to a friend or family member? Are you willing to have a difficult conversation or ask a courageous question?

Where are your opportunities for boldly communicating your ideas, expectations, and/or questions?

_____

_____

_____

Leadership NOW! . . . Teamwork

How can you be a team leader? What can you do to set and achieve high standards? How can you hold your teammates accountable? How can you help your team be positive and stay clear of gossip and other negative energy?

How will you challenge yourself this week to be a star team leader (whether the team is your family, a group in your science class, a sports team, or a club)?

_____

_____

_____

Leadership NOW! . . . Ethics

What standards of behavior are important to you? Is it being honest or trustworthy? Maybe it involves keeping an open mind with a willingness to listen to others' points of view.

What behaviors are you willing to commit to today to use as a compass for all your actions and decisions?

_____

_____

_____

Condense the answers you came up with and write them in abbreviated form in each of the respective areas marked in the circle: vision, critical and creative thinking, respect, communication, teamwork, and ethics. This diagram can serve as a snapshot of your leadership action plan.

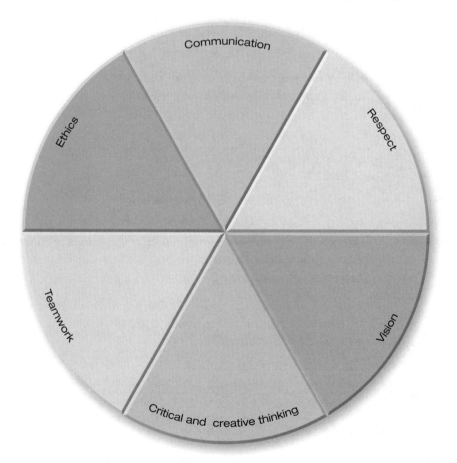

LEADING TOMORROW

H opefully, you have just brainstormed several ways you can practice your leadership skills today, whether in your home, school hallways, or on the streets of your community. Making an effort to lead today, in simple ways, will help you evolve as a leader for tomorrow.

As you continue to practice these elements of leadership, take time for self-reflection, which will guide and inspire your leadership roles for tomorrow.

One of the great commands from the Greek philosopher, Socrates, is "know thyself." These words still ring true for developing leaders today. But what exactly does it mean to know thyself?

It involves knowing your strengths and weaknesses. It means understanding why you feel the way you do. It requires processing the critical experiences in your life and understanding the influence these experiences have on your outlook, your goals, and your attitudes. It means connecting the stories of your past to your dreams for the future. Taking time to know yourself will ultimately help you shape your leadership vision and goals. Take Howard Shultz, the chairman and CEO of Starbucks, for example.

Howard Schultz's personal story has been a driving force behind the development and success of one of the world's most recognized coffee brands. As a child growing up in Brooklyn, New York, Schultz was accustomed to making do with very little. His father worked as a diaper-service delivery driver and money was never plentiful. However, when his father broke his ankle and lost his job, things went from uncomfortable to downright unlivable. At the time, most employee benefits like health insurance weren't available to people in low-paying jobs. Schultz's father was no exception. Without income, either from his job or insurance, Schultz' family quickly fell into poverty.

This event stayed with Schultz into adulthood. As an executive at Starbucks, he developed a plan inspired by the events from his early life. Schultz created a company that offers full-coverage healthcare benefits to both full- and part-time employees, a rarity today. The effort has benefitted the company as well, helping it attract committed employees who stay with the organization for years. With low employee turnover, Starbucks is able to save on training costs for new hires, which in turn has helped cover the costs for healthcare benefits.

In an interview, Schultz explained how his personal story affected his leadership. "I saw firsthand the debilitating effect that [not having health insurance or benefits] had . . . on our family. I decided if I was ever in the position to make a contribution to others in that way, I would. My greatest success has been that I got to build the kind of company my father never got to work for."[2]

The lesson? Never underestimate the power of your personal story. Retain your experiences and aim to gain new ones. You never know how an event can change the course of your leadership and make a difference for those around you.

So what is your own story? What personal experiences define you? What relationships have influenced who you are and who you yearn to become? You may have a personal story steeped in tragedy and difficulty. Or you may have a story blessed with privilege, opportunity, beauty, or excellence. Know that it isn't the story itself, but what you take from it, and what you choose for inspiration that make all the difference.

In the space on the opposite page, record some of the defining moments in your life. Don't worry about complete sentences or fully developed ideas. The point is to simply brainstorm. Include the people who shaped your outlook, who have influenced your attitudes, hopes, and dreams. Draw pictures. Connect images and words. Doodle if it helps. This space is for you to create a montage of your experiences.

At the end of the chapter, you'll be asked to write your personal story based on some of the ideas you just included here. It won't need to be long—three to five minutes when read aloud is plenty. You aren't striving for a linear description of your life: *I was born in Indiana; my family moved to England; I have three siblings*; and so forth. Instead, you'll focus on key events or aspects of your life that define the essence of who you are. We all have a personal story, and like Howard Schultz, we can all be guided by the wisdom that comes from our stories.

IDENTIFYING CORE VALUES
FOR LEADERSHIP

T aking the time to reflect on your personal story will help you identify values that are important to you. These values, in turn, will inform your leadership. For Howard Schultz, the value of having a safety net when tragedy strikes clearly emerged from his childhood experiences. Providing such a safety net for others then became central to his leadership vision.

What is important to you as a result of your experiences? Is it having a tightly knit family or living a life of adventure? Perhaps it is having financial security, or integrating into a foreign culture. Take a moment to identify ten values that are important to you. If you need some help, refer to the following list. However, feel free to use your own values that might not be included on this list.

VALUES

Acceptance	Affluence	Awareness	Beauty
Bravery	Cleverness	Closeness	Compassion
Creativity	Dignity	Discipline	Education
Excellence	Family	Fun	Happiness
Health	Humility	Honor	Independence
Imagination	Intelligence	Justice	Joy
Love	Loyalty	Perseverance	Popularity
Power	Punctuality	Recognition	Reliability
Security	Spirituality	Success	Support
Teamwork	Truth	Wisdom	Wealth

YOUR TOP TEN VALUES

_____   _____

_____   _____

_____   _____

_____   _____

_____   _____

As we've noted earlier, the most effective leaders are able to align their actions to their core values. As an emerging leader, this is where you can begin to draw the lines between your personal experiences, the values that are born from these, and the actions they then inspire. Your greatest leadership moments will stem from your inspired actions.

Personal Story → Core Values → Inspired Actions

Tennis great, Venus Williams, took such action at the 2010 Dubai Tennis Championships. The prior year, the country's officials denied Israeli player Shahar Peer entrance into Dubai because of political strife between the Arabs and Israelis. Williams, who has experienced her share of prejudice, fought the discrimination on the grounds that all tennis players should have access to the international competitions and that

politics should not be played out on the tennis courts. She made a public statement that she would not defend her championship title in 2010 if Shahar Peer was again denied access to the tournament. Influenced by Williams's stance, government officials agreed to let Peer into the country for the 2010 tournament.[3] Williams emerged as a true leader whose core values inspired her to take a stand and put her championship title on the line while the world watched.

Where to Lead . . . *at home*

As you reflect on your personal experiences and define your core values, you may begin to wonder where you can channel the inspired actions that result. Where can you emerge as a blossoming leader? The first place to explore is your home and family environment. If one of your core values is health and fitness, what actions can you take to help your family develop a healthier lifestyle? Can you lead the efforts to have more nutritious meals or to exercise together by taking family walks and bike rides on the weekends? If you value compassion, what can you do at home to encourage your family members to act with kindness toward one another? Can you each draw names out of a hat and for one week shower compassionate acts upon your recipient? Or can you decide as a family one compassionate gesture that you will all practice as a team for the upcoming week? Engaging your family around inspired actions is a great way to fine-tune your leadership skills.

The following story is an example of a young woman who had a simple, yet profound, personal experience that triggered her value of justice, and in turn inspired her and her family to take bold action.

While waiting at a traffic light during a drive home from a slumber party with her father, fourteen-year-old Hannah Salwen noticed a man begging for food on one side of the intersection and a new Mercedes on the other. Taken by the two extremes, Salwen said, "Dad, if that man had a less nice car, that man over there could have a meal." When she brought up the discussion again at home, her mother responded, "What do you want to do? Sell our house?"[4]

And that's exactly what they eventually did. Hannah's realization of such injustices triggered a great deal of dialogue for her family. After realizing that they had more space than they needed, the Salwen family

decided to sell their large house, donate half of the sale price to charity (which ended up being eight hundred thousand dollars), and use the other half to buy a more modest, family-centered home.

With the eight hundred thousand dollars set aside, the Salwens went to work determining how best to donate the money. They spent months researching various charities and eventually decided on the Hunger Project—a New York City-based international development organization focused on eliminating global poverty. With the charity decided, the Salwens pledged the entire amount. The money sponsored health, development, and food programs for forty villages in Ghana.

What did the Salwens get in return? "We essentially traded stuff for togetherness and connectedness," Kevin Salwen, Hannah's father, said in an interview. "I can't figure out why everybody wouldn't want that deal."[5]

Have you ever been struck by the injustice of something? You and your family might not be in a position to sell a house or donate a month's worth of rent, but you can lead with small actions.

When have you witnessed something that went against your core values?

_____

_____

_____

What is one way you can lead your family to take action?

_____

_____

_____

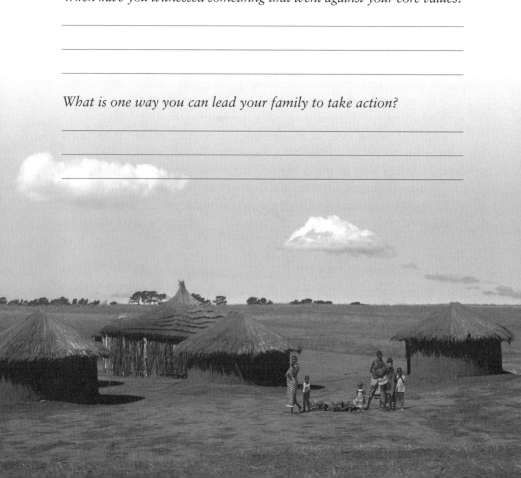

Where to Lead . . . *at school*

School is the next obvious place to explore your leadership potential. Be creative. If you enjoy your visual art class, why not ask fellow students to submit their favorite pieces they've created and then produce an art show? You can hang the artwork in the lobby, invite guests to come and view the pieces on a Friday night, serve light refreshments, play soft music in the background, and have the artists on-hand to talk about their work.

Or you can even take it a step further. Why not ask local art galleries in town to collaborate with you on a student art show? If you live in a community with several art galleries close-by, have people walk from gallery to gallery and see student work, along with the professional work hanging in the gallery, and make it a fun, invigorating evening. The galleries receive more exposure and the students get to experience their work being shown next to professionals—a win-win for all.

If art isn't your thing, what about video taping one student, teacher, or administrator a week at school? Ask what they love to do, what their favorite time in history is, what they hope for the future, and other questions to learn more about them. For the rest of the week, play your interview on a screen in the school lobby for all students to see. It's a great way for students to learn more about the people in the building and an innovative way to create community.

You can take this idea a step further and host a talk show on your public access television station. Create a forum for people in your school and community to talk and debate issues important to you and your peers. Once you get started, the possibilities are endless.

If assuming roles like these feels overwhelming, start small. Step up as a leader when working on a class project. Organize dates and times where your group can meet to work. Solicit input from all members. Clarify the assignment and delegate responsibilities.

Many students consider the athletes and student council members in their schools to be leaders. But even students in these high-profile positions have to stretch themselves and develop an awareness of the many opportunities that exist for them to be peer leaders. Joe Ehrmann's story about coaching his high school football team is a great example.

When Joe Ehrmann began playing professional football for the Baltimore Colts in the 1970s, he had little on his mind besides the game. His attitude quickly changed when his brother was diagnosed with cancer. After his brother died, Ehrmann questioned his priorities in life.

After retiring from football, Ehrmann was invited to coach a boys-only preparatory school in Baltimore. Ehrmann jumped at the chance. With his new priorities, he reentered the game with a different perspective.

Ehrmann was determined to make his players leaders both on the field and in life. "All of us ought to have some kind of cause, some kind of purpose in our lives that's bigger than our own individual hopes, dreams, wants, and desires. At the end of our life, we ought to be able to look back over it from our deathbed and know that somehow the world is a better place because we lived, we loved, we were other-centered, other-focused."[6]

On the field and in the locker room, Ehrmann pursued this dream through community-centered discussions with the players. He instilled a code of conduct: accepting responsibility, leading courageously, enacting justice on behalf of others. These attributes were practiced daily by Ehrmann's team and enforced strictly—even in the cafeteria, where Ehrmann expected his athletes to never let a student sit alone, player or not. "How do you think that boy feels if he's eating all alone?" Ehrmann asked his players. "Go get him and bring him over to your table."[7]

How does this type of leadership play out on the field? Very well, as it turns out. Ehrmann's players have remained undefeated for three out of the past six seasons. In 2002, the team ranked number one in Maryland and fourteenth in national standings.

Even these football players, who are often looked up to by their peers, had to stretch beyond their comfort zone, to be "other-focused" as their coach said, to look for opportunities to include others, and think beyond their own needs and desires.

List one leadership action you can take today that stretches you beyond your comfort zone to make a difference for someone at your school.

_____

_____

Making an effort to invite someone new to join you at the school assembly, to practice a difficult sports move with a teammate who is struggling, or to help a substitute teacher who is being given a hard time are all individual ways you can lead as a peer. But what happens when you join your leadership initiative with other teens in your school?

The students at Overlake School in Redmond, Washington did just this, changing the lives of teenagers on the other side of the world. Through bake sales, car washes, talent shows, and other fundraising efforts, the students galvanized support to raise thirteen thousand dollars for the American Assistance for Cambodia organization. These funds were then matched by the World Bank and the Asian Development Bank to create a new school in Pailin, a Cambodian town on the Thai border. The students learned that Cambodian men go to school on average for only 2.6 years, and women only 1.7 years. Their goal was to make education available to students, especially to young girls who are often sold into slavery to support the sex trade. These student leaders from Overlake didn't stop once the school in Cambodia was built. Instead, they continued to lead their community in raising funds to send resources, books, and even teachers to help educate the Cambodian students.[8]

There is great power when leaders band together in schools to make a difference. What can you and your school peers do collectively to create positive change in the world?

_____

_____

_____

Where to Lead . . .
in your community and the world

The students at Overlake demonstrate how you can band together and make a significant difference, not just in your school, but across the world. Raising thirteen thousand dollars is a big step and takes time and commitment. But you can start small. Gathering a group to pick up trash along the roadside, singing carols at a nursing home, or staging a theatrical production at a low-income daycare center are all ways to make a difference in your community. Perhaps you know of others already working toward a cause you value. If so, research the work being done, volunteer your time, and get involved.

> ### Keys for Leadership
>
> **ENDURANCE:** Leadership takes time. It calls for dedication and a willingness to commit to a vision, even when the vision seems impossible. It demands that you don't give up, but remain steadfast with conviction. It requires endurance.

As a high school student, Pamela Escobar did just this, and changed the fate of many by working fervently to address and solve problems affecting people around the world—all between classes, homework, and extracurricular activities. During her sophomore year, she designed and implemented a tutoring program for ESL students called Tutoring Academic Peer Services (TAPS). Frustrated after learning about the plight of child labor in developing countries, she passed a school policy ensuring that gym uniforms were not purchased from these factories or sweatshops. Her passion for the issue continues today with her involvement with Free the Children, an international organization aimed at ending child labor.

However, her biggest accomplishment was also the most controversial. Disturbed by the number of illegal immigrants dying from dehydration while crossing the desert into the United States, Escobar knew she wanted to help. Working with the American Civil Liberties Union of Southern California and Jovenes, Inc., a grassroots organization, she helped place water at locations across the desert. Her choice to participate wasn't politically driven; it was simply a desire to help people seriously in need of aid. Because of her leadership work, Ms. Escobar won a Milken scholarship to attend college at Brown University.[9]

Assuming leadership roles in the community and world can be daunting. But, by getting involved and joining others, you can develop your leadership voice, whether it's through speaking, writing, or, like our Pioneering Young Leader for this chapter, dancing.

PIONEERING young leaders

JACKIE ROTMAN, EVERYBODY DANCE NOW!

Jackie was only twelve when inspiration first struck. Onstage, performing in a packed auditorium for people with disabilities, she heard  audience members chanting for more. Instead of ending the show, Jackie and her fellow dancers brought some of the audience members up onstage where they danced and celebrated together as a community. Jackie didn't realize this special moment's power would shape her future.

When she turned thirteen, she wanted to serve others and to find something specific to make life meaningful. The memory of building community through dance surfaced. She understood the power dance has to build students' self-esteem. She also realized that creating the opportunity for kids with disabilities to dance and gain access to the arts would allow her to share her gifts and passion in a powerful way. At that point, her idea for Everybody Dance Now! was born.

The following year, she launched her organization. Starting small, she gathered a team of three dancers and began offering free dance classes in her local community. Four years later, the organization was offering close to fifteen classes a week for students throughout the community, providing performance opportunities for the more serious dance students, and paying high school and college dancers market wages for teaching these classes.

A professional from the local arts community noticed what Jackie was trying to

do and decided to mentor her, helping her find funding to grow her organization. "Kids underestimate what they can do," Rotman says. "When you're a teen you have time to serve. You're not challenged with a full-time job or taking care of a family. And when you ask adults for help they are usually more than willing to support what you are trying to do!"[10]

Jackie is now a full-time student at Stanford University. But due to her incredible leadership skills, Everybody Dance Now! is still going strong. She has trained student leaders to take over her former role and manage the organization, suc-ceeding at one of the most difficult leadership challenges: passing the leadership baton on and keeping the company sustainable. In addition to overseeing Everybody Dance Now! from afar, Jackie also serves as co-president of Right to Education for All, an organization dedicated to increasing access to education around the world.

It took courage for Jackie to assume a visible leadership role in her community at such a young age. Dancers, parents, and other community leaders watched as she forged ahead and brought her vision to life. Any mistakes she made along the way both off and onstage were out in the open for people to see.

Yet mistakes are an inevitable part of leadership. President Theodore Roosevelt's words from a speech he gave in 1910 offer encouragement for young leaders:

> It is not the critic who counts: not the man who points out how the strong man stumbles or where the doer of deeds could have done better. The credit belongs to the man who is actually in the arena, whose face is marred by dust and sweat and blood, who strives valiantly, who errs and comes up short again and again, because there is no effort without error or shortcoming, but who knows the great enthusiasms, the great devotions, who spends himself for a worthy cause; who, at the best, knows, in the end, the triumph of high achievement, and who, at the worst, if he fails, at least he fails while daring greatly, so that his place shall never be with those cold and timid souls who knew neither victory nor defeat.

Will you stand on the sidelines with those *"cold and timid souls who knew neither victory nor defeat,"* or will you choose to step into the arena and *"spend yourself for a worthy cause?"* This is the ultimate leadership question.

AVOIDING COMMON MISTAKES LEADERS MAKE

 s Roosevelt expressed, by stepping into the arena there will be errors, some avoidable and some not. This saying applies to peer leaders and world leaders alike. And while mistakes are a part of any learning process, it is helpful to try to avoid the preventable ones.

Following is a list of common mistakes peer leaders make. In essence, it's a summary of the points we've talked about throughout the book to help you avoid common errors in leadership.

Top 12 Mistakes Peer Leaders Make:

MISTAKES OF VISION

- Lacking the courage to stand up for an idea, especially when it is unpopular
- Not having a clear idea of what needs to be accomplished

MISTAKES OF CRITICAL AND CREATIVE THINKING

- Failing to think critically about a problem and instead acting on impulse
- Giving up before finding creative solutions when faced with challenges or obstacles

MISTAKES OF RESPECT

- Having an attitude of superiority
- Not behaving, dressing, or carrying themselves in a way that commands respect

MISTAKES OF COMMUNICATION

- Neglecting to listen to others' input
- Failing to clearly explain plans or expectations, and not discussing problems when they arise

MISTAKES OF TEAMWORK

- Ignoring and not recognizing the contributions of others
- Lacking trust in others' abilities to get the job done

MISTAKES OF ETHICS

- Believing that whatever has to be done to accomplish a goal is okay, even if it is wrong or destructive
- Acting as if rules don't apply to them

As you practice leading in various areas of your life, be mindful of these pitfalls and do what you can to avoid these common mistakes.

Leading from Your Inheritance to Your Legacy

Over the course of nine chapters, we have shared what it takes to be a leader, what the key elements of leadership are, and how you can begin to lead yourself, your family, your school, and your community. We've also talked about how your personal experiences can inspire your actions and leadership. As we wrap up our discussion, we'd like to encourage you to continue thinking about your role as a leader both for today and for the years to come.

You've read about leaders from antiquity to today and have seen connections in their leadership. Now it is time for you to think about your own ancestors and the leadership goals you have for your future. You might be surprised by the connections you make regarding the gifts your ancestors passed on to you and the legacy you hope to leave for future generations.

Take a few moments to reflect on the gifts you received from your ancestors. What have you been given as a result of being born where you were, to the family you have, with your heritage?

Write down your ideas as they come to mind in the space below.

_____

_____

_____

_____

Now take a moment to imagine the future. What gifts do you want to give to future generations? What do you hope to pass along to those who follow you? What do you want your legacy to be? Perhaps it is a passion for dance, like Jackie Rotman, or a desire to make education accessible to others, as Juan Pablo Romero Fuentes did.

Write down your ideas as they come to mind in the space below.

_____

_____

_____

_____

Do you see any connections? How can you lead in a way that connects the gifts you've received in life with your hopes for what you can leave for others? For some, it might be the gift of having plenty to eat and drink or a choice of clothes to wear. For others, it might be the experience of reading, of language, and of communicating. If there isn't an obvious connection for you, do not worry. Keep your eyes open. Listen to those around you. Take note of leaders who inspire you. And most importantly, keep the ideas about your ancestors and your legacy in your mind so they can evolve. In time, you will know what you are called to do.

ENDURING leaders

CONNECTING YESTERDAY TO TOMORROW

WE ARE THE WORLD

Dedicated musicians for hunger and earthquake relief

It is said that music is a universal language, and when leaders step up to the plate to create, produce, and distribute it across the globe, this universal language has the power to save lives.

This is just what Quincy Jones, Michael Jackson, and Lionel Ritchie did in 1985 to raise money for the famine victims in Ethiopia. These men co-wrote and produced the hit single "We Are the World," which became one of the best-selling songs of all time and successfully raised millions of dollars for hunger relief. Over forty recording artists, including Stevie Wonder, Bruce Springsteen, and Tina Turner, lent their voices to the effort, truly demonstrating the powerful effect leaders can have when they come together for a joint cause.

The concept endured. Twenty-five years later, after Haiti experienced a massive 7.0 magnitude earthquake killing hundreds of thousands, Quincy Jones and Lionel Ritchie came together again, this time with the next generation of leaders in the music

business. With eighty-five musicians, they recorded a remake of the original "We Are the World" to raise money for the devastated country of Haiti. "We Are the World 25 for Haiti" aired on American television during the coverage of the 2010 Winter Olympics Opening Ceremony. Artists including Justin Bieber, Miley Cyrus, Pink, and Lil' Wayne performed on the track that includes a tribute to Michael Jackson.

The leadership effort was beneficial to both the artists and the victims in Ethiopia and Haiti. "What you pray for your entire career," says Ritchie, "is that besides all of the hit records and all of the money you plan on making, that you actually leave some kind of mark on the world." [11]

If you'd like to participate in the mark they are leaving, you can log on to their official website at www.wearetheworldfoundation.org to follow their work and international relief efforts.

SUMMARY

I n this chapter, you looked at your core values and learned that great leadership is inspired by these values. You reflected on ways to lead today and tomorrow, in your home, schools, and community. Finally, you read about common mistakes leaders make but were encouraged to take risks and embrace a bold vision for your leadership.

building leadership skills

FOR THE TWENTY-FIRST CENTURY

Success and Failure

ANALYZING LEADERSHIP IN ACTION

Think of a leader who's experienced both failure and success. Choose someone you know personally or a person whose work you can research. You might look to a coach from the NBA, your state legislator, or a business owner from your community.

List your leader's name, one noteworthy success they've experienced, and one noteworthy failure in the following chart.

Now, think through each of the leadership elements we've covered and reflect on your leader's actions in regard to these elements. How did his or her vision (critical and creative thinking, communication, etc.) influence the success or contribute to the failure? Did holding on to the vision, when everyone else doubted it, help your leader succeed? Or, did a lack of clarity around vision contribute to your leader's particular failure. Record your impressions in the chart. You might not be able to comment on each element of leadership with regard to one single failure or success, but try best to assess their work in each of these areas.

After you are done, share your observations with your classmates.

Leader's name: _____

SUCCESS   **FAILURE**

_____

_____

Vision

_____

_____

_____

Critical and creative thinking

_____

_____

_____

Respect

_____

_____

_____

Communication

_____

_____

_____

Teamwork

_____

_____

_____

Ethics/Integrity

_____

_____

_____

What can you take away from this exercise and apply to your own leadership strategies?

_____

_____

_____

_____

_____

_____

Leading in Your Own Life

FINDING YOUR SOURCE OF INSPIRATION

Now it's time to write your personal story based on some of
the ideas you brainstormed in the chapter. Keep it short—three
to five minutes when read aloud is plenty. Remember, the purpose of
your story isn't to give all the facts about your life. It's to focus on
the experiences that have made you who you are today. We all have
a personal story; some are happy, some are funny, some intriguing,
and others heart-wrenching. But, like Howard Schultz, we can all be
guided by the wisdom that comes from our story.

Take time to write your story on a separate piece of paper. If you
are comfortable with sharing, read your story aloud to your class. If
not, it's okay. The goal is for you to connect with the experiences that
define you and will someday fuel your leadership. It's not about making a presentation today to the class.

Teamwork for Effective Leadership

EVALUATING YOUR WORK

Now that you've acted on your vision and implemented your plan,
it's time to evaluate both your process and the results of your work.

Meet with your leadership team and answer the following questions to reflect on the work you've done.

1. *What worked well in your planning process (your communication, teamwork, etc.)?*

   _____

   _____

   _____

2. *Where did you struggle while planning to execute your vision?*

   _____

   _____

   _____

3. *If you were to start over and plan for your project again, how would you plan differently?*

_____

_____

_____

4. *What was the outcome of your leadership project?*

_____

_____

_____

5. *Did it meet your expectations? How or how not?*

_____

_____

_____

6. *On a scale of one to ten (one being low, ten being high) how successful do you feel your project was?*

_____

_____

_____

7. *How could you have improved the overall project?*

_____

_____

_____

8. *If someone else was going to attempt to do what you did, how could you mentor him/her? What advice would you give?*

_____

_____

_____

9. *What do you wish you would have known before you implement-*
   ed your vision that you know now?

   _____

   _____

   _____

   _____

   _____

   _____

   _____

10. *What are you going to take away from this*
    experience?

    _____

    _____

    _____

    _____

    _____

    _____

    _____

Organizations, Clubs, and Events

Here is a list of organizations and events that offer leadership opportunities. You will find organizations listed under the following headings: Personal Development, Community Service, Career Interest, Interpersonal Dynamics, and Personal Interest.

PERSONAL DEVELOPMENT

 These organizations are committed to developing leadership skills in young people.

Camp Rising Sun

www.lajf.org

This seven-week-long summer camp is an international, full-scholarship event for gifted and talented students ages 14 to 16. The program focuses on learning through peer interaction and problem solving. Students who are accepted into the program participate in debates, outdoor experiences, group councils, and a musical theater production.

Challenge Leadership Program

www.challengeleadership.com

The Challenge Leadership Program is a six-hour event comprised of 80 students and school representatives. The goal is to increase student body involvement and enthusiasm in school activities and events. Candidates must be nominated by a teacher or principal.

Contact: 800-492-1370

Do Something

www.dosomething.org

Do Something believes in the power of teenagers to facilitate positive change. The organization acts as a support system for high school students who want to take action. All products and programs are free.

Contact: Ben Millard 212-254-2390 ext. 236;
e-mail: bmillard@dosomething.org

Family, Career and Community Leaders of America

www.fcclainc.org

FCCLA's mission is to "promote personal growth and leadership development through Family and Consumer Sciences education." The organization focuses on the roles of family, wage earners, and community leaders in character development and interpersonal communication.

Growing Leaders

www.growingleaders.com

Growing Leaders' mission is to "equip and mobilize one percent of the world's population under the age of 25 (30 million students) to think and act like authentic, life-giving leaders." It strives to help teens identify personal talents and purposes and put those gifts into action for service.

International Leadership Association

www.ila-net.org, www.ilaspace.org

"The ILA promotes a deeper understanding of leadership knowledge and practices for the greater good of individuals and communities worldwide. The ILA is the global network for all those who practice, study, and teach leadership." The organization also provides a member forum to network with other active leaders.

Contact: Josh Tarr, Coordinator of Conferences & Member Communities,
301-405-5218; e-mail: jtarr@ila-net.org

International Youth Leadership Institute

www.iyli.org

The IYLI provides several ways for teens to experience leadership—through volunteering, international study, seminars, community service, and a school partnership program. Young leaders also gain opportunities for mentoring and college preparation through this program. IYLI is based in New York.

Contact: 718-246-2620

LeaderShape

www.leadershape.org

LeaderShape is a six-day program that builds interpersonal and leadership skills. Students ages 17 to 25 participate in activities overseen by facilitators. They then develop a plan for change in their communities to be executed within the 9-12 months after the program.

Contact: 217-351-6200; e-mail: lead@leadershape.org

National Youth Leadership Conference

www.cylc.org

This government-run program is designed to give high school students an understanding of their roles in democracy and the responsibilities of leadership. Students work in Washington with lobbyists, members of Congress, journalists, and others responsible for the continuation and communication of democracy.

COMMUNITY SERVICE

ome high schools require students to fulfill community service hours before graduation. These organizations give students an opportunity to do community service, while also encouraging camaraderie among participants.

4-H

4-h.org

Originally an agricultural organization for youth, 4-H has evolved to include a focus on personal growth and positive change. 4-H places a special emphasis on science, technology, citizenship, and health.

Contact: National Council at 301-961-2934

Americorps

www.americorps.gov.

Americorps is a national program that allows students to exchange a year of community service for college funding. Service opportunities are available for students ages 17 and older.

Contact: 202-606-5000; e-mail: questions@americorps.org

Boy Scouts and Girl Scouts

www.scouting.org, www.girlscouts.org

The Boy Scouts provide an annual National Advanced Youth Leadership Experience, a weeklong leadership experience for 14- to 17-year-old boys, including workshops in teamwork and ethics. The Girl Scouts program is based on three key leadership principles: discover, connect, and take action. High school girls can join troops at the senior level (grades 9 and 10) or ambassador level (grades 11 and 12).

Hugh O'Brien Youth Leadership (HOBY)

www.hoby.org

This organization encourages students to develop their own unique perspectives and then apply these perspectives to a community activity. Students are appointed by their schools to participate in global leadership-building experiences. Adults may also volunteer for workshops and seminars.

Contact: 818-851-3980

Interact

www.rotary.org

Interact is Rotary International's service club for young people ages 14 to 18. Run by local Rotary chapters, it aims to help students develop personal leadership, demonstrate respect for others, understand the value of hard work, and advance international goodwill through two service projects per year.

Key Club International

www.keyclub.org

Key Club is a student-led organization that belongs to Kiwanis International. Students are provided with community service and leadership opportunities, including career development, service-learning, and college scholarships.

Contact: 317-875-8755

Me to We

www.metowe.com

Me to We works with students and educators to individualize the leadership learning experience. Through its programs Volunteer Now, Youth and Philanthropy Initiative, and Global Leadership Seminars, Me to We stresses the importance of thinking globally and acting on the community level.

Contact: leadership@metowe.com

National Beta Club

www.betaclub.org

The National Beta Club is an honors organization for fifth through twelfth graders with an emphasis on community service. The club aims to promote the concepts of honesty, morality, ethical conduct, service, and leadership.

National Youth Leadership Council

www.nylc.org

NYLC is a service-learning organization that emphasizes the role of youth in society and community. It also teaches critical thinking and seeks to address problems with solutions derived from educational curriculum.

Contact: 651-631-3672

Rotary Clubs

www.rotary.org

Students under age 30 can join Rotary clubs to build leadership skills. Education about ethics, service, and fellowship are central to Rotarian values. The Youth Exchange program allows students to participate in study abroad while acting as cultural ambassadors to other countries.

Contact: Rotary Youth Leadership Awards program, 847-866-3436; e-mail: ryla@rotary.org

Youth Service America

www.ysa.org

YSA "seeks to improve communities by increasing the number and diversity of young people, ages 5-25, serving in important roles." The nonprofit center provides a means of implementation for innovative service ideas. YSA has a partnership with international organizations in more than 100 countries to promote youth service worldwide.

Contact: 202-296-2992

CAREER INTEREST

F or students interested in combining their leadership opportunities with their career goals, career-based organizations can be a great resource. Many of these groups offer competitions, awards, scholarships, and conventions to members. Additionally, they can provide useful networking opportunities long before the job search and interview.

American Medical Student Association

www.amsa.org

The AMSA is considered the voice of physicians-in-training across the United States. Run by student members, the group focuses on activism in the healthcare field by working to eliminate health disparities, advocate for diversity in medicine and fight for universal healthcare. Additionally, the group contributes more than one million hours of community service each year.

Business Professionals of America

www.bpa.org

The BPA is an organization dedicated to students pursuing careers in business management, office administration, and information technology. By participating in conferences and programs offered by the group, members are prepared to succeed in real-world business situations.

Distributive Education Clubs of America (DECA)

www.deca.org

This is the high school level of Delta Epsilon Chi. DECA membership spans across educational curricula incorporating marketing, business, and finance principles into areas such as work, community service, and business leadership.

Contact: 703-860-5000

Future Business Leaders of America/Phi Beta Lambda

www.fbla-pbl.org

FBLA is the high school branch of Phi Beta Lambda. The association prepares students for business careers and helps them develop their leadership skills through meetings, seminars, competitive events, publications, and conferences, including the National Leadership Conference.

Contact: 800-325-2946; e-mail: general@fbla.org

Future Scientists and Engineers of America

www.discoverycube.org/fsea.aspx

FSEA is an after-school program designed to motivate and inspire students through hands-on projects that relate education to career possibilities. Members earn points over time, which can be redeemed for anything from a gift certificate to a tuition stipend for college.

Girls Going Places Entrepreneurship Award Program

www.girlsgoingplaces.com

This program rewards the enterprising spirit of 15 young women ages 12 to 18. Cash prizes are given to those demonstrating budding entrepreneurship, taking the steps toward financial independence, and making a difference in their communities and schools.

Health Occupations Students of America (HOSA)

www.hosa.org

HOSA is a national student organization aimed at promoting career opportunities in the healthcare industry and delivering quality healthcare to all people. The organization focuses on providing education opportunities and leadership development to students through competitive activities at the local, state, and national levels.

Junior Engineering Technical Society

www.jets.org

JETS' goal is to help students explore, assess, and experience engineering first-hand. The program utilizes assessment tools, career exploration, and student competitions to encourage students to discover their potential for engineering.

Junior State of America (JSA)

www.jsa.org

JSA is nationally administered but locally run organization geared toward students interested in government, politics, foreign affairs, the law, and education. It offers networking opportunities and the exchange of ideas through debates, talks, problem solving, conventions, and conferences—all of which are organized by students.

National FFA Organization (Future Farmers of America)

www.ffa.org

The group's mission is to develop student potential for leadership, personal growth, and career success through agricultural education. Members are connected to careers in the science, technology, and business of agriculture.

ROTC Clubs (Reserve Officers' Training Corps)

Air Force	www.afrotc.com
Army	www.usarmyjrotc.com
Marines	www.mcjrotc.org
Navy	www.njrotc.navy.mil

Junior ROTC clubs are funded by the United States Armed Forces. The clubs focus on instilling the values of citizenship, service to the United States, personal responsibility, and leadership through understanding opportunities in the military. These clubs continue on in college with full-fledged ROTC organizations and can offer scholarships.

SkillsUSA-VICA

www.skillsusa.org

SkillsUSA-VICA is a national organization dedicated to young people enrolled in trade, industrial, technical, and health education programs. Through community service activities, the group nurtures realistic career goals, ethics, and dignity of work in members.

Technology Student Association

www.tsaweb.org

The TSA is a student organization devoted to students interested in technology. In local chapters, members compete in state and national competitions in such areas as biotechnology, Web site design, flight challenge, and film technology.

INTERPERSONAL DYNAMICS

T hese organizations address the cultural and social dynamics associated with environment, tradition, and culture. Academic, political, and religious clubs fall under this category.

National Honor Society

www.nhs.us

NHS recognizes outstanding high school students (grades 10-12) in scholarship, leadership, service, and character. If your school does not belong to a local NHS chapter, ask your principal where you can join one. Review the membership requirements online before applying.

Contact: 703-860-0200

National Association of Student Councils

www.nasc.us

NASC boosts the benefits of being involved with student government by providing a national network with other schools. Benefits include scholarships, awards, and recognition for achievement and conferences. To join, schools must submit an annual application and initiation fee.

Contact: 703-860-0200

Political Organizations:

National Teen Age Republicans — republicanteens.org
High School Democrats of America — highschoolyda.org
Young Democratic Socialists — ydsusa.org
New American Independent Party — newamericanindependent.com

Religious Organizations:

Campus Crusade for Christ International — ccci.org
The Foundation for Jewish Campus Life — hillel.org
Muslim Students Association — msanational.org

Student Pagan Organizations	collegewicca.com
Life Teen for Catholic Teenagers	lifeteen.com
Latter-Day Saints Student Organizations	lds.org/institutes/organizations

PERSONAL INTEREST

Sometimes the best way to develop leadership skills is by being involved with something you're passionate that isn't necessarily focused on academic, career, or community involvement. These organizations reflect personal interests and are not necessarily just for high school students.

Animal Behavior Society	animalbehavior.org
American Quarter Horse Association	aqha.com
American Historical Association	historians.org
American Mathematical Society	ams.org
Costume Designers Guild	costumedesignersguild.com
USCF Mechanics Program	promechanics.com
American Society of Interior Decorators	asid.org
Motion Picture Association of America	mpaa.org
American Society of Cinematographers	theasc.org
Art Directors Guild	artdirectors.org
Online Film Critics Society	ofcs.org
Writers Guild of America	wga.org
American Culinary Federation	acfchefs.org
American Society of Psychical Research	aspr.com
International Laser Tag Association	lasertag.org
Society of American Magicians	magicsam.com
Entertainment Software Association	theesa.com
National Association of Broadcasters	nab.org
United Brotherhood of Carpenters and Joiners of America	carpenters.org
Society of Children's Book Writers and Illustrators	scbwi.org

Society of Illustrators	societyillustrators.org
National Demolition Association	demolitionassociation.com
American Fitness Professionals & Associates	afpafitness.com
Greeting Card Association	greetingcard.org
Handwriting Analysts Group	handwriting.org
Photographic Society of America	psa-photo.org
Toastmasters International	toastmasters.org
American Federation of Musicians	afm.org
Drum Circle Meetup Groups	Drumcircle.meetup.com
The Nature Conservancy	nature.org
National Farmers Union	nfu.org
Screen Actors Guild	sag.org
International Thespian Society	itothespians.com
Stuntmen's Association of Motion Pictures	stuntmen.com
Stuntwomen's Association of Motion Pictures	stuntwomen.com
Association of Performing Arts Presenters	artspresenters.org

APPENDIX B

Further Reading and Resources

The 21 Irrefutable Laws of Leadership

John C. Maxwell

Maxwell shares insight by exploring successes and failures in business, politics, sports, religion, and military conflict.

Building Everyday Leadership

Mariam Macgregor

Macgregor defines leadership and explains the importance and benefits of action. Lessons include: what makes a good leader, doing the right thing, turning conflict into cooperation, and thinking creatively.

Combinations: Opening the Door to Student Leadership

Ed Gerety

Gerety, a professional leadership trainer, provides stories, strategies, and challenges for students interested in leading.

John P. Kotter on What Leaders Really Do

John P. Kotter

Kotter offers a look at real experience and issues in leadership and shows the consequences of organizations and communities lacking leaders.

Leadership

James Macgregor Burns

Political science professor James Burns discusses leadership in relation to world history and American politics. Complexities with economic, political, and social relationships between leaders are also addressed.

The Leadership Challenge

James M. Kouzes and Barry Z. Posner

This book helps readers become leaders through methods supported by extensive research, especially in the business world. The book takes the stance that *everyone* should lead, using the motto "Leadership is Everyone's Business."

Leadership from the Inside Out: Becoming a Leader for Life

Kevin Cashman

Research, case studies and coaching methods on leadership are included in this guide. Personal awareness, commitment, and practice are three key tools Cashman employs to develop leadership skills.

Leadership Is An Art

Max De Pree

De Pree approaches leadership philosophy as a means to building strong relationships, presenting valuable ideas, and creating a long-lasting impact within society. The author emphasizes generosity and the "whys" of corporate life.

Leadership Rocks

Jay Strack

Dr. Strack's program aids students in achieving their own leadership potential, highlighting the importance of good, young leaders. Aspects such as endurance, enthusiasm, moral courage, and selflessness are part of the process.

Letters from Leaders

Henry O. Dormann

Dormann provides a collection of letters from 79 different leaders around the world, from Walter Cronkite to Muhammad Ali. Advice includes goal-setting, achievement, leadership, and public service, and is addressed to the young generation of today.

Now, Discover Your Strengths

Marcus Buckingham and Donald O. Clifton

This book separates personality types into 34 different profiles, based on personal tendencies and desires. The profiles encourage users to develop individual talents and strengths. An online quiz segment is included to determine your individual profile.

On Becoming A Leader
Warren Bennis

Bennis helps readers develop their own strategies for leading and gives examples of leaders in times of conflict and uncertainty.

On Leadership
John William Gardner

Gardner's goal is to encourage the human race, despite past failures, to use vision to achieve any possibility "...to live up to the best in our past and to reach the goals we have yet to achieve."

Primal Leadership: Learning to Lead with Emotional Intelligence
Daniel Goleman

This book is an excellent resource that highlights the connection between personal tendencies and the ability to take charge and make a difference in the lives of others.

The Secret for Teens Revealed
Andrea Samadi

This workbook emphasizes the importance of current decisions on future outcomes. Each section contains a pre-test, lesson, review, and extension exercises. Special modes of thinking and behavior for successful leadership are discussed.

Strengths-Based Leadership
Tom Rath, Barry Conchie

Authors Rath and Conchie present the results of extensive field research, asking real-world leaders what they admire in other leaders. Three keys to effective leadership are discussed along with ideas for action.

To Lead or Not to Lead: Leadership Development Studies
Phi Theta Kappa

This text is comprised of case studies on leadership including Plato, Machiavelli, and Martin Luther King Jr. The book is a great read for examples of changing leadership throughout history.

APPENDIX C
Leader Biographies

Chapter 1
BECOMING A LEADER

TITLE PAGE:

Oprah Winfrey (1954–PRESENT)

Television host and producer, magazine founder, philanthropist

Oprah Winfrey's life is the epitome of the "rags-to-riches" story, as she overcame childhood poverty to become a household name through her self-titled talk show. Winfrey started her own production company and talk show as a result of her success as a radio and television host in cities such as Nashville and Chicago.

The Oprah Winfrey Show quickly became the highest-rated talk show in the United States and is broadcasted worldwide. Winfrey has been ranked on the Forbes list of billionaires and as the richest African-American of the twentieth century. In addition to her production company, Winfrey has established her own magazine as well as various international charities.

http://www.oprah.com/pressroom/Oprah-Winfreys-Official-Biography/6

LEADERS DISCUSSED IN THE TEXT:

Hannah Teter (1987–PRESENT)

Olympic gold medalist in snowboarding

When she's not riding the slopes and securing Olympic medals, Teter is known for her dedication to worthy causes around the world. Her charity work includes bringing fresh water to the people of Kirindon, Kenya, and supporting the infrastructure and humanitarian needs of Africa.

http://www.notablebiographies.com/newsmakers2/2006-Ra-Z/Teter-Hannah.html

Frederick Douglass (1817–1895)

Abolitionist, orator, statesmen

After escaping from slavery, Douglass made significant contributions to the abolitionist movement by becoming a respected African-American speaker and writer. His achievements included being chosen as an advisor to Abraham Lincoln during the Civil War.

http://www.biography.com/articles/Frederick-Douglass-9278324

Confucius (ca. 551 B.C.–ca. 479 B.C.)

Chinese teacher, philosopher

A legendary figure in China, Confucius founded the school of Confucianism or Ju philosophy. Confucius believed that the primary task of a ruler was to achieve the well-being and happiness of the people of his state and to lead by example.

http://www.notablebiographies.com/Co-Da/Confucius.html

Ishmael Beah (1980–PRESENT)

After a tumultuous childhood as a boy soldier in Sierra Leone, Beah served as a representative in the United Nations First International Children's Parliament, wrote a book about his experiences, and partnered with Starbucks and UNICEF for child welfare in war.

http://www.alongwaygone.com/

Chapter 2
CREATING A VISION

TITLE PAGE:

Erik Weihenmayer (1968–PRESENT)

Adventurer, motivational speaker, author

In 2001, Erik Weihenmayer became the first blind person to climb to the top of Mount Everest. He wrote the memoir Touch the Top of the World: A Blind Man's Journey to Climb Farther Than the Eye Can See, to document his achievements. Weihenmayer is also a former teacher and wrestling coach, skier, mountaineer, skydiver, and marathon runner. He has also won an ESPY award and has been inducted into the National Wrestling Hall of Fame. To learn more about Erik Weihenmayer, visit his Web site, **www.touchthetop.com,** and find curriculum to accompany his memoir.

http://www.touchthetop.com/about.htm

LEADERS DISCUSSED IN THE TEXT:

Roy Kroc (1902–1984)

Businessman

As the founder of the McDonald's Corporation, Kroc was the first businessperson to apply the principles of mass production to a service industry. Under his leadership, McDonald's grew to become the largest food chain in the world.

www.mcdonalds.com

Christopher Reeve (1952–2004)

Actor, activist

Best known for his role as "The Man of Steel" in the movie *Superman*, Reeve became equally famous for his tragic equestrian accident in 1995 that left him paralyzed. Rather than be deterred by his situation, Reeve became the face of spinal cord injuries and challenged doctors around the world to conquer the complex mysteries of the central nervous system.

www.chistopherreeve.org
www.christopherreevehomepage.com

Herb Brooks (1937–2003)

Hockey coach

Brooks made history when he led the American hockey team to upset the powerful Soviets and then win the gold medal in the 1980 Olympics in what was later called the "Miracle on Ice." A determined, challenging man, Brooks expected and cultivated the best from his players.

www.herbbrooksfoundation.com

Sir Albert Howard (1873–1947)

Organic farmer

Unimpressed by the scientific approaches to agriculture of his time—which encouraged overspecialization—Howard set out to grow a healthy crop using conventional methods: sun, water, and soil. His determination to utilize the teachings nature provided resulted in the early organic farming movement.

http://www.journeytoforever.org/farm_library/howard_memorial.html

Jim Collins (1958–PRESENT)

American business author, consultant

Collins studies the success and failures of companies. He's written several books on the sustainability and growth of companies and has served as a consultant to more than one hundred corporations, including some in the social sector.

http://www.jimcollins.com/about-jim.html

William Kamkwamba (1987–PRESENT)

Inventor

When his family was hit hard by a famine, Kamkwamba looked for a way to alleviate some of the strain on his family. After finding an old textbook on energy at the library, he set out to make a windmill capable of providing electric power using spare parts around his family's home. Since then, he's built a solar-powered water pump for his village and two other windmills.

http://movingwindmills.org/story

Chapter 3

CRITICAL AND CREATIVE THINKING

TITLE PAGE:

Yo-Yo Ma (1955–PRESENT)

Cellist, composer

At the age of four, Yo-Yo Ma picked up a cello for the first time, and he is now a Grammy award-winning cellist and world-renowned orchestra composer. Ma played the cello for Presidents Kennedy and Eisenhower during his childhood and studied at the prestigious Julliard School of Music before earning a bachelor's degree at Harvard University. He is known for adding an eclectic twist to classical music and for working on more than seventy-five albums, including fifteen Grammy winners. Ma has also been honored as a Messenger of Peace for the United Nations, and in 2009 he was appointed by President Obama to the President's Committee on the Arts and Humanities.

http://www.yo-yoma.com/yo-yo-ma-biography

LEADERS DISCUSSED IN THE TEXT:

Caroline Moore (1994–PRESENT)

Amateur astronomer

On November 7, 2008, at the age of 14, Moore became the youngest person to discover a supernova.

http://www.nsf.gov/discoveries/disc_summ.jsp?cntn_id=115097

Archimedes of Syracuse (ca. 287 B.C.–ca. 212 B.C.)

Greek mathematician

In addition to being a mathematician, Archimedes was an accomplished physicist, engineer, inventor, and astronomer. His list of inventions and discoveries is long, and he is generally considered one of the greatest minds of antiquity.

http://www.biographyshelf.com/archimedes_biography.html

Galileo Galilei (1564–1642)

Italian physicist

A major player in the Scientific Revolution, Galilei was best known for his improvements to the telescope and his support of Copernicanism. He is considered the father of modern physics and astronomy.

http://www.biography.com/articles/Galileo-9305220

Guirand de Scevola (1871–1950)

French painter

Working as a telephone operator for a French artillery unit during the First World War, de Scevola realized that cubist painting techniques could be used to hide infantry on the ground through the use of earth tones and netting.

Johannes Kepler (1571–1630)

German astronomer

German astronomer Johannes Kepler's discovery of three basic laws governing the motion of planets made him one of the chief founders of modern astronomy (the study of the universe and its stars and planets).

http://www.notablebiographies.com/Jo-Ki/Kepler-Johannes.html

Jacques-Yves Cousteau (1910–1997)

French explorer, scientist, ecologist

A respected underwater explorer, photographer, and inventor of diving devices, Cousteau was responsible for bringing the sea to television sets around the world and educating others about the damaging effects of pollution.

http://www.notablebiographies.com/Co-Da/Cousteau-Jacques.html
http://www.cousteau.org/about-us/jaques

Stephen Hawking (1942–PRESENT)

English scientist, physicist, mathematician

Hawking is considered one of the world's foremost authorities on cosmology—the study of the origins, structure, and space-time relationships of the universe. His contributions have helped shape the way we look at the rules of the universe.

http://www.hawking.org.uk/index.php/about-stephen/briefhistory

Henrietta Swan Leavitt (1868–1921)

American astronomer

While working at the Harvard College Observatory, Leavitt made several discoveries regarding how to determine the magnitude of a star and, later, the theory of period-luminosity. Her contributions influenced the work of later astronomers including Edward Hubble in determining the age of the universe.

http://www.womanastronomer.com/hleavitt.htm

Chapter 4
EARNING RESPECT

TITLE PAGE:

César Chávez (1927–1993)

Farm worker, civil rights activist

César Chávez and his family endured years of discrimination and poverty due to their Mexican-American heritage, which later led him to establish his own organization to fight for the rights of migrant workers. His family moved from Arizona to California during the Great Depression, where they and other Mexican-American citizens experienced low wages and unfair working conditions.

After he completed eighth grade, he quit school to work in the California vineyards and later joined the Navy. Once he completed a tour of duty during World War II, Chávez established the National Farm Workers Association to improve working conditions for migrant workers and farmers. Chávez led strikes over the years to boycott the California agriculture industry to draw attention to the struggles of migrant workers and the use of pesticides. The National Farm Workers Association (NFWA) later became known as United Farm Workers.

http://www.ufw.org/_page.php?menu=research&inc=history/07.html

LEADERS DISCUSSED IN THE TEXT:

Mother Teresa (1910–1997)

Albanian nun

Mother Teresa's devotional work among the poor and dying of India won her the Nobel Prize for Peace in 1979. She is also known as the founder of the only Catholic religious order still growing in membership.

http://www.notablebiographies.com/Mo-Ni/Mother-Teresa.html
http://nobelprize.org/nobel_prizes/peace/laureates/1979/teresa-bio.html

Bernard Madoff (1938–PRESENT)

American stock broker, financial advisor and chairman of NASDAQ

Madoff was a successful financial advisor and stockbroker. Though he rose to the ranks of NASDAQ chairman, his shady dealings and poor choices resulted in his charge of running the largest Ponzi scheme in history.

Andrei Sakharov (1921–1989)

Russian physicist and reformer

Andrei Sakharov was one of the Soviet Union's leading physicists and is regarded in scientific circles as the "father of the Soviet atomic bomb." He also became one of Soviet Union's most prominent political dissidents (a person who holds political views that differ from the majority) in the 1970s.

http://www.notablebiographies.com/Ro-Sc/Sakharov-Andrei.html

Greg Mortenson (1957–PRESENT)

American humanitarian, writer, and activist

Greg Mortenson is a proponent of community-based education programs in the mountainous regions within Pakistan and Afghanistan. He is also a U.S. Army veteran and was a Nobel Peace Prize nominee in 2008 and 2009.

http://www.gregmortenson.com/biography/

Dina Astita (1957–PRESENT)

Indonesian teacher, survivor of 2004 Indian ocean tsunami

Dina Astita is a teacher who lost her three sons in the 2004 tsunami, which killed 90 percent of her village. Educators chose her to restart the local education system where she taught orphans.

http://www.time.com/time/subscriber/2005/time100/heroes/100astita.html
http://www.bbc.co.uk/worldservice/lg/programmes/2009/12/091215_
tsunami_journalist.shtml

King Jigme Singye Wangchuck (1955–PRESENT)

Former king of Bhutan and political reformer

Jigme Singye Wangchuck is the former ruler of Bhutan who sequentially gave up his power. In 1998 he relinquished his absolute power, and in 2005 he issued a constitution to his people that allowed for his impeachment. He enacted the country's first democratic elections after he resigned.

http://www.time.com/time/magazine/article/0,9171,1186840,00.html

Beryl Markham (1902–1986)

British-Kenyan aviator, author, equestrian

Beryl Markham was a British-Kenyan pilot, who was the first to fly solo across the Atlantic Ocean from east to west. She wrote a successful book detailing her adventure across the ocean. She was also the first woman in Kenya to receive her pilot's license.

http://www.karenblixen.com/gale.html

David Greenberg (1943–PRESENT)

American businessman, aviator

1943-present
David Greenberg is an American aviator credited with helping diffuse the Korean Air problems. He was hired by Korean Air in 2000 to help improve its image after a passenger plane veered into Soviet air space and was shot down.

http://www.usatoday.com/news/sept11/2002-08-12-koreanair_x.htm

Sir Ernest H. Shackleton (1874–1922)

British explorer

Ernest Shackleton was a pioneering explorer in the early twentieth century who, with his Nimrod Expedition team, explored further to the South Pole than anyone at the time.

http://www.south-pole.com/p0000097.htm

Jessica Watson (1993–PRESENT)

Australian sailor

Jessica Watson is an Australian sailor who was the youngest to sail solo, unassisted, and nonstop around the world.

http://jessicawatson.com.au/index.htm

http://www.abc.net.au/news/stories/2009/10/18/2717160.htm?section=justin

Dorothy Height (1912–2010)

American social service worker, activist

As the president of the National Council of Negro Women, Height was an integral part of the fight for desegregation and developing leadership programs for youth.

http://www.biography.com/articles/Dorothy-Height-40743

Nydia Velazquez (1953–PRESENT)

Puerto Rican-American politician

Velazquez's political career has been full of firsts: In 1992, she became the first Puerto Rican woman elected to the U.S. House of Representatives. In 1998, she became the first Hispanic woman to serve as a ranking member on a House committee, and in 2006, she became the first Latina to chair a full congressional committee.

http://www.house.gov/velazquez/about/bio.html

Wade Davis (1953–PRESENT)

Canadian anthropologist, ethnobotanist, author

As an author and photographer of indigenous cultures, Davis has spent a lot of time in North and South America. His work has focused on the traditional uses and beliefs associated with psychoactive plants.

http://www.nationalgeographic.com/field/explorers/wade-davis.html

Chapter 5

COMMUNICATION

TITLE PAGE:

Wilma Mankiller (1945–2010)

Cherokee chief, activist, author

Wilma Mankiller was elected the first female chief of the Cherokee Nation in 1985 and has written and collaborated on books about Native American and Cherokee culture. Mankiller's family moved from Oklahoma to California when she was young, and she attended San Francisco State University, where she became active in San Francisco's Indian Center. She moved back to Oklahoma to aid in the economic and political advancement of the Cherokee nation.

Mankiller faced adversity once she became chief because of her gender, but she did not allow it to inhibit her from improving the Cherokee community through community programs and enlisting the assistance of the federal government. She strengthened ties between the Cherokee Nation and the federal government and improved the nation's infrastructure and economic growth. Mankiller was awarded with the Presidential Medal of Freedom in 1998.

http://www.notablebiographies.com/Lo-Ma/Mankiller-Wilma.html

http://www.biography.com/articles/Wilma-Mankiller-214109

LEADERS DISCUSSED IN THE TEXT:

Heini Hediger (1908–1992)

Swiss zoologist

Heini Hediger was a Swiss zoologist credited with helping form modern zoo biology after studying animal and human communications.

http://www.ut.ee/SOSE/sss/articles/turovski_28.htm

Christine Stevens (1951–2002)

American animal rights activist

Christine Stevens was the founder of the Animal Welfare Institute, an organization designed to protect animals from inhumane treatment.

http://www.awionline.org/ht/d/sp/i/208/pid/208

Monty Roberts (1935–PRESENT)

American equestrian

Monty Roberts is an American horse trainer who gained international recognition for being able to communicate with horses. His training program is known for helping to build relationships with horses and train them with more human methods.

http://www.montyroberts.com/ab_about_monty.html

Rachel Carson (1907–1964)

American ecologist, writer, biologist

Rachel Carson was an American ecologist who fought against pesticides in 1960s and played a pivotal role in the banning of DDT, a synthetic pesticide, in 1972.

http://www.rachelcarson.org/default.aspx

Jane Goodall (1937–PRESENT)

British primatologist, environmentalist, anthropologist, animal rights activist

Jane Goodall is a British primatologist who spent many years studying chimpanzees in Tanzania. She also founded the Jane Goodall Institute.

http://www.janegoodall.org/jane-goodall

Shadrach Meshach

Tanzanian humanitarian

After meeting Jane Goodall as a young man in Tanzania, Meshach has dedicated his time and energy toward making the world a better place for people in need through programs like the ACACIA Female Leadership Initiative.

http://www.femaleleadership.org

Chapter 6
TEAMWORK

TITLE PAGE:

Cal Ripken Jr. (1960–PRESENT)
Baseball player, author

Retired Baltimore Orioles player Cal Ripken Jr. holds many records after his 21 years of playing professional baseball, including the most consecutive games played. Ripken played 2,632 consecutive games and hit 431 home runs in his career, and he was inducted into the National Baseball Hall of Fame in 2007. Aside from his Major League Baseball career, Ripken has written five books, some of which are best-sellers. He has also established his own nonprofit organization named after his father, Cal Ripken Sr. The organization aids at-risk and underprivileged children through sports programs.

http://www.ripkenbaseball.com/calripken/bio/

LEADERS DISCUSSED IN THE TEXT:

Steve Case (1958–PRESENT)
American businessman

Steve Case is an American businessman responsible for launching the popular Internet software America Online.

http://www.achievement.org/autodoc/page/cas1bio-1

Franklin D. Roosevelt (1882–1945)
32nd president of the United States

Following the Great Depression, Roosevelt—along with his team of trusted advisors—enacted the New Deal, which reinvigorated the job market and economy.

http://www.whitehouse.gov/about/presidents/franklindroosevelt

Henry Ford (1862–1947)
American engineer, inventor, businessman

Fascinated early on by internal combustion engines, Ford devoted most of his adult life to the design, production, and distribution of a reasonably priced, reliable, efficient automobile, the Model T.

http://www.hfmgv.org

Nick Graham (1993–PRESENT)

American entrepreneur, businessman

By buying his small town's failing grocery store, Nick Graham, a 17-year-old from Truman, Minnesota, rejuvenated the local economy and the spirits of the citizens who live there.

http://www.americanprofile.com/kids/article/25009.html

Anne Mulcahy (1952–PRESENT)

American businesswoman

Starting out at a field sales representative in 1976, Mulcahy rose through the ranks of Xerox Corporation to eventually become chairman of the board and CEO of the company.

http://www.sec.gov/spotlight/xbrl/2006/ammulcahy_bio.pdf

James Cameron (1954–PRESENT)

Canadian filmmaker

Though having always had an interest in film, young Cameron was unsure of his path until he saw *Star Wars*. From there, he devoted himself to the study of film, borrowed money from friends for equipment, and eventually landed a small job with Roger Corman. Within three weeks of being hired, Cameron had his own department and was hiring employees. The rest, as they say, is history.

http://www.achievement.org/autodoc/page/cam0bio-1

Chapter 7

ETHICS

TITLE PAGE:

Sonia Sotomayor (1954–PRESENT)

U.S. Supreme Court Justice

In August 2009, Sonia Sotomayor was appointed as the first Hispanic and third female justice in the Supreme Court. She grew up underprivileged in the Bronx, New York, and defied the odds to graduate summa cum laude from Princeton University in 1976. She went on to Yale Law School and passed the bar in 1980. Her career in law led her from public cases as an assistant district attorney in New York City to working in private practice. In 1991, Sotomayor was appointed to the U.S. District Court of Southern New York City as its youngest judge, and in 1998, she became the first Hispanic judge in the U.S. Second Circuit Court of Appeals. Sotomayor has also taught as an adjunct professor at New York University and Columbia University and holds honorary degrees from various universities.

http://www.whitehouse.gov/the_press_office/Background-on-Judge-Sonia-Sotomayor/
http://www.biography.com/articles/Sonia-Sotomayor-453906?part=1

LEADERS DISCUSSED IN THE TEXT:

Sandra Day O'Connor (1930–PRESENT)

U.S. Supreme Court Justice

In 1981, Sandra Day O'Connor became the first woman to serve as a justice on the U.S. Supreme Court. In 2009, she was awarded the Presidential Medal of Freedom, the highest civilian honor.

http://www.biography.com/articles/Sandra-Day-O%27Connor-9426834

Sister Helen Prejean (1938–PRESENT)

Roman Catholic nun

Sister Prejean is an American nun who has become one of the leading advocates for the abolition of the death penalty.

www.prejean.org

Nelson Mandela (1918–PRESENT)

South African president and political activist

Nelson Mandela is a South African leader who spent years in prison for opposing apartheid, the policy by which the races were separated and whites were given power over blacks in South Africa. When he was finally released, he became president and ended apartheid in his country.

http://www.notablebiographies.com/Lo-Ma/Mandela-Nelson.html
http://nobelprize.org/nobel_prizes/peace/laureates/1993/mandela-bio.html

Bono (Paul Hewson) (1960–PRESENT)

Irish singer, activist

Aside from his success as the front man for the Irish rock group U2, Bono works to generate awareness about a variety of issues, including AIDS, poverty, and debt relief for developing countries.

http://www.biography.com/articles/Bono-16257407

Juan Pablo Romero Fuentes

Guatemalan founder of Los Patojos school

As a young man in Guatemala, Fuentes struggled with a language barrier that prevented him from communicating with English-speaking employers. From that experience, Fuentes founded the Los Patojos school, which is dedicated to teaching English to young people and creating community awareness.

http://www.justworldinternational.org/projects.cfm

Victor Frankl (1905–1997)

Austrian neurologist, psychiatrist

The father of logotherapy, Frankl proposed that humans can undergo a tremendous amount of strain if they can identify a purpose and meaning in life.

http://www.worldofbiography.com/9124-Victor%20Frankl/ataglance.htm

Chapter 8
PEER MENTORING

TITLE PAGE:

Steve Jobs (1955–PRESENT)

Entrepreneur/CEO of Apple, Inc.

Steve Jobs' success story is an atypical one, as he became a multibillionaire despite dropping out of college. He and high school friend Steve Wozniak built a personal computer and established Apple Computers after Jobs quit Reed College in Oregon and worked for video game company Atari. They dedicated themselves to creating technology that was smaller, cheaper, and easy to use. Apple technology has revolutionized the design and use of computers and portable devices, with innovations such as Mac computers, the iPod, iPhone and various software programs. Jobs is also the co-founder and CEO of Pixar Animation studios, which has created movies such as *Toy Story* and *WALL-E*.

http://www.apple.com/pr/bios/jobs.html

http://www.biography.com/articles/Steven-Jobs-9354805?part=2

LEADERS DISCUSSED IN THE TEXT:

Daniel Garcia

American peer leader

After attending the leadership program College Summit during high school, Garcia discovered that he enjoyed working with at-risk youth to achieve their academic and professional goals. He is now an alumni leader for College Summit and working through college.

http://www.collegesummit.org/regions/southern-california/sca_peer_leaders_alumni

Ngahihi O Te Ra Bidois

Maori motivational speaker, educator, business professional

After succeeding in the business world by age 26, Bidois decided that to be happy, he needed to reconnect with his Maori roots. Today, Bidois works in the education sector, guiding young people to achieve their dreams by connecting with their identity.

http://www.ngahibidois.com/index.html

Lee Kuan Yew (1923–PRESENT)

Former prime minister of Singapore

Among his many reforms, Yew is well-known for his emancipation of women and the industrialization of Singapore, making it the most prosperous nation in Southeast Asia.

http://www.biography.com/articles/Lee-Kuan-Yew-9377339

Lee Hsien Loong (1952–PRESENT)

Current prime minister of Singapore

Eldest son of former Prime Minister Lee Kuan Yew, Loong has focused his leadership on social issues like the aging population of Singapore and the globalization of the country.

http://www.cabinet.gov.sg/CabinetAppointments/Mr+Lee+Hsien+Loong.htm

Howard Schultz (1953–PRESENT)

American businessman, entrepreneur

Captivated by the notion of bringing the traditional Italian coffeehouses to the United States, Schultz combined his love of coffee drinks and his innate knowledge of real estate to create one of the most successful brands in the world, Starbucks.

http://www.starbucks.com/about-us/our-heritage

Chapter 9

MAKING A DIFFERENCE

LEADERS DISCUSSED IN THE TEXT:

Venus Williams (1980–PRESENT)

American tennis player, businessperson

In addition to be a champion athlete, Williams has dedicated herself to a number of causes around the world, including UNESCO; promoting gender equality; the development of her own clothing line, EleVen; and an interior design company, V Starr Interiors.

http://www.biography.com/articles/Venus-Williams-9533011?part=0

Hannah Salwen

American author, humanitarian, student

One fateful morning, Salwen noticed a man on the street begging for food. Seeing an expensive car across the street, she was moved by the inequality of the situation and decided to live on less and help more. Since then, she's coauthored a book on the subject and still works with the Hunger Project on solving global hunger.

http://www.thp.org/learn_more/news/latest_news/ power_of_half_new_book_from_thp_investors_kevin_and_hannah_salwen

Joe Ehrmann (1949–PRESENT)

American football coach, former football player

After playing professional football for the Baltimore Colts and the Detroit Lions, Ehrmann turned his attention to helping others. Becoming a football coach for a small boys' school, he implemented a code of conduct designed to make his players better on the field and in life.

http://www.parade.com/articles/editions/2004/edition_08-29-2004/featured_0

Pamela Escobar

American student, human rights activist

Escobar's contributions to humanitarian efforts include designing and implementing a peer tutoring program, passing a school policy ensuring the responsible production of gym uniforms, and working with Free the Children, an international organization aimed at ending child labor. She also worked with the American Civil Liberties Union and Jovenes, Inc. to place water throughout the desert for dehydrated immigrants.

http://www.mff.org/newsroom/news. taf?page=f&_function=detail&id=452

Jackie Rotman (1991–PRESENT)

Founder of Everybody Dance Now!

Rotman founded Everybody Dance Now! to provide opportunities to dance and perform to members of her community. Rotman has since passed her leadership baton on to other young leaders and is now studying at Stanford University.

http://www.everybodydancenow.org/

Quincy Jones (1933–PRESENT)

American music conductor, producer, arranger

Having worked with musical legends like Ray Charles and Michael Jackson, Jones is known as a mover and shaker in the industry. His credits include everything from hit records to film scores to sitcom theme songs.

http://www.achievement.org/autodoc/page/jon0bio-1

APPENDIX D

World's Greatest Problems

B ecoming a leader today at school is a great way to develop skills for tackling some of the problems facing your community, your country, and world. As you prepare to lead in the future, consider some of the following global problems that have been defined by J.F. Rischard in his book, *High Noon: 20 Global Problems—20 Years to Solve Them*. Which issues inspire you and call you to action?

Sharing our planet:
Issues involving the global commons

Global warming. Since the mid-20th century, the Earth's average temperature has increased 0.74 ± 0.18 degrees C (1.33 ± 0.32 degrees F) and is projected to continue. Most believe the cause to be the increasing concentrations of greenhouse gases.

Biodiversity and ecosystem losses. Biodiversity is the variation of life forms within a given ecosystem and is often used to measure the health of biological systems. Ecosystem losses, especially those certain species humans depend on for food, could result in extinction.

Fisheries depletion. Often caused by overfishing, it affects the ecosystem of that particular body of water and jeopardizes the food supply and economic stability of coastal populations.

Deforestation. Trees provide oxygen for every living organism to breathe, and serve as habitats for many creatures. When forests are burned to clear land, large amounts of CO_2 are released, contributing to global warming.

Maritime safety and pollution. Globalization has increased trade, and there is now more shipping across oceans. Ships pollute the air and water and directly affect coastal areas, impacting biodiversity, climate, food, and human health. There are also issues as to who is responsible for governance at sea.

Water deficits. The human population has nearly tripled over the last fifty years, but factors such as industrial pollution and poor civic planning have decreased the overall water supply.

Sharing our humanity:
Issues requiring a global commitment

Massive step-up in the fight against poverty. Poverty refers to living conditions without access to basic human needs such as clean water, nutrition, healthcare, education, clothing, and shelter. Poverty affects millions of people around the world. Six million children die of hunger every year—17,000 every day.

Peacekeeping, conflict resolution, combating terrorism. With today's technological advancements, it is important to maintain peace to avoid a potentially catastrophic World War III.

Education for all. Education is a privilege provided to children in most developed countries but not accessible for many children living in third-world countries or in poverty.

Global infectious diseases. Today's modern modes of transportation make it possible for a person to travel to a foreign land, contract a disease, and not have any symptoms of illness until after they get home, exposing others along the way and spreading disease faster than ever before.

Digital divide. There is a gap between people with access to digital and information technology and those with little to no access. This gap affects how people communicate, gather information, and navigate their lives in the twenty-first century.

Natural disaster prevention and mitigation. As Hurricane Katrina in 2005 and the destruction in Haiti in 2010 have shown, preparing for disasters before they occur, having quick response and support plans once they occur, and knowing how to best rebuild communities after disasters strike are vitally important.

Sharing our rule book:
Issues needing a global regulatory approach

Reinventing taxation for the twenty-first century. With an increasing uneven distribution of wealth and the mounting government debt, current taxation rules might need to be reassessed.

Biotechnology rules. Biotechnology is a field of biology that uses microorganisms such as bacteria and yeast to solve problems and make useful products. Because biotechnology can be used for destructive purposes, rules are needed to govern how the technology is used and implemented.

Global financial architecture. Due to the global economy, one country's financial stability is connected to another's. With the current economic crisis, policymakers are working to help financial markets function better by adopting frameworks that prevent future crises and help economies maintain resilience during financial turbulence.

Illegal drugs. Illegal drugs cause a host of problems, from creating a global black market for their cultivation and distribution, to dire societal consequences such as health issues, socio-economic conflicts, and political instability.

Trade, investment, and competition rules. Globalization is changing the way businesses trade, invest, and compete.

Intellectual property rights. Under intellectual property law, owners have certain rights to intangible assets such as musical works, literary pieces, artistic works, and ideas. Instant publishing and increased public access through the Internet have made these assets harder to regulate.

E-commerce rules. Electronic commerce is the buying and selling of products and services over electronic systems like the Internet. With the technological advances of today, e-commerce rules will become increasingly important to protect buyer's accounts and identities and ensure payment to the seller.

International labor and migration rules. People leave their home countries for various reasons, including economic opportunities, family, political conditions, and education. With growing populations and the current global economic crisis, international migration is sure to increase, creating the need for international labor rules, taxation laws, and guidelines for access to various countries' health and education benefits.

Source: Rischard, J.F. *High Noon: 20 Global Problems—20 Years to Solve Them.* New York: Basic Books, 2002. 66.

Leadership
NOTES

Chapter 1

1. Lewin K., Lippitt R., and White, R.K. "Patterns of Aggressive Behavior in Experimentally Created Social Climates," *Journal of Psychology*, 10 (1939), 271-301.
2. Larry Hedrick, ed., *Xenophon's Cyrus the Great: The Arts of Leadership and War* (New York, St. Martins Press, 2006), XI.
3. Larry Hedrick, ed., XIII.
4. Larry Hedrick, ed., 29.
5. Retrieved April, 2010 from http://www.pbs.org/wgbh/aia/part4/4p1539.htm.
6. Retrieved January, 2010 from http.//www.beahfound.org.
7. Retrieved January, 2010 from http://www.iranchamber.com/history/cyrus/cyrus_charter.php.
8. Retrieved April, 2010 from http://www.plato.stanford.edu/entries/confucious.

Chapter 2

1. Retrieved April, 2010 from http://data.worldbank.org/data-catalog/world-development-idicators/wdi-2007.
2. Silverberg, Robert. *The Seven Wonders of the Ancient World*, (London, Crowell-O Collier Press, 1961).
3. Larry Hedrick, ed., 64.
4. Retrieved April, 2010 from http://www.k2news.com/erik.htm.
5. Larry Hedrick, ed. 2.
6. Darren Rovell, "Miracle on Ice, One on One with Al Michaels, 30 Years Later," *CNBC*, February, 22, 2010, from http://www.cnbc.com/id/35520760/Miracle_on_Ice_One_on_One_with_Al_Michaels_30_Years_later.htm.

7. Retrieved July, 2009 from http://www.pbs.org/empires/medici/renaissance/brunelleschi.html.

8. Retrieved October, 2009 from http://www.web.mit.edu/tac/docs/kamkwamba-bio.pdf.

9. Martin Luther King Jr., "I Have a Dream," 1963, quoted in *To Lead or Not to Lead: Leadership Development Studies*, (Phi Theta Kappa, Inc., Jackson, MS, 1995), p. 2.3.

Chapter 3

1. Larry Hedrick, ed., 192.

2. Jeffrey Kluger and Jim Lovell, *Apollo 13* (New York, Houghton Mifflin Company, 1994), and Retrieved March, 2010 from http://www.science.ksc.nasa.gov/history/apollo-12.html.

3. Retrieved March, 2010 from http://webpages.charter.net/dkessler/files/kessys.html.

4. Retrieved March, 2010 from http://www.nasa.gov/mission_pages/station/main/index.html.

5. Retrieved March, 2010 from http://library.thinkquest.org/27948/archimede.html.

6. Retrieved March, 2010 from http://www.nsf.gov/discoveries/disc_summ.jsp?cntn_id=115097.

7. Retrieved March, 2010 from http://conferences.ted.com/TED2010/program/speakers.php.

8. Retrieved March, 2010 from http://history.nasa.gov/sts51l.html.

9. Retrieved March, 2010 from http://www.all-art.org/artists-g.html.

10. Jane Wardell, "Hawking Changes His Mind on Black Holes," *MSNBC*, 16 July 2004 at http://www.msnbc.msn.com/id/5452537/.

11. Retrieved March, 2010 from http://www.pbs.org/wgbh/aso/databank/entries/baleav.html.

Chapter 4

1. Robert D. McFadden, "Edmund Hillary, First on Everest, Dies at 88," *The New York Times*, Jan 10, 2008, http://www.nytimes.com/2008/01/world/asia/11cnd-hillary.html.

2. Jonathan M. Karpoff, "Charles Francis Hall," *The Encyclopedia of the Arctic* retrieved April, 2010 from http://faculty.washington.edu/karpoff/Research/Hall.pdf.

3. "Bernard L. Madoff," *New York Times*, Nov 3, 2009, from http://nytimes.com/top/reference/timestopcs/people/m/bernard_l_madoff/index.html.

4. "'Step by Step:' Interracial Education in the Y.W.C.A." retrieved April, 2010 from http://www.smith.edu/library/libs/ssc/ywca2/case2.html.

5. Larry Hedrick, ed., p. 13.

6. Retrieved April, 2010 from http://www.house.gov/velazquez/about/bio.html.

7. Retrieved March, 2010 from http://nobelprize.org/nobel_prizes/peace/laureates/1975/sakharov-autobio.html.

8. "Lang Lang," *New York Times*, May 19, 2010 from http://topics.nytimes.com/top/reference/timestopics/people/l/lang_lang/index.html.

9. Greg Mortenson and David Olive Relin, *Three Cups of Tea: One Man's Mission to Promote Peace...One School at a Time*, (New York: Penguin Group, 2006).

10. "A&S Interview: Sully's Tale," *Air & Space Smithsonian*, 18 Feb 2009, Retrieved March, 2010 from http://www.airspacemag.com/flight-today/Sullys-Tale.html.

11. Bachu Phub Dorji and Anne Marie Schreven, "Gross National Happiness and Good Governance: Civil Service Reform towards Achieving Gross National Happiness," retrieved March, 2010 from http://www.gnh-movement.org/papers/schreven.pdf.

12. Simon Elegant, "Dina Astita: A Survivor's Story," Jan 10, 2005 from http://www.time.com/time/subscriber/2005/time100/heroes/100astita.html.

13. Mary S. Lovell, *Straight on Till Morning: A Biography of Beryl Markham*, (New York: St. Martin's Press, 1987).

14. Kristen Gelineau, "Teen Completes Solo Sail around World," *The Denver Post*, 15 May 2010, sec. A, p. 2.

15. Malcolm Gladwell, Outliers: The Story of Success, (New York, Little, Brown and Company, 2008).

16. "Shackleton's Voyage of Endurance," *PBS*, Retrieved March, 2010 from http://www.pbs.org/wgbh/nova/shackleton/.

Chapter 5

1. Retrieved February, 2010 from http://www.awionline.org/ht/d/ContentDetails/id/11892/pid/2515.

2. Retrieved February, 2010 from http://www.awionline.org/ht/d/ContentDetails/id/11892/pid/2515.

3. Retrieved February, 2010 from http://www.navajocodetalkers.org/.

4. Heini Hedinger, *Man and Animal in the Zoo*, (London: Routledge and Kegan Paul, 1969).

5. Monty Roberts, *The Man Who Listens to Horses*, (New York: Random House, 1996).

6. Monty Roberts, *The Man Who Listens to Horses*, (New York: Random House, 1996).

7. Dorothy McLaughlin, "Silent Spring Revisited," *Frontline Online* at http://www.pbs.org/wgbh/pages/frontline/shows/nature/disrupt/sspring.html.

8. Retrieved from http://www.janegoodall.org/.

9. Retrieved from http://www.janegoodall.org/.

10. Julie Coburn, "A Report on the Jane Goodall Institute Global Youth Summit," at http://www.janegoodall.ca/JuliasReport.php.

11. Bhalin Singh and Mark Szotek "Jane Goodall Institute Hosts the 'Academy Awards' of Conservation" December 16, 2009, from http://news.mongabay.com/2009/1216-szotek_jgi_awards.html.

Chapter 6

1. Retrieved May, 2010 from http://www.evc.org/about/alumni/christine-l-mendoza.

2. "Youth Focused Grant Making in Action: The Time Warner Youth Advisory Board," *Innovate*, Fall, 2004, p.1. at http://www.theinnovationcenter.org/docs/innovate_fall2004.pdf.

3. Leslie Gaines-Ross, "Xerox: A Textbook Turnaround", *Bloomberg Businessweek* at http://feedroom.businessweek.com/index.jsp?fr_story=b15c08eaa1c171f6c72a3a1f08837bb7999aa6f5.

4. Phil Rockrohr, "Anne Mulcahy Tells How She Resurrected Xerox," *Chicago Booth News,* 20 September 2006, at http://www.chicago-booth.edu/news/2006-09-20_xerox_ceo.aspx.

5. James Cameron, *Ted2010: What the World Needs Now*, 13 Feb 2010 at http://conferences.ted.com/TED2010/program/speakers.php.

6. Evan Carmichael, "Lesson #5: Teamwork is an Essential Tool for Success" *Motivations and Strategies for Entrepreneurs* from http://www.evancarmichael.com/Famous-Entrepreneurs/810/Lesson-5-Teamwork-is-an-Essential-Tool-for-Success.html.

7. Robb Murray, "17-Year-old Reopens Truman's Main Street Market," 4 Nov 2006, *The Mankato Free Press* at http://mankatofreepress. com/local/x519259818/17-year-old-reopens-Truman-s-Main-Street-Market?start:int=0.

8. Bob Faw, "Teen Aims to Save His Minnesota Town," *Nightly News with Brian Williams*, 26 Jan 2007, at http://mankatofreepress.com/ local/x519259818/17-year-old-reopens-Truman-s-Main-Street-Market?start:int=0.

9. Tom Withers, "LeBron James Wins MVP in Landslide," 2 May 2010, *The Huffington Post* at http://www.huffingtonpost.com/2010/05/02/ lebron-james-wins-mvp-in-_n_560310.html.

10. "Crisis Communication Strategies," *Department of Defense* at http://www.ou.edu/deptcomm/dodjcc/groups/02C2/Johnson%20 &%20Johnson.htm.

11. Retrieved January, 2010 from http://www.ideafinder.com/history/ inventors/ford.htm.

12. Retrieved January, 2010 from http://www.ideafinder.com/history/ inventors/ford.htm.

Chapter 7

1. "Enron Scandal at a Glance," *BBC News World Edition*, 22 Aug 2002 at http://news.bbc.co.uk/2/hi/business/1780075.stm?story Link=%23.

2. "China: Tainted Milk Suppliers Charged," *CNN:Asia*, 16, Sept 2008 at http://www.cnn.com/2008/WORLD/asiapcf/09/16/china. formula/.

3. Eric Hoover, "Truth and Admissions: Former MIT Dean Seeks to Reclaim Her Name," *The Chronicle of Higher Education*, 6 Dec 2009 at http://www.cnn.com/2008/WORLD/asiapcf/09/16/china. formula/.

4. Joey Nowak, "Plagiarizing Speech Costs Valedictorian," *The Co-lumbus Dispatch*, 6 June 2008 at http://www.dispatch.com/live/ content/local_news/stories/2008/06/06/circlevilleval.ART_ART_ 06-06-08_B3_M2ADU5S.html.

5. Larry Hedrick, ed., p. 89.

6. Institute of Government and Political Affairs, University of Illinois, Retrieved April, 2010 from http://igpa.uillinois.edu/ethics/person/ sandra-day-oconnor.

7. Retrieved May, 2010 from http://www.prejean.org/.

8. John Carlin, "Nelson Mandela Unites a Nation with his Choice of Jersey," *The Observer,* 7 Jan 2007, at http://www.guardian.co.uk/sport/2007/jan/07/rugbyunion.features1.

9. "Obama: 'I screwed up' in Daschle Withdrawal," *MSNBC*, 3 Feb 2009 at http://www.msnbc.msn.com/id/28994296/.

10. Edna Gunderson, "U2 Singer to be Feted in New York," *@U2*, 2 Feb 2003, at http://www.msnbc.msn.com/id/28994296/.

11. Retrieved March 2010 from http://www.lospatojos.org.gt/ingle/ingle.swf.

12. Victor E. Frankl, *Man's Search for Meaning* (New York: Touchstone Books, 1984).

Chapter 8

1. Duane Bourdeaux, interview by author, Salt Lake City, Utah, 17 May 2010.

2. P.D. Stanley and J.R. Clinton, *Connecting: The Mentoring Connections*, (Colorado Springs, Colorado: Navpress, 1992).

3. Retrieved February, 2010 from http://www.collegesummit.org/region/southern-california/scu_peer_leaders_alumni.

4. Retrieved February, 2010 from http://www.collegesummit.org/region/southern-california/scu_peer_leaders_alumni.

5. Retrieved February, 2010 from http://www.collegesummit.org/region/southern-california/scu_peer_leaders_alumni.

6. "Peer Educators Mentor Teens," *USAID from the American People*, Retrieved April, 2010 from http://www.usaid.gov/stories/dominican-republic/ss_dr_teens.html.

7. Ngahihi O Te Ra Bidois, *Ancient Wisdom, Modern Solutions* (Auckland: Spot On Publications Ltd., 2009).

8. Larry Hedrick, ed., p. 294.

9. "Founding Father Lee Kuan Yew to Mentor Son's Cabinet" *Singapore Window*, 10 August 2004 at http://www.singapore-window.org/sw04/040810a1.htm.

10. Malcolm Gladwell, *Outliers: The Story of Success*, (New York: Little Brown and Company, 2008).

11. Tom Dirks, "The History of Film, The 1970s" at http://www.filmsite.org/70sintro.html.

Chapter 9

1. Addy Dugdale, "The Young App-rentices: Five App Developers Ages 16 and Under," 20 April 2010 at http://www.fastcompany.com/tag/jonah-grant.

2. Bill George, *True North* (New York: Gildan Media Corp, 2008), CD.

3. "Venus Williams Ends Peer's Run to Defend Dubai Title," Associated Press *USA Today*, 19 Feb 2010 at http://www.usatoday.com/sports/tennis/2010-02-19-dubai-tennis-championships_N.htm.

4. Nicholas D. Kristof, "What Could You Live Without?" *The New York Times*, 24 Jan 2010, at http://www.nytimes.com/2010/01/24/opinion/24kristof.html.

5. Nicholas D. Kristof, "What Could You Live Without?" *The New York Times*, 24 Jan 2010, at http://www.nytimes.com/2010/01/24/opinion/24kristof.html.

6. Jeffrey Marx, "He Turns Boys into Men," *Parade Magazine*, 29 Aug 2004, Retrieved Feb 2010 from http://www.racematters.org/joeehrmann.htm.

7. Jeffrey Marx, "He Turns Boys into Men," *Parade Magazine*, 29 Aug 2004, Retrieved Feb 2010 from http://www.racematters.org/joeehrmann.htm.

8. Mark Litke, "US Teens Share Eductation with Kids in Cambodia," *ABC News/World News*, 1 Feb 2007, at http://abcnews.go.com/WNT/story?id=2842703.

9. Retrieved Feb 2010 from http://www.mff.org/newsroom/news.taf?page=f&_function=detail&id=452.

10. Jackie Rotman, interviewed by author, Palo Alto, CA, 22 Feb 2010.

11. Cecily Hilleary, "Charity Song, 'We are the World' Remembered 25 Years Later," Voice of America, 25 Dec 2009 at http://www1.voanews.com/english/news/africa/we-are-the-world-79429907.html.

Leadership
BIBLIOGRAPHY

SELECTED BIBLIOGRAPHY

Beah, Ishmael. *A Long Way Gone: Memoirs of a Boy Soldier*. New York: Farrar, Straus and Giroux, 2007.

Bidois, Ngahihi o t era. *Ancient Wisdoms, Modern Solutions*. Auckland: Spot On Publications, 2009.

Carson, Rachel. *Silent Spring*. New York: Houghton, Mifflin Company, 1962.

Davis, Wade. *The Wayfinders: Why Ancient Wisdom Matters in the Modern World*. Toronto: House of Anansi Press, 2009.

Dormann, Henry, ed. *Letters from Leaders*. Connecticut: The Lyons Press, 2009.

Gerber, Robin. *Leadership the Eleanor Roosevelt Way*. New York: Penguin Books, 2003.

Gladwell, Malcolm. *Outliers: The Story of Success*. New York: Little, Brown and Company, 2008.

Gladwell, Malcolm. *The Tipping Point*. New York: Little, Brown and Company, 2000.

Hawking, Stephen. *A Brief History of Time*. Toronto: Bantam Books, 1998.

Hedrick, Larry. *Xenophon's Cyrus the Great*. New York: St. Martin's Press, 2006.

Howard, Albert. *An Agricultural Testament*. New York: Rodale Press, 1973.

Krakauer, Jon. *Into Thin Air*. New York: Villard, 1997.

Lovell, Mary S. *Straight on Till Morning*. New York: St. Martin's Press, 1987.

Mortenson, Greg, and Relin, David O. *Three Cups of Tea*. New York: Viking Penguin, 2006.

Prejean, Helen. *Dead Man Walking: An Eyewitness Account of the Death Penalty in the United States*. New York: Vintage, 1994.

Roberts, Monty. *The Man Who Listens to Horses*. New York: Random House, 1996.

DID YOU KNOW?

As of 2008, there are still 776 MILLION adults globally who are unable to read or write.

Our world is facing a crisis: Illiteracy. According to the United Nations Educational, Scientific and Cultural Organization (UNESCO), there are currently 103 million children without access to school and who are not learning to read, write or count. Without intervention, their situation will only get worse.

They need YOUR help!

Join us this Friday in the gymnasium after school for a rally to raise money for this important cause! Your participation is essential for our success. With your help, we hope to raise $3,000 for Literacy for All, an organization dedicated to providing education services to those in need. There will be food, games, live music, and a chance to win a guitar donated by Charlie's Rock Emporium! Admission is $5 and all proceeds go straight to the cause.

You can't make it?

- *No problem!* We're accepting donations all week. Just visit the Student Council Lounge to pick up a donation envelope. We'll be accepting cash, checks, and money orders. You can even donate online at: **www.literacy forall.org/bethesdahighschool**

You want to know where your money is going?

- *Understandable.* To track the progress of your donation, visit **www.literacy forall.org**. An interactive map allows you to see which village receives help from your donation. And after three months, check back to the progress from your contribution!

You want to know if illiteracy is a real problem?

- *Don't believe us?* Believe this: Illiteracy was listed as the third worst problem facing developing nations in our lifetime. Illiteracy contributes to low human development as well as low life expectancy rates. For more on the epidemic, visit: **www.unesco.org**.

Join us and join the cause!

This flyer represents one of many ways teenagers can make a difference. See page 131.